Exploring the explorers

SPANIARDS IN OCEANIA,
1519–1794

Mercedes Maroto Camino

Manchester University Press
Manchester and New York
distributed in the United States exclusively by Palgrave Macmillan

Copyright © Mercedes Maroto Camino 2008

The right of Mercedes Maroto Camino to be identified as the author of this work has been asserted by her in accordance with the Copyright, Designs and Patents Act 1988.

Published by Manchester University Press
Oxford Road, Manchester M13 9NR, UK
and Room 400, 175 Fifth Avenue, New York, NY 10010, USA
www.manchesteruniversitypress.co.uk

Distributed in the United States exclusively by
Palgrave Macmillan, 175 Fifth Avenue, New York,
NY 10010, USA

Distributed in Canada exclusively by
UBC Press, University of British Columbia, 2029 West Mall,
Vancouver, BC, Canada V6T 1Z2

British Library Cataloguing-in-Publication Data
A catalogue record for this book is available from the British Library

Library of Congress Cataloging-in-Publication Data applied for

ISBN 978 0 7190 7779 1 *hardback*

First published 2008

17 16 15 14 13 12 11 10 09 08   10 9 8 7 6 5 4 3 2 1

Typeset
by SNP Best-set Typesetter Ltd., Hong Kong
Printed in Great Britain
by CPI Antony Rowe, Chippenham, Wiltshire

Exploring the explorers

Manchester University Press

Contents

List of figures		*page* vii
Preface and acknowledgements		ix
Introduction: writing history		1
1	Navigation and the Pacific: Magellan and Spanish voyages prior to 1567	16
2	Spanish voyages to the Pacific 1567–1606	36
	2.I Mendaña and the Solomons (1567–68)	36
	2.II Mendaña and the Santa Cruz (1595)	66
	2.III Quirós and Vanuatu (1606)	82
3	Voyaging and the Pacific 1606–1770s	103
4	Spanish voyages to the Pacific 1770–94	123
	4.I González and Easter Island (1770)	123
	4.II Boenechea and Tahiti (1772)	133
	4.III Máximo and the padres in Tahiti (1774–75)	146
	4.IV Mourelle and Vava'u (1781)	181
	4.V Malaspina and Vava'u (1793)	195
5	Viewing the Pacific	210
Appendix: notes on sources and English translations		223
Bibliography		228
Index		239

List of figures

1.1	Claudius Ptolemaeus (Ptolemy), World Map. © National Maritime Museum.	*page* 22
2.1	Itinerary of the voyage of Álvaro de Mendaña to the Isles of Solomon (1567–68). By Iain MacIntyre.	37
2.2	Itinerary of the voyage of Álvaro de Mendaña to the Isles of Santa Cruz (1595). By Iain MacIntyre.	68
2.3	Abraham Ortelius, 'Typus Orbis Terrarum' (1570). From *Theatrum Orbis Terrarum*. © National Maritime Museum.	83
2.4	Itinerary of the voyage of Pedro Fernández de Quirós to Vanuatu (1605–6). By Iain MacIntyre.	85
3.1	*Umete* or sacred bowl of Taputapuatea, c.1770. Museo Nacional de Antropología (Madrid).	116
3.2	'The Two Worlds of Omai'. Courtesy of E. H. McCormick Research Library. Auckland Art Gallery Toi o Tamaki.	117
4.1	Itinerary of the voyage of Felipe González de Haedo to Easter Island (1770). By Iain MacIntyre.	125
4.2	Itinerary of the voyage of Domingo de Boenechea to Tahiti (1771–72). By Iain MacIntyre.	135
4.3	Itinerary of the voyage of Domingo de Boenechea to Tahiti (1774–75). By Iain MacIntyre.	148
4.4	Itinerary of the voyage of Francisco Mourelle de la Rúa to Vava'u (1780–81). By Iain MacIntyre.	182
4.5	Itinerary of the voyage of Alejandro Malaspina to Vava'u (1793). By Iain MacIntyre.	197
5.1	Diego de Prado y Tovar, 'The Bay of St Philip and St James' (1606). Archivo General Simancas (M. P. y D. VIII–82).	214
5.2	Juan Hervé, 'Plano de Ysla de Amat llamada por sus naturales Otajeti' (1772). Museo Naval (Madrid).	215

5.3 Juan Hervé, 'Plano de Enzenada de Matabay' (1772). Museo Naval (Madrid). 217
5.4 Diego de Prado y Tovar, 'People of the Bay of St Philip and St James'. Archivo General Simancas (M. P. y D. XVIII–81). 218

Preface and acknowledgements

The exploration of 'new worlds' is a challenging subject whose interest and complexity have not diminished for me. Indeed, the title of the first article that I published, 'Mapping *terra incognita*', has inspired much of my later work, including the present book. Teaching and investigating colonialism have been important in my career, although I have not dealt directly with the meetings between the explorers and the 'explored' in print until now. It has thus been a long voyage in search of a location from which to speak, and that journey has rewarded me with insights into unexplored landscapes. Needless to say, I have needed the guidance of many maps along the way and it is now a pleasure to be able to recognise some of those who made them.

It was with some trepidation that I started in 1998 to investigate Spanish voyages into the Pacific, thanks to an invitation to participate in the celebrations surrounding the anniversary of Vasco da Gama's voyage. That journey was followed by a white winter at the Newberry Library in Chicago, a place that has twice offered me a home, and has always been an unending source of inspiration. In the years that followed, I realised that early navigation to the Pacific was a subject worth tackling anew, if only to redress some imbalances or the sheer lack of material available.

This book owes a great debt to those who have studied some of the paradoxes in representing the past and different cultures, including Michel de Certeau, James Clifford, James Boon, Johannes Fabian, Hayden White, Stephen Greenblatt, Anthony Pagden and Tom Conley. I am also indebted to The University of Auckland who, over many years, offered economic and logistic support for the research involved by way of grants and sabbatical leave. Having to move to the other side of the world while writing the book was made easier by my new institution, Lancaster University, and, especially, by David Whitton. The support from the Faculty of Arts and Sciences and from my own department enabled me to access some material, as well as to commission the graphics of the voyages, for which I am grateful to the painstaking, patient and professional work of Iain MacIntyre.

A number of trusts and institutions have provided the necessary funding for the research that is pertinent to this project. Groundwork for early modern voyages was enabled thanks to support from the Newberry Library (Chicago), the National Maritime Museum (Greenwich), the American Geographical Society (Milwaukee) and the Spanish Ministry of Foreign Affairs. The Royal Society of New Zealand gave me a Marsden Grant in 2002–3 to expedite the study which resulted in my book, *Producing the Pacific*, in 2005. Fortunately, the society's support continued with a second Marsden Grant as part of a team formed by Anne Salmond. The writing of this book owes much to the visits to various archives, as well as the time made available by the society's contribution towards teaching relief, and the efficient research assistantship of Gwyn Fox, who has also indexed this book.

Thanks to the generosity of a Holzheimer-Woodward Fellowship I was able to investigate the wonderful facilities of The Institute for Research in the Humanities of the University of Wisconsin-Madison during two spring months in 2005, when the structure of the book was planned. The late David Woodward and, in his stead, Matthew Edney, helped me make my time profitable, as did Arthur and Janet Holzheimer.

Colleagues from various institutions and at different conferences have provided invaluable feedback, as well as comments on some portions of book. Among them, I wish to mention the Australia and New Zealand Medieval and Early Modern Studies Conference (2005), the Australian Map Circle (2005), the History Department at Lancaster University (2006) and The University of Auckland (2007). The Spanish Consulate, Monash University and the University of Melbourne kindly invited me to speak at the Symposium they hosted to celebrate the anniversary of Quirós-Torres' voyage in 2006. Fredric Angleviel from the University of New Caledonia also issued an invitation on behalf of the European Union to participate in the commemorations held in Vanuatu to which I contributed a written paper.

Librarians working in various archives have shown enormous patience and generosity with their time and resources. I owe a special debt to those who have kindly agreed to allow me to use photographs of their maps, namely, the National Maritime Museum (Greenwich), and *Archivo de Simancas, Museo Nacional de Antropología* and *Museo Naval* of Madrid. Staff at the Celsus Kelly Library in Melbourne kindly gave me access to his collection, as well as his annotated notebooks. I wish to thank especially Pilar Romero de Tejada from the *Museo Nacional de Antropología* (Madrid), Thea Roche from the Celsus Kelly Library (Melbourne), Jose María Burrieza and José Luis Rodríguez de Diego from the *Archivo General de Simancas* (Valladolid), María Luisa Martín Merás, Carmen Zamarrón and José María Moreno from the *Museo Naval* (Madrid), Bob Karrow, Art Holzheimer and James Akerman from the Newberry Library (Chicago), Chris Baruth from the American Geographical Society (Milwaukee), Judith A. Leimer and Matthew Edney from the History of Cartography Project (Madison), Esther González

Ibarra from the *Real Academia de Historia* (Madrid) and Nigel Rigby from the National Maritime Museum (Greenwich). Francisco Mellén from the *Asociación Española de Estudios del Pacífico* has kindly shared his unending wisdom about these voyages. Malcolm Read of State University of New York at Stony-Brook and Jonathan Tittler of Rutgers University have kindly supported my work throughout a good many years and I take this opportunity to show my appreciation.

In terms of comments and editing suggestions, my greatest debt is to Chris Arkinstall and, especially, to Dave MacIntyre, who read the whole manuscript tirelessly, providing many incisive observations. The staff at Manchester University Press, especially Emma Brennan, have been efficient, kind and cooperative in this painstaking process, always addressing queries and problems in an efficient and professional manner. My deepest thanks also to Patrick Williams, for his perceptive comments, editorial accuracy, encouragement and patience. Peter Hulme and Glyn Williams read some sections, generously sharing their wisdom while discreetly pointing out some obvious blunders. Needless to say, errors and inconsistencies are all my own.

Last but not least, I owe an immense debt to my sister, as well as to my parents, siblings, *sobrinas*, friends, students, ex-students, colleagues and ex-colleagues, who have patiently supported me with food, love and friendship. To name some, thanks are due to Carmen, Bene, Luis, Geoff, Fiona, Rosa, Ali, Ian, Chris, Gwyn, Lara, Sarah, Elena, Antonio, Jayne, Mariajo, Kathy, Walescka, Pilar, John, Owen and the late Paula. Each step of the process met with Dave's support and encouragement and this book is dedicated to him.

Introduction: writing history

As the subtitle of this introduction suggests, this study is underpinned by ideas expounded in history, anthropology, ethnography and cultural studies during the last decades of the twentieth century. Especially after the 1970s, researchers in these disciplines not only redefined what history and culture are but also questioned what it means to represent the past and 'others' in relation to 'us' and our present time. Subsequently, some schools of thought, such as New Historicism or Cultural Materialism, discredited the aspirations to detachment and objectivity which disguised biases, as well as power relationships, inherent in historical or ethnographical accounts.[1] By that time, moreover, the remains of the evolutionary perspective, which placed our predecessors, as well as members of different cultures, along a continuum of development, had been largely put to rest.

These parameters are of importance to this study of Pacific voyages, not only in regard to the selection of material, but also in the way that it is interpreted. This is because writing historical or ethnographic accounts implies a way of selecting and ordering information that inevitably foregrounds one reality over other possible options. The events that are singled out and the manner in which they are described determine our perception of different times and peoples, and any account, whether of factual or fictional deeds, needs to construct a narrative, offering a plausible interpretation that may be implicitly or explicitly suggested. In spite of the interpreter's best efforts to provide an objective and detached perspective, history and ethnography, even when transmitted in visual or aural form, always rely on developing a storyline, using rhetorical designs and strategies.[2]

Cultural histories thus build stories with beginnings and ends, which rely not just on knowledge of facts but also on the imagination and skill of the writer. In practical terms this means that narrative effectively recreates the past in a dialectical negotiation between representation and invention, in Eric Hobsbawm's use of the term.[3] Accordingly, the present ethnohistorical study cannot but be enabled by the exclusion of certain events and of alternative readings, a process that is even more evident when, as is the case here, there are few descriptions and no individual or comparative interpretation of those events singled out for analysis. In other words, writing about Spanish voyages of the Pacific effectively makes them history.

This book looks at eight Spanish voyages to the Pacific, most of which are hardly known beyond, or even within, the Spanish borders, and concentrates on the journeys and encounters with indigenous peoples in order to illuminate aspects of the early modern ethnography of world exploration and the cultural traits that underscore it. I have, therefore, considered the past as (an)other place: an alien territory that can be incorporated into the present only through the narratives that necessarily define and colour it. Such a standpoint takes as given that the act of writing involves the use of literary devices such as metaphors, similes and allegories, as well as a teleological design. Hence, my work acknowledges the plurality of historical or cultural interpretations, along parameters originally expounded by, among others Clifford (1988), James Boon (1982) or Michel de Certeau (1988) and, in relation to the Pacific, Bronislaw Malinowski (1922), Marcel Mauss (1923–24), Greg Dening (1980 and 1996), Bronwen Douglas (1993), Nicholas Thomas (1997) or Anne Salmond (2003 and 2005).

Cultural plurality, as I attempt to demonstrate in this work, applies to all aspects of these voyages: the explorers and the indigenous peoples encountered.[4] While the differences among the indigenous peoples were acknowledged by the explorers at the time, the Spaniards, who are often treated as one entity, were, in fact, a heterogeneous mix, which included Iberians, Europeans, Latin American Creoles, Africans and *mestizos* of Spanish and Amerindian descent. Starting with Iberians, Africans and Creole Spanish in the sixteenth century, voyagers to Oceania went on to include mixed-race Spaniards, as well as other Europeans whose fleets, like the previous ones, were made up of people of various social classes, regional and ethnic backgrounds. This means that the categories 'Spanish' and 'Pacific islanders' should be considered as multifaceted, varied and culturally dynamic. These differences inform their attitudes towards one another, as well as the representations of those attitudes, as shown in the chapters that follow.

Culture is, therefore, seen throughout this analysis as both a system of knowledge, which embraces the cognitive processes that may be shared by a certain community, and a set of behaviours and practices. The view of culture applied to the texts examined in this book is the plural one that has become instrumental in the development of cultural studies.[5] The intended plurality of one's approach is, however, restricted by the information available. Although there are a numbers of extant sources about the Spanish voyages to the Pacific in archives, publications or translations, it is also apparent that there are some noticeable gaps in the journals. This is nowhere more clearly illustrated than when investigating aspects that we nowadays consider important, including the composition and attitude of the crews, or customs of the host cultures, where the parties involved left little or no trace in the existing narratives.

In relation to the largely unknown crews, it is worth highlighting that the majority of the voyages studied here were, by and large, organised, prepared and staffed from the South American mainland and that, while their crew members were mostly Iberian and South American sailors, they also included other Europeans and an unknown number of African slaves. This means that many explorers were already living in the Americas, and were thus already removed from their own homelands, while others had never so much as landed in Europe, and had spent most of their lives in direct contact with Creole, African or Amerindian cultures. Prejudices notwithstanding, these sailors or settlers often had at their disposal a broader spectrum of ways with which to picture, or engage with, a new society. Settling and living in the Americas provided expatriates, Creoles or *mestizos* with a multifaceted notion of social groupings that could be used to face up or to describe the complexity and novelty of those encountered in the Pacific. As this study suggests, it also helps to explain, for example, some attitudes towards the land or indigenous peoples, or the desire from men and women to settle in an unknown and unexplored island group in the Pacific thousands of miles away from their 'civilised' 'homes' in Europe, the Philippines or the Americas. These characteristics, which became more widespread in later voyages, were not, however, free from stereotypes or ethnocentrism, as shown throughout this book.

With regard to the inhabitants of the Pacific, it is worth stressing that, as described in journals about these voyages, the explorers faced up to heterogeneous groups of island cultures. Moreover, as the Spaniards were able to corroborate, indigenous geographical and environmental knowledge was often considerable owing to their having been adept navigators. In fact, large geographical displacements were not limited to the Spanish or European ships traversing the stretches of sea now constituting the

South Pacific. People had travelled for centuries, if not millennia, in the 'sea of islands' that makes up Oceania.⁶ Well before Portuguese and Spanish ships rounded the Cape of Good Hope or landed in the Americas, the length and breadth of the Pacific, which takes up nearly one third of the world's surface, had been navigated by waves of explorers and migrants. These navigators investigated the world around them, preceding European curiosity in their zeal to discover, explore or settle new lands or, rather, in their case, an island world which stretches from Madagascar to Easter Island. Their deeds, however, were not written down and have, therefore, been excluded from historical documents, being reconstructed instead by anthropologists through ethnographic or linguistic data and archeological evidence.

By contrast, explorers and missionaries from the voyages studied here produced a variety of written descriptions which, though less familiar to English-speaking readers, had clear practical and political uses at that time. My interpretation, therefore, relies on a number of sources, the conditions of whose production entailed some biases and limitations that coloured them, and have not been scrutinised to date.⁷ The influence of these circumstances are stressed in this work, which questions the degree to which explorers portrayed what they expected to encounter, using analogies from their known world, or were equipped to deal with an unknown universe in its own terms. This is probed in various sources, whenever available, in an attempt to draw attention to alternative ways of comprehending the world and new peoples.

For these reasons, this book attempts to give a voice to different historical actors, though I have not been able to account for all those taking part. This difficulty is even more apparent with regard to recordings of encounters with indigenous peoples, where no account exists from the host cultures and few, if any, from the sailors or the soldiers. Nonetheless, a consistent effort has been made to highlight absences, silences or partialities that may be relevant to a twenty-first-century reader.

The first limitation encountered by Spanish voyagers was not, however, one of describing peoples but of coming to terms with the idiosyncrasies of an ocean of which they knew nothing. Whereas Polynesian navigators had learned to negotiate some of the problems that Pacific navigation presented, the early modern Spanish fleets were ill-prepared to do likewise. The many obstacles and challenges that sailing the length and breath of the largest ocean in the world presented are sketched in the first chapter of this book, 'Navigation and the Pacific: Magellan and Spanish voyages prior to 1567'. Outlined there are the serious handicaps that would hamper sailing ships for centuries, and which began to be fully appreciated in the round-the-world journey led by Ferdinand Magellan (1519–21).

In spite of the considerable loss of life, much was achieved in terms of geographical knowledge in Magellan's voyage, which was completed by Juan Sebastian Elcano following the former's death in the Philippines. The trials and tribulations of this long journey are summarised in this chapter, which clarifies how, in spite of the terrible difficulties faced by early explorers, the Pacific was gradually incorporated into the European sphere of influence from the sixteenth century onwards. With minimal input from Pacific islanders, the handful of largely ill-fated attempts to traverse the Pacific which followed Magellan's, and are itemised in the chapter, are essential for understanding the three important voyages that followed.

Chapter 2, 'Spanish voyages to the Pacific 1567–1606', analyses three interesting, though largely ignored or misrepresented, Pacific journeys which departed from the western coast of South America. They were initiated by the arduous, first-ever voyage of South Pacific exploration during which the Solomon Islands were discovered in 1567. Álvaro de Mendaña led this journey, studied in the section devoted to 'Mendaña and the Solomons (1567)', where some of the engagements between the visitors and the islanders are scrutinised. This description of Mendaña's original voyage sets the general tone of a study which strives to avoid the pitfalls of simplifying a complex, sophisticated and shifting subject. In practical terms, this means that the European perspective is exposed or (to use the term chosen for this book's title), 'explored', in the same manner that Europeans have looked at others, especially since the Enlightenment.[8]

The difficulties inherent in trying to represent fairly all the parties taking part in these voyages is not the only complication faced by this book as regards the selection and assessment of the material from which its overarching narrative is constructed. Using extant sources, which may even be limited in scope, the attempt to remain unbiased is often revealed as a utopian objective for, inevitably, sympathies or disgust cannot but be exposed in circumstances where, for example, those seen to be victimised are given no voice with which to present their side of events in the available documents. In other words, this analysis of events proceeds not just from the existing information about the voyages but also from inferences made from the writer's vantage point, which has been shaped by previous historical narratives, as well as, for instance, ethnicity, social class, gender and professional position.[9] As with any ethnographic or historical account, I effect a process of cultural translation in order to come to terms with events, societies or groupings that are partly or totally alien to me. By so doing, the opaque is rendered transparent and meaning may be attached to actions, extracting an intended message, as well as a plausible explanation – a process which Clifford has famously associated to allegory within the ethnographic paradigm of participant observation (1986a: 109).

In describing past events and cultures, this book is subject to the strengths and weaknesses of participant observation. As the name suggests, participant observation requires that one take part in the cultures described, while attempting to accept them on their own terms. Nonetheless, as Clifford remarks, observers cannot but be outsiders who must, of necessity, remain beyond the cultures under scrutiny (1988a: 93).[10] In other words, in spite of the participant observer's best intentions, the relationship with one's object of study can never be one of total empathy. It is, instead, always and inevitably, a negotiation between distance and implication, which is, at best, underwritten by a sincere wish to value others and the cultures that they inhabit. Therefore, a process of involvement and estrangement runs through this book's attempts to represent and explain some events or their motivations.

These premises are tested again in the two difficult voyages that followed Mendaña's, the first of which included women and men from the Latin American mainland, intending to settle the Solomons. Although the islands would not be located again for another two hundred years, Mendaña tried to find and settle them in his next voyage, some tragic encounters of which are summarised in the second section of Chapter 2, 'Mendaña and the Santa Cruz (1595)'. Plagued by malaria, many voyagers died during this journey, including Mendaña, who lost his life in the Santa Cruz archipelago. He was survived by his wife, Isabel Barreto, the first-ever female admiral who, with Pedro Fernández de Quirós as pilot, directed the few survivors of this journey back to the Philippines.

Mendaña's pilot, Quirós, who was to become one of the most popular early Pacific navigators, led the only seventeenth-century Spanish voyage to the South Pacific in 1606. With Luis Vaez de Torres as commander of one of the two ships, Quirós landed in *Austrialia del Espíritu Santo*, today's Vanuatu, separating there from Torres, who travelled across the strait that today bears his name. The interesting engagements of these voyagers with the people of Vanuatu's Santo and other islands from the group formerly known as New Hebrides are examined in the third and last section of Chapter 2, 'Quirós and Vanuatu (1606)'.

The description of the spatial displacements involved in these three voyages and their motivations is complemented in their respective sections by analyses of engagements at the point of contact. These engagements, which have been ignored or overlooked in the few historical works on these voyages and are largely disregarded in contemporary ethnographies of the islands visited, become the focus of my attention. Scenes of arrival, barter, gift-giving and exchange are quoted and examined, for they reveal a good degree of interaction which, even if unequal, shows power being challenged or negotiated and gives a salient role to the dialogue obtaining between the parties. Altogether, the terms and conditions of barter and gift-giving denote a discontinuous and often inconsistent effort on the part of the Spaniards to communicate with and understand different cultures.

Barter and gift-giving are appropriate scenarios in which to observe cross-cultural engagements because they involve a degree of mutual satisfaction. In the cases studied here, bartering also meant that some control was exerted by locals, who were acknowledged to have held the upper hand in a number of exchanges. This, however, was sometimes reversed by the explorers, who assumed the right to coerce the islanders before a deal could be struck, especially when they were denied the food that they craved, which often happened during those early encounters. Like the islanders, the voyagers exchanged items that might be of practical or decorative use, seeking in return some artefacts that had material value for them or were precious curiosities. Consequently, different values and criteria converged during these exchanges, resulting in both the Spaniards and the locals believing that they were getting a good deal.

The attitudes and thought processes of both Spanish explorers and Pacific island peoples are, therefore, illuminated throughout this book by focusing on engagements, many of which were economic in nature. There were, however, other exchanges that were concerned not with material goods, but with language, knowledge or the mutual participation in rituals and ceremonies pertaining to one of the groups, and these are also highlighted throughout this book. These exchanges provide some important information about indigenous peoples and, above all, the European perception of others and, as suggested in this book's title, of themselves.

These parameters are also used to scrutinise the eighteenth-century explorations that make up the second half of this book. The chronological leap of around 170 years from the early to the later voyages is due to the fact that, after the beginning of the seventeenth century, there would be no planned journey of exploration from Spain to the South Pacific until the last third of the eighteenth century. Nevertheless, other European powers – especially the Dutch, English and French – made the Pacific a focus of their enterprises, which are summarised in Chapter 3, 'Voyaging and the Pacific 1606–1770s'.

By the eighteenth century, however, an increased knowledge of, among other things, the world and other cultures, had exposed inadequacies in the deterministic view of peoples or human history held by the likes of Quirós. A summary of the political, economical and philosophical thoughts that informed those changes and influenced the men taking part in contemporary journeys, as well as those sponsoring them, is sketched in this chapter. An outline of some of the ideas arising from the French Enlightenment, with the focus on reason and, eventually, on cultural evolution, is complemented here, with a summary of improvements in navigational techniques, geographical and physical knowledge.

One obvious difference between the mindset of eighteenth-century explorers and their predecessors is that throughout the settlement of the Americas, and as a result of the subjugation of the great Aztec and Inca empires, early Spanish voyagers, by and large, believed in a providential view of the world and of humanity. Unlike their 'enlightened' followers, sixteenth-century explorers could justify colonisation by claiming that they were instruments of the divine will to extend Christianity's kingdom. This notion persisted even when the difficulties of incorporating the discovered worlds into a universal Christian paradigm became immediately apparent to many, and the contradictions inherent in that outlook remained contested and unresolved. One example is given by Pedro Fernández de Quirós who led the 1606 voyage and who, as his contemporaries noted, was imbued with ideas from the early conquest and settlement of the Americas, more than a century after Christopher Columbus's arrival in 1492. In fact, Quirós was rightly compared with Columbus and he continually stressed the supposedly innate innocence of indigenous peoples, very much in line with the views of Bartolomé de las Casas.[11] This was in contrast with the presentation of indigenous peoples as possessing inhuman brutality, exemplified by the practice of human sacrifice or cannibalism.[12]

Following upon the new era of Pacific exploration, which was heralded by the important eighteenth-century voyages of George Anson (1740–44), Samuel Wallis (1766–68), Louis Antoine de Bougainville (1766–69) and, especially, James Cook (1769–71, 1772–75 and 1776–79), the Spaniards took a renewed interest in this part of the globe, which they had until then considered as their own 'lake'. During the last part of the eighteenth century, besides the better-known scientific journey of Alessandro Malaspina (1789–94), four significant explorations took place. The study of these five voyages, four of which were sponsored by the Spanish crown and organised by the Viceroy of Peru, Manuel de Amat, makes up Chapter 4 of this book. It was from the Peruvian port of El Callao in Lima that the ships from four of these five voyages departed, with the first one directed towards today's Rapa Nui or Easter Island in 1770. This expedition was commanded by Felipe González de Haedo, with Juan Hervé, who produced some remarkable bird's-eye views of the island, as pilot. Contact with the locals during this voyage was rather minimal, as the ships remained at the island for only a few days. Nevertheless, the instructions given and the attitude of the officers and the men on board were very much in line with what would be the tenor of the following voyages, and are looked at in the first section of Chapter 4, 'González and Easter Island (1770)'.

The next two Spanish-sponsored voyages were to Tahiti, and took place in 1771–72 and 1774–75, respectively. During the first voyage, there were some interesting engagements, which are investigated in the second section of Chapter 4, 'Boenechea and Tahiti (1771–72)'. However, it was after this voyage that the most interesting cultural and economic exchanges in the Pacific were to take place, with the transfer to Lima of four Tahitians – two of whom died before reaching their destination. This is because the two surviving Tahitians learned Spanish while they were there and, in turn, taught their language to the person who would become an interpreter in the next voyage, Máximo Rodríguez. This voyage, which is the focus of the third section of Chapter 4, 'Máximo and the Padres in Tahiti (1774–75)', also departed from Lima and is of particular interest because of the length of the stay on Tahiti of Máximo, two Franciscan friars and one sailor. Their sojourn, which lasted nearly a year, ended when Tomás de Gayangos repatriated the 'mission' back to Peru.

The last two voyages of Spanish exploration to the Pacific reached the Vava'u group of islands in the Tongan archipelago. The earliest of these was led in 1780–81 by Francisco Mourelle de la Rúa, the first European ever to land on those islands. Although little known, this voyage contains some interesting descriptions of the inhabitants of the islands and the rituals in which they participated with the Spaniards. For the Vava'u islanders, this was the very first cultural/commercial exchange with Europeans, and they seem to have welcomed and enjoyed it, as described in 'Mourelle and Vava'u (1781)'.

The same group of islands was visited in the most 'enlightened' eighteenth-century Spanish voyage to the Pacific: the scientific journey led by Alessandro Malaspina in 1789–94, which is examined in the last section of Chapter 4, 'Malaspina and Vava'u (1793)'. The description of the islands and the attitude of the voyagers, as explained throughout this section, very much follow the pattern set out in the voyages of James Cook, and provide an eloquent summary of the journeys investigated in this book. This brief look at a segment of Malaspina's interesting voyage is followed by the conclusion, 'Viewing the Pacific', which offers an evaluation of the journeys, reassessing to what extent explorers 'invented' what they were seeing, in order to fulfil expectations, or displayed a lack of tools with which to describe an unknown universe. In order to explain this, I juxtapose one bird's-eye view and one drawing of indigenous peoples from Quirós's journey with two views selected from the two or three score of them produced during one of the eighteenth-century voyages to Tahiti. This final chapter also remarks on how, in both the earlier and later voyages, Spaniards replayed their own internal problems, especially class conflicts, which were often translated as ethnocentrism.

Alongside navigation or scientific knowledge, there were some substantial transformations from the earlier to the later voyages in the ways exchanges with indigenous peoples were conducted and understood. John Pocock (2000) sums up these shifts, showing how after the 1700s the evolution of commerce offers a commentary on the participating cultures and the individual's place in society. The way Europeans organised trade and commerce, according to Pocock, meant that individuals came to be understood in terms of their relationships with property; so that the self became 'transactional'.[13] Commerce might be defined not just as a social exchange, but involved also the individual human being, who became first and foremost a proprietor. Unlike the previous feudal landholder, this 'individual' owned mobile goods, exemplified by the gold that could be exchanged. This is the notion of trade and commerce that informed the voyages studied here and which was intimately linked with the increasing importance of the individual in the capitalist and mercantile economies developing in Western Europe.

These definitions have a bearing on our understanding of the relationship between the new worlds and the economic, political and social developments taking place in Europe from the early modern era onwards. That economic factors underscored the colonial enterprise and had an effect in the old world is never questioned by scholars of different backgrounds and outlooks, although the relationship between cause and effect remains a subject of some contention. Whereas, for some, imperialism was a prerequisite of capitalist development in Western Europe, for others, empires were the outcome of economic developments obtaining there. For the former thinkers, Europe's economies developed in the way they did because the colonies provided the necessary gold and cheap labour.[14] By contrast, for the latter school of thought, as Doug Munro puts it, 'imperialism was a political act that arose out of the economic activities of Europeans' (1993: 115). As far as the present study goes, to what degree colonialism was the producer or the product of capitalism is a moot point, as both reciprocally inflected one another throughout the colonial era. Nevertheless, this study assumes that all past and present societies gradually came to be integrated within what Immanuel Wallerstein has labelled a 'world system' (1974, 1980 and 1989).

If the economic and cultural parameters within which Europeans operated changed during this time, it is only logical to assume that the indigenous parties participating in these exchanges also changed in ways that the explorers could hardly ascertain. Sadly, we have little autochthonous information about these peoples, and we can only infer from Spanish information how the islanders understood the alien cultures or valued the goods that they received or traded. Nonetheless, besides evaluating carefully the descriptions given in the available sources, observations from modern anthropologists, who have analysed oral histories, shed some light on these encounters. In particular, twentieth-century investigations about bartering and gift-giving in Pacific societies can be useful in assessing past exchanges, especially because many studies have incorporated considerable input from Pacific peoples following on from Marcel Mauss's pioneering *The Gift: Forms and Functions of Exchange in Archaic Societies* (1967 [1923–24]).[15] It is reasonable to infer from these sources that throughout the Pacific, exchanging gifts was an important social ceremony that could bind or separate peoples, and which was marked by rules and obligations that are not comparable to capitalist accumulation.[16]

The fact that exchanges took place does not mean that there was reciprocity either in the sixteenth or in the eighteenth centuries, even if both parties might be portrayed as having been pleased with the end result. Not only would the notion of 'reciprocity' suggest a level of complicity with the explorers on the part of those who would be colonised, but it can also serve to mitigate the sense of guilt that has hampered much European thought. Henry Louis Gates has delineated the conundrum faced by the scholar who wants to highlight the agency of the local inhabitants in the face of European arrival on their shores. Even if this position, as Gates argues, implicitly dismisses many aspects of the devastation often visited on the colonised, one also needs to steer clear of the alternative and to 'play up the absolute nature of colonial domination, and be open to charges of negating the subjectivity and agency of the colonized, thus textually replicating the repressive operations of colonialism' (1991: 462).

The difficult equilibrium between these positions is partly addressed by the terminology used in this book, including 'cross-cultural engagement', which has been selected in order to underline the fact that agency by no means rested solely with one of the parties involved in the meetings.[17] Instead, especially in the journeys to Tahiti investigated in the latter part of this book, it could easily be said that, in spite of European technological advances, the locals had the upper hand in many of the exchanges. The use of the word 'engagement' also implies an attempt to redress the imbalance that would render indigenous peoples subjects with no purchase on the way their history is written. Furthermore, unlike idioms such as encounter or contact, engagement implies a level of intercultural dialogue and, as suggested above, of negotiation. This is clearly more prominent in the later voyages and accounts, particularly in the 'mission to Tahiti' sponsored by the Viceroy of Peru, Manuel Amat, in 1774–75, as shown. For the remaining sections, especially for the sixteenth- and seventeenth-century voyages, terms such as encounter, or even 'fatal encounter', could give a reasonable idea of the relationships established.

My choice of terms is, above all, designed to avoid the deterministic pitfalls of the so-called 'fatal impact' theory.[18] Nevertheless, there is no ideal selection, as shown, for example, by the way that Mary Louise Pratt has redefined 'contact', taking into account hierarchical relations and inequalities. Throughout Pratt's book, *Imperial Eyes*, 'contact zone' is used 'to refer to the space of colonial encounters, the space in which peoples geographically and historically separated come into contact with each other and establish ongoing relations, usually involving conditions of coercion, radical inequality, and intractable conflict' (1992: 6).[19] Like the qualifications Pratt exposes, my own preference for the term 'engagement' does not suggest that there was equality in places where the harquebus might have the ultimate word. I differ from Max Quanchi's proposal that: 'Europeans and islanders were *equally* brutal and gratuitous in their excessive use of force against "others"' (2000: 49; my italics). Equality of this sort assumes that indigenous peoples had more agency than they normally had before European military technology, and may even imply that the islanders condoned the occupation that frequently followed voyages of exploration. Pacific peoples were by no means acquiescent in the wishes of the voyagers, although they often had few means with which to counter the effect of European weapons.

Finally, the study of these journeys seeks to offer a glimpse of what Marcel Mauss famously described as 'lunes mortes', or pale moons, in the 'firmament of reason' (1924: 309). I make my own Clifford's remarks in relation to Mauss's words when he says that: 'the "reason" referred to is not a parochial Western nationality but the full human potential for cultural expression' (1988: 129). In other words, the attempt to bring to light some events or points of view which may not have received much attention to date is, to the present writer, an effort to counter parochialism. Also, and perhaps more importantly, it is not so much a representation of the 'full human potential for cultural expression' as a search for it.

NOTES

1 The subtitle of my introduction echoes the title of the collection of essays edited by James Clifford and George Marcus, *Writing Culture: The Poetics and Politics of Ethnography* (1986b).
2 Hayden White highlights the importance of narrative in the writing of history (1987: 24 and *passim*). Similarly, Jane Marcus argues that: 'The writing of history is all a matter of the construction of more or less plausible plots' (1989: 133).
3 Hobsbawm defines 'invented tradition' as 'a set of practices ... which seek to inculcate certain values and norms of behaviour by repetition, which automatically implies continuity with the past. In fact, where possible, they normally attempt to establish continuity with a suitable historic past.' 'Invented traditions' embrace 'both "traditions" actually invented, constructed and formally instituted and those emerging in a less easily traceable manner within a brief and dateable period' (1983: 1).
4 Thomas warns against 'the suggestion that cultural dynamism arising from intersocial contact only occurred after European contact' (1997: 191). To illustrate his argument, he mentions Pacific islanders who, like Tupaia and Omai, travelled back to Europe, or to other islands (1997: 194). More will be said in the sections devoted to eighteenth-century voyages to Tahiti about the islanders who travelled on Spanish ships.
5 Culture, Clifford posits, 'in the mid nineteenth century ... referred to a single evolutionary process ... By the turn of the century, however, evolutionist confidence began to falter, and a new ethnographic conception of culture became possible. The word began to be used in the plural, suggesting a world of separate, distinctive, and equally meaningful ways of life' (1988: 92–3).
6 The expression 'sea of islands', now widely used, was coined by Epeli Hau'ofa, for whom, 'it was continental men, Europeans and Americans, who drew

imaginary lines across the sea, making the colonial boundaries that, for the first time, confined ocean peoples to tiny spaces' (1993: 8).

7 Focusing on written texts can seem to imply that, as Edmond remarks, 'European descriptions unproblematically created colonial subjects' (2000: 238).

8 These points are summed up by Paul Rabinow, when he urges that: 'We need to anthropologize the West: show how exotic its constitution of reality has been; emphasize those domains most taken for granted as universal (this includes epistemology and economics); make them seem as historically peculiar as possible; show their claims to truth are linked to social practices and have hence become effective forces in the social world' (1986: 241).

9 In Louis Montrose's words, 'the histories we reconstruct are the textual constructs of critics who are, ourselves, historical subjects' (1989: 23).

10 The standard method of fieldwork, which was first set down by Malinowski in the Trobriand Islands (1922: 25), requires the presence of the ethnographer, who observes and participates in the culture, learning and speaking the language.

11 Las Casas, who was born in Seville in 1484, became a Dominican friar and an outspoken advocate of the rights of Amerindians throughout his life. He engaged in theological debates with Juan Gines de Sepúlveda, which culminated in the great debate of 1550 in Valladolid, where Las Casas defended the humanity and rights of Amerindians with passion. The publication of his *Brevísima relación de la destrucción de las Indias* (*A Brief Account of the Destruction of the Indies*) (1552), galvanised public opinion against the methods used by conquistadors and *hacendados* to subdue the Amerindian population.

12 'A Europe newly convinced of the innate sinfulness of man, and increasingly conscious of the need for a powerful state organization to restrain the forces of disorder had little inclination to idealize the virtues of primitive societies' by the seventeenth century (Elliott 1970: 103).

13 At this point, as Pocock puts it, 'we encounter the very interesting suggestion that it is precisely commerce that shapes the mind in this way; defined as the constant interchange of goods, words, ideas, and emotions, commerce presents both the world perceived and the mind perceiving as transactional ... [T]his perception ... anticipated later materialism by depicting the personality as shaped in a universe of moveable goods' (2000: 27).

14 Elliott describes the 'formulation of modern European history in which the discovery and exploitation of American plays a crucial role in promoting economic and social change [and is] ... intimately associated with the rise of European capitalism' as the theory of which Adam Smith and Karl Marx were 'its patron saints' (1970: 55). Elliott addresses these schools of thought in Chapter 3, 'The New Frontier' (1970: 54–78).

15 For Mauss, according to Boon, '[t]he circulation of commodities is the starting point of culture' (1982: 88).

16 A common idiosyncrasy of Pacific communities has been 'a stress on exchange of material objects and food in preference to accumulation or storage' (Douglas 1993: 16). Before Europeans arrived in the Pacific 'trading was usually limited to customary visits between neighbouring groups. During such visits the islanders exchanged local products for reason of ritual and friendship rather than for economic necessity' (Diamond 1993: 58).

17 Robin Torrence and Anne Clark define engagement as 'the active involvement of both sides ... Engagement also implies that both sides have made a conscious decision to be involved ... By assuming that the Indigenous groups were active participants, new interpretations of old behaviour become possible' (2000b: 16).

18 Cultural contact, for Paul Rainbird, 'relates to meetings between Europeans and indigenous people ... and includes accounts of the colonial experience. All too often these accounts have been viewed from a European perspective, usually one of perceived domination ... and of "fatal impact" for the indigenes' (2000: 32–3).

19 'A "contact" perspective emphasizes how subjects are constituted in and by their relations to each other. It treats the relations among colonizers and colonized, or travelers and "travelees" ... in terms of copresence, interaction, interlocking understandings and practices, often within radically asymmetrical relations of power' (Pratt 1992: 7).

1 Navigation and the Pacific: Magellan and Spanish voyages prior to 1567

By the time Europeans arrived in the Oceanic archipelagos, most of the islands were populated by indigenous peoples, many of whom were great navigators.[1] Nonetheless, the way we know the ocean and its division into the island groups of Micronesia, Melanesia and Polynesia are very much European constructions. In fact, it was not until Europeans charted and represented the Pacific world that the dimensions and features of the ocean we know today took shape. As Oskar Spate points out, it was only after Ferdinand Magellan had traversed the large expanse of water, at that time known as the South Seas, that the Pacific was 'born'.[2]

The conceptualisation of 'the Pacific' and its discursive production were part and parcel of a European design which started with Vasco Nuñez de Balboa's discovery and naming of the great expanse of sea, which he saw from Darien in Panama in 1513. It gained its greatest momentum after Magellan's journey (1519–21) and it was finally delimited by James Cook in the latter half of the eighteenth century. The sheer size of the ocean and its difficult currents meant that, in spite of the remarkable achievements of Magellan's journeys and those who dared to follow him, it took more than two hundred and fifty years before the map of the Pacific was fully drawn and for the coordinates of its islands to be permanently fixed. And, just over one hundred years after Cook completed the map of the Pacific all its islands were all annexed by various European powers. This colonial hold started to loosen after the Second World War, though it is certainly far from complete or satisfactory, and its effects are, in many places, ineffaceable.

Probably one of the most resilient and insidious sequels of European colonialism is the division of the Pacific islands between Micronesia, Melanesia and Polynesia. This eighteenth-century classification obeys what, for contemporary ethnographers, are xenophobic grounds. For, whereas the label Micronesia refers to the size of the islands and Polynesia to the great number of them, Melanesia is a term coined to denote the skin tone of its inhabitants. The original references and attribution of these labels belongs to the eighteenth-century explorer Jules-Sébastien-César Dumont d'Urville, who first used the term Melanesia. Regarding the 'Melanesians', D'Urville disparagingly wrote, 'En masse, like all members of the black race of Oceania, these people are disgustingly lazy, stupid, savage, greedy and without any good qualities or virtues that I know of' (Qtd. Douglas 1993: 25).[3] Indeed, the diverse groups encountered in what is known as Melanesia were perceived and classified as darker, uglier, wilder and 'debased'.[4]

The division between Polynesia and Melanesia, which was typical of evolutionism and prejudice during the Enlightenment, is still alive today.[5] However, as early modern travellers observed, the ethnic differences among peoples in different islands of so-called Melanesia, or even within the same island, were considerable. Likewise, their languages and dialects were also varied, as were the ways in which they either welcomed or tried to repel those who arrived on their shores. Consequently, in relation to this division, Bronwen Douglas concludes that Polynesia should be considered 'a subclass of Melanesia ... because Melanesia combines unrelated languages and peoples and is not made up of groups possessing any shared ancestral history' (1993: 18).

Like Douglas, other contemporary scholars have argued eloquently for the need to reject such categories, stressing that what seemed to be 'backward' traits during one historical era may be apprehended differently in other times and places. For example, the social organisation of the groups living in what became known as Melanesia, which was perceived as less evolved, being composed of smaller groups with more equal members, is one such case, with Marshall Sahlins (1963), for example, disparaging the absence of hierarchy, while Nicholas Thomas has praised its egalitarianism (1997: 132).

Using the work of archaeologists and historical linguists, Patrick Vinton Kirch has summarised the effects of the labels given to Oceania, warning against taking them as 'meaningful segments of cultural history'. Instead, Kirch endorses the terminology proposed by Roger Greene, namely, Remote Oceania and Near Oceania, which includes New Guinea, the Solomons and Bismarcks (2000: 5).[6] In spite of the fact that it may be difficult to extend its use, Greene's division would do away with the misrepresentation of 'Melanesians', whose classification does not conform to any shared cultural traits, according to historical and archeological data.

It is with regard to these notions that I have chosen to treat all the islands which the Spanish sighted or visited as part of the Oceanic world, with no apparent differentiation other than their geographical location, roughly south of the Equator. This study, therefore, only considers the Philippines briefly as landings for early voyages because they are not normally deemed to be part of the Oceanic island world but as part of South East Asia. Also, encounters in the Philippines were soon followed by settlement, making it a long-term colony that was ascribed to Spain for over three hundred years and, therefore, not comparable with the visits studied here. This study looks at the contact zones established in voyages to the Oceanic of the South Pacific, from the sixteenth to the eighteenth century, with some brief references to areas north of the Equator, as, for example, the Philippines or Magellan's 'Ladrones' (Marianas) whenever relevant.

If cultural differences among Pacific islanders were hard to fathom for early modern travellers, the sheer geographical distance between the islands was no less daunting for them. From the perspective of the Spanish voyages studied in this book, navigation in this area of the world was undoubtedly fraught with many difficulties. This was not just because they had grossly underestimated the size of the ocean, but also, and perhaps more importantly, because of the Pacific's complicated systems of winds, which make it impossible to navigate from west to east during much of the year. This challenging system of winds, known as trade winds, blows from east to west most of the time, and reduces the possibility of sailing eastwards to narrow bands in the northern hemisphere during the summer months of July and August, which is why some of the early journeys of exploration to the South Pacific often returned to the North American coast.[7] The problems arising from these adverse winds were only effectively understood following Miguel de Legazpi's return voyage, led by Andrés de Urdaneta, from the Philippines in 1565, which sailed north of the belt created by the trade winds, reaching the Californian coast.[8] This was the route that would be followed thereafter by the Manila galleon, which carried precious metals to the Philippines to trade for spices and Asian merchandise. From Legazpi's time onwards, the Manila galleon would sail north before heading east in order to avoid the trade winds.[9]

Although wind systems became increasingly known and manageable after 1565, other hardships, including piracy, hunger and scurvy, remained as challenging handicaps. Nevertheless, the greatest problem for navigation in the Pacific was the location or, rather, the relocation, of places previously visited. In spite of the fact that, by the eighteenth century, many parts of the ocean had already been sighted, especially by Portuguese, Spanish and Dutch expeditions, the exact location of those findings remained a mystery for subsequent travellers. Before the development of the chronometer, which enabled sailors to calculate longitude accurately in the late eighteenth century, even places known to exist were hard to find again.

Longitude was the most difficult problem to solve and, up to the late eighteenth century, its estimation was an arduous and imprecise task. By contrast, latitude started to be determined fairly accurately from the late fifteenth century onwards, using astrological observations or instruments such as the quadrant and the astrolabe. Spate summarises the means and timeframe to determine latitude, noting that: 'before 1480 the astrolabe and the quadrant had been adapted for use at sea (possibly by Prince Henry's Jewish expert, Master Jacome of Majorca), and tables of latitude had been drawn up for points as far south as the Equator – using the sun, for the Pole Star was too low to be easily observed as far south as Guinea' (1979: 21).

Latitude was, therefore, easily fixed by calculating the distance to the sun at midday, which was achieved with the cross-staff, the astrolabe or the quadrant. However, with imprecise clocks, it was impossible to determine longitude, and highly inaccurate methods, including dead-reckoning, compensated for this absence. Glyndwr Williams sums up the 'complicated series of observations and calculations' or guesswork involved in dead-reckoning, which consisted in estimating 'the distance covered by the ship in a certain time, noted the compass courses steered, and then plotted the vessel's track on a chart' (1966: 152). In fact, the pitfalls of dead-reckoning are nowhere better illustrated than in the failure to reach the Solomons after Álvaro de Mendaña's first voyage in 1567, as shown below.[10] The problems arising from the different readings of longitude were partly addressed early in the eighteenth century by the calculation of lunar distances – the method used by James Cook on his first voyage (1768–71). However, it was only effectively solved in the last third of the century with the development of John Harrison's timepiece.[11]

The sixteenth-century expeditions which immediately preceded those of Mendaña faced up to these challenges with various degrees of success or, more often, lack of it. In fact, the disappearance of many ships from those navigations gave way to the myths and mysteries that persist to this day. Although largely unfortunate, these explorations created the environment for subsequent voyages to develop, preparing the ground for the European entry into the Oceanic world. The summary of those explorations contextualises the main voyages studied in this book and illuminates the origins of these legends.

Before the expeditions of Álvaro de Mendaña and Pedro Fernández de Quirós, which took place between 1567 and 1606, there were other important, though largely unsuccessful, journeys directed to the South Pacific. Because of the trade winds mentioned above, most of the brief landfalls from these voyages took place north of the Equator and the contacts with indigenous peoples were minimal. Nevertheless, it is interesting to note their reach, how they were conducted and the type of instructions to which the explorers adhered.

With regard to the South Pacific, the most important journey was the circumnavigation led by Ferdinand Magellan, and completed by Juan Sebastián Elcano (1519–21). Indeed, Magellan's journey is the most significant after Columbus, whose landing on the Americas had signalled a turning point in Spain's position in world exploration. Before Columbus's voyage, Portugal had led the march towards unseen lands throughout most of the fifteenth century. However, it was Spain that pioneered the exploration of the Atlantic and, subsequently, the South Seas, following Núñez de Balboa's discovery of the ocean, when Spain claimed for itself all the islands and continents found in the South Pacific. This declaration endured well into the seventeenth century, making the ocean effectively a 'Spanish Lake', as Spate puts it. Voyages to the area started soon after Núñez de Balboa's sighting, encountering so many difficulties that they were discontinued from the early seventeenth century.[12]

Although perhaps self-explanatory to many contemporary cultures, the zest to explore and discover lands beyond the confines within which Europeans had lived comfortably for centuries was something reasonably new during the fifteenth and sixteenth centuries. Several hypotheses have been put forward to account for this desire to push back the boundaries of the known world. This European aspiration has been attributed to the growing migration to cities, which made a larger number of products available and desirable. Also, urban centres facilitated the exchange of ideas with regard to social reform and the possible upgrading of living conditions so that self-improvement became a possibility and a wish for many.

On a practical front, there was a growing need for spices because of their value in preserving food. Salt and smoke had been used to preserve meat, but pepper, ginger, nutmeg, clove and cinnamon were useful ingredients to disguise the smell and taste of meat that had started to deteriorate (Landín 1992: 1. 90). Commerce in spices, the precious products from 'the

East', meaning India and China, was at the time the monopoly of Venice and Genoa, whose traders and explorers travelled east via Egypt (Alexandria) and Istanbul (then called Constantinople). However, the difficulties in using that route increased with the fall of the Byzantine Empire to the Ottomans in 1453 and this provided the stimulus for the journeys of Bartolomeu Dias (1488), Columbus (1492) and Vasco da Gama (1498), in search of new routes. Once Vasco da Gama traced the route to the Indies by sailing east via the Cape of Good Hope, which had been rounded four years earlier by Bartolomeu Dias, the Portuguese settled in India's Calicut (Calcutta) in 1512 and Lisbon became the spice centre for Europe. Spain was thus left to explore the western route, which it did, increasingly, following Columbus' four voyages.

The desire to seek lands beyond the *non plus ultra* ('there is nothing beyond'), which Charles V significantly altered to *plus ultra* in his motto in order to endorse exploration, has also been assigned to moral, religious and spiritual values associated with the Renaissance.[13] Samuel Y. Edgerton, for example, has cogently suggested that a sense of spiritual loss on the part of Christians inflected the need to expand the boundaries of the known world (1987: 14). For Edgerton, the fact that the centre of the Christian spiritual universe, Jerusalem, seemed to be forever in Muslim hands in spite of the various attempts to recover it by Crusaders, was a source of constant frustration for Christians. It was, Edgerton suggests, partly as a result of Christian dissatisfaction that the wish to explore the world grew exponentially. This growth was stimulated by new development in architecture and planning, which had a speedy effect on mapping through the use of the grid (1987: 29).

Equally influential in the stimulus to travel and chart the lands beyond the known universe was the recovery in the fifteenth century of the geographical knowledge of the Greek Claudius Ptolemaeus (Ptolemy). Indeed, Ptolemy's worldview was among the most important factors behind the design of Columbus's voyage, for it shaped the cartographic developments needed for the discovery of new lands (Figure 1.1). Various renditions of world maps derived from Ptolemy's studies flourished from the later part of the fifteenth century onwards, and they were used with different additions, such as the opening up of the Cape of Good Hope, well into the following century.[14]

The expansion into unknown worlds thus reached the South Seas under the auspices of kings Charles V (1516–56), Philip II (1556–98) and Philip III (1598–1621).[15] First, Magellan discovered and landed in the Marianas and the Philippines in the first round-the-world circumnavigation,

1.1 Ptolemy's World Map. Appearing in many different editions, Ptolemy's worldview dominated mapmaking for over fifty years, until Magellan's voyage (1519–21).

completed by Juan Sebastián Elcano (1519–21). Next, Gonzalo Gómez de Espinosa's journey probably landed in the western Carolines in 1522, while in the following expedition (1525–27), García Jofre de Loaísa's crew found a portion of the Marshall archipelago, after the death of their captain. The last surviving ship of this fleet, *La Florida*, commanded by Álvaro de Saavedra (1527–29), found islands from the Marshalls, Carolines, Admiralty, Schouten and Aroe groups.

Subsequent to these frustrated enterprises, Hernando de Grijalva's fleet either saw or landed in the Revillagigedo, the Southern Espórades, Gilbert, Carolines and Mapia Islands (1536–37). Also departing from New Spain, which was the name of the Spanish viceroyalty in Mexico and Central America, Ruy López de Villalobos landed again in the Revillagigedo, Marshalls, Carolines and Belau (1542–45). Offshoots from this expedition were the discoveries by Bernardo de la Torre (1543) and Íñigo Ortiz de Retes (1545), which are itemised below. Both these captains tried unsuccessfully to return to New Spain from the Philippines and the Moluccas respectively, and found the groups of Vulcano and Bonin, also sighting the north coast of New Guinea.

The last Spanish expedition into the Pacific before Mendaña's quest for the Solomons in 1567 was led by Miguel López de Legazpi to the Philippines, with Andrés de Urdaneta as pilot (1564–65). Although on the way to the Philippines these explorers found new islands of the Marshall, Caroline and Palau groups, the most important aspect of this journey was the discovery of the route for return journey to New Mexico, between 37° and 39° of latitude north, avoiding the trade winds that blew to the south.[16]

As mentioned, it was Ptolemy's knowledge, or, rather, the gaps in it, especially in relation to the size of the Atlantic and the non-existence of the Pacific, that spurred the discoveries of Columbus in the Caribbean. And it was the underestimation in contemporary maps of the distance between the Americas and the Spice Islands (Moluccas), which created the environment for Charles V's support of Magellan's aspirations. Consequently, on 20 September 1519, Magellan left Spain from San Lúcar de Barrameda, which was the port of Seville, with some 243 men in five ships: *Trinidad, San Antonio, Concepción, Victoria* and *Santiago*. They were searching for a way westward to the Spice Islands in order to demonstrate that these islands fell within the Spanish side of the line of demarcation, as Magellan had indicated in his proposal to Charles V.[17]

This famous or infamous line, normally referred to as the Bull of Demarcation, was drawn by Pope Alexander VI in the *Intercoetera* of 1493. The bull separated the Portuguese and Spanish claims of the world newly discovered by tracing a line 30° west of the island groups of the Azores and Cape Verde. It assigned to Portugal everything east of the line and to Spain everything west. However, not only was the line ambiguous, but nobody knew at the time that the Pacific, the largest ocean in the world, existed.

The leader of the round-the-world journey, Fernão de Magalhães – anglicised as Ferdinand Magellan – was a Portuguese aristocrat born c.1480, who had been brought up as a page in the royal court. He entered the Marine Department established by King Manuel I when he was sixteen years old. In 1505, he sailed as a volunteer on the expedition to the Orient led by Francisco d'Almeida, from which he returned wounded, and was thereafter promoted to the rank of captain. Magellan participated in the war between Portugal and Morocco in 1513, where he received another wound that left him lame for the rest of his life. He was then accused of trading with the Moors and King Manuel refused to employ him again in spite of his denials. Magellan, like Columbus before him and Pedro Fernández de Quirós thereafter, offered his services to Spain and was employed by Charles V to command the important journey that would circumnavigate the world for the very first time.

The most important sources for Magellan's journey are the journals of Francisco Albo and of the Italian gentleman Antonio Pigafetta of Vicenza, who joined the expedition voluntarily.[18] If Magellan kept a journal, which he must have as captain, it has not come to light; nor did the journals or notes of the captains who succeeded him. Similarly, no writing from Elcano has survived, even though he was in command of the *Concepción* and took over the leadership of the journey after Magellan's death in August 1521.[19]

Magellan's expedition was ill-fated from the beginning, as many of the crew on board resented being led by a Portuguese. While sailing around the coast of South America, he managed to subdue a mutiny, killing the leader, Gaspar de Quesada, and marooning two of the main instigators, Juan de Cartagena and Pero Sánchez de la Reina, in Patagonia. Magellan then sent the *Santiago* to explore the area but the ship was lost in a storm. However, the people on board managed to reach the coast and returned to San Julián on foot. Magellan then discovered and named the Cape of the Eleven Thousand Virgins, which is located at the eastern entrance to the strait that Magellan named *Todos los Santos* (All Saints) and is today known by his own name. The whole area around this strait is extremely difficult to navigate, as it harbours many small islands and strong currents. One of the ships, the *San Antonio*, was forced to return to Spain after failing to get through. The remainder of the fleet took thirty-eight days to find their way out, which they did finally via a cape suitably named *Cabo Deseado* (Desired Cape).

The hardships of the journey were not over yet, increasing daily as the fleet traversed an ocean the dimensions of which were broader than any had contemplated. Members of the crew were dying from scurvy practically every day, and Pigafetta narrates how they were constantly hungry and thirsty, going so far as to sell to each other rats as delicacies. Leaving Magellan's Strait, Pigafetta notes, the ships entered the

> Pacific Sea, where we remained three months and twenty days without taking on board provisions or any other refreshments, and we ate only old biscuit turned to powder, all full of worms and stinking of the urine which the rats had made on it, having eaten the good. And we drank water impure and yellow. We ate also ox hides which were very hard because of the sun,

rain, and wind. And we left them four or five days in the sea, then laid them for a short time on embers, and so we ate them. And of the rats, which were sold for half an écu apiece, some of us could not get enough. (1969: 57)

On the long and painful way towards the north-western Pacific, Magellan's ships sighted islands, which they named *San Pablo* and *Isla de los Tiburones* (Shark Island). These have today been identified as Fakahina, which is an atoll of the Tuamotus, and Flint Island, located north of Tahiti.[20] As these islands seemed to the explorers to be dry and uninhabited, they called them *Las Desaventuradas* (Unfortunate Islands).[21]

Three months after they had entered the ocean, Magellan's fleet finally saw some islands, which looked fertile, in the southern Marianas and the fleet landed on one of them, which was probably Guam.[22] There, in what was the first contact between Europeans and Micronesians, the islanders gave Magellan's men water and food. The Marianese, however, soon started to take everything they could, including a skiff, from the ship and their islands were consequently christened *Islas de los Ladrones* (Isles of Thieves). To recover the skiff, Magellan landed with forty armed men and burned houses, destroyed canoes and killed seven men. This, indeed, was the first 'fatal contact' between Pacific islanders and Europeans.

From the Marianas, the three-ship fleet arrived in Samar, now the Philippines, which were named by the explorers, *Islas de San Lázaro*, as it was St Lazarus' day. Just over two decades later, these islands were rechristened with the name still used today, the Philippines, in honour of King Philip II.[23] In the Philippines, Magellan's men landed in Cebu and signed a treaty of friendship with its ruler or rajah, Humabón. To demonstrate their friendship, Magellan committed himself and his men to fighting Humabón's enemy in Mactán, with dire results for the Spaniards. As the fighting broke out, the explorers had to run for their ships and, to the dismay of his crew, Magellan was hacked to death. Pigafetta's words, though somewhat overwrought, are often quoted to signal that event: 'On this all at once rushed upon him with lances of iron and of bamboo and with these javelins, so that they slew our mirror, our light, our comfort, and our true guide' (1969: 88).

After Magellan's death, which perhaps followed the betrayal of the slave Enrique de Malacca, the rajah of Cebu hosted a banquet for the Spanish, during which some of the officers were killed. The remaining officers departed, seeing from the ships one of their own, Juan Serrano, tied up and cursing them for abandoning him to his fate. There were now so few survivors that they could not operate the three remaining ships, and were forced to burn one, the *Concepción*. In the *Trinidad* and *Victoria*, the rest of the crew reached the Moluccas by way of Brunei, and there the *Trinidad* had to be left behind to be repaired in Tidore. Juan Sebastián Elcano, who had been chosen as captain of the *Victoria* after Magellan's death, took the remaining men back to Spain. The ship, which had left the Moluccas with, according to Pigafetta, some forty-seven Europeans and thirteen Indians, arrived back in San Lúcar de Barrameda with a mere eighteen men and three Indians on 6 September 1522. There, they were to savour the glory of being the first world circumnavigators, as well as receiving a handsome sum of money following the sale of their cargo of spices.

While the *Victoria* made its way to Spain via the Cape of Good Hope, the *Trinidad*, after having undergone the necessary repairs, attempted to return to Mexico. The voyage was arduous and ill-fated, because of the trade winds and the monsoon season. As they could not progress, the Spaniards asked for asylum in Tidore, where the Portuguese put them in prison and seized their journals, documents and maps. After four months of incarceration, the captain, Gómez de Espinosa, and some of his men started the journey to Spain via Asia overland. Gómez de Espinosa was next heard of from Cochin (Indochina) in 1525, from where he directed a letter to the Holy Roman Emperor, Charles V, informing him that he had been a prisoner for ten months. After a total of two years in Cochin, Gómez de Espinosa arrived in Lisbon in 1526, where the Portuguese put him in prison for a further seven months. Fortunately, Gómez de Espinosa lived several more years to enjoy the yearly pension awarded to him by the emperor for his loyal services.

In spite the catastrophic loss of life, Magellan's journey stands out as one of the most impressive sea voyages of all time. The geographical and navigational knowledge gained from the journey remained quite unparalleled, and was not to be furthered for many decades, if not centuries.[24] After this outstanding journey, the following expeditions have faded into insignificance in many books dedicated to Pacific exploration, even though they are certainly remarkable in many aspects. The first expedition sent to the Pacific after the return of Magellan's *Victoria* was led by the Commander of the Order of Santiago, Fray García Jofre de Loaísa. Also sponsored by the Spanish crown, Loaísa led a disastrous mission from La Coruña in Spain, where a *Casa de Contratación* (house of trade) for dealing with the colonies and destined specifically for the Spice Islands was briefly set up to supplement Seville's *Casa*. The seven-ship fleet, directed to the Moluccas and the Philippines along the Magellanic route, left on 24 July 1525, with Juan Sebastián Elcano as second-in-command and pilot. Loaísa led the *Capitana*, named *Santa María de la Victoria*, which was the largest of them all, and Elcano, the *Sancti Spiritus*. The remaining ships were: *Anunciada, San Gabriel*, the caravels, *Santa María del Parral* and *San Lesmes*, and the pinnace ('patache') *Santiago*.²⁵

Among Loaísa's crew was Andrés de Urdaneta, working as an accountant. Later, as an Augustinian friar, Urdaneta accompanied Miguel López de Legazpi to the Philippines in 1565 and became famous for directing the westward voyage to New Mexico. By way of contrast, Loaísa's expedition across the Atlantic was a complete failure. Contact was lost with the *Capitana* after a storm and Elcano commanded the remaining ships into Rio Gallegos where the whole fleet ran aground, surviving thanks to the favourable tide. In the strait, his own ship, *Sancti Spiritus*, beached and was lost, so that its men had to be distributed among the other ships. As bad weather continued, the *Anunciada* and the *San Gabriel* turned back and the *San Lesmes* was dragged by the prevailing winds to 55° south, discovering on the way the southernmost tip of South America, thereafter named Cape Horn.

Misfortune continued after Loaísa's fleet left the strait. Following another storm, the *Santiago* decided to head for New Spain, where it arrived on 25 July 1526. The *San Lesmes* disappeared, never to be seen again, and the *Santa María del Parral* was shipwrecked on Sanguin Island, between the Isles of Celebes and Mindanao. Only three ships survived and were picked up by an expedition sent for the purpose, which was led by Álvaro de Saavedra. Indeed, Loaísa's whole voyage was 'a succession of disasters', as Spate indicates in his eloquent summary of the ill-fated journey:

> The *Sancti Spiritus*, with Elcano, was wrecked at the Cape of the Eleven Thousand Virgins, though all but nine men were saved; two ships deserted; the caravel *San Lesmes* was driven to 55°S and saw what 'appeared to be the end of the land', presumably the first sighting of Staten Land, so named by Schouten and Le Maire in 1616. The *San Lesmes* rejoined, and four ships entered the Pacific, to be scattered within a few days by a great tempest. The pinnace *Santiago* made its way to New Spain; the *San Lesmes* disappeared, and its wreck on Amanu in the Tuomotus [sic] may be taken as proven by the discovery there of four cannon. Another caravel, *Santa Maria del Parrel* [sic], reached Mindanao on its own; the few survivors of wreck and mutiny became captives of the islanders, and of the three picked up by Saavedra one was hanged for mutiny and one went bush. (1979: 90)

The fate of the *San Lesmes* has been the focus of much debate, especially following Robert Langdon's hypothesis. Langdon believed that the ship's survivors became the ancestors of many Polynesians living now in various island groups, whose difference in skin colour would be due to their Mediterranean genes. Although the case has neither been proved nor disproved, Langdon's account remains far fetched, and his material evidence was rather slim. Nonetheless, remains of shipwrecks and survivors from some of these voyages are more than possible, even if the men did not multiply with the fervour that Langdon attributed to them.[26]

From this voyage, as far as we know, only one island, Taongi, in the Marshalls, which was called by the Spaniards *San Bartolomé*, was sighted and, although this afforded some new geographical knowledge, no engagements with Pacific islanders took place there. The *Santa María de la Victoria* reached Tidore on 1 January 1527, after another laborious lap in which Loaísa, Elcano and others died. During this part of the journey, the fleet sighted Taongi, in the Marshall archipelago, and landed on the Marianas. There, they rescued a sailor lost from Magellan's expedition, who proved useful to them because of his knowledge of the local language. Their struggle to survive continued and, once in the Moluccas, the Spaniards fought with the Portuguese before being rescued by the expedition led by Álvaro de Saavedra y Cerón, returning to Spain in 1536, some seven years after the Moluccas had been sold to Portugal in 1529.

The rescuers of the remainder of Loaísa's fleet were led by a cousin of Mexico's most famous conquistador, Hernán Cortés, the aforementioned Álvaro de Saavedra. On orders of the Emperor Charles V, Cortés armed a fleet of three ships and around 110 men to be commanded by his kinsman, now newly promoted to captain, to search for the lost ships of Loaísa's journey. Thus, two years after Loaísa's expedition, in 1526, Cortés sent Saavedra from New Spain (Mexico) to the Moluccas and then on to New Guinea (1527–29). Besides discovering the fate of Loaísa's ships, the main objective of the expeditions was to ransom Juan Serrano in Cebu if he were still alive. The total cost was met by Hernán Cortés, and, for all we know, was not repaid during his lifetime.

In the letters that Cortés wrote to Saavedra, he urged him to treat the indigenous peoples with consideration as vassals of the emperor (Landín 1992: 1, 227).[27] This goodwill was to be facilitated by the accompanying cargo, which included an abundance of artefacts and trinkets for barter and gifts. Altogether, the cost of these items was nearly as much as that of the weapons or the food on board, which corroborates the importance attached to the possible exchanges with locals.[28] Saavedra's fleet left Zihuatanejo (Mexico) on 31 October 1527, soon losing sight of two of its ships. Only one, the *Florida*, reached the intended destination in the Moluccas, where the men had to fight against the Portuguese. They tried to return to New Spain with cloves, but could not do so because of the contrary winds, and turned back to Tidore. Around New Year, Saavedra found several islands, namely, the Kepulaun Schouten, one island off Papua-New Guinea, Admiralty, Bismarck, Truk, one island from the Carolines' group and New Guinea. Repeating Loaísa's error, Saavedra unsuccessfully tried to land in Guam, reaching Mindanao on 1 February 1528.

After he had the ship repaired, Saavedra departed on 3 May 1529, attempting to return to New Spain a second time. He passed by Ponape Island, which he named *Los Pintados*, as well as another island, which he named *Los Jardines*. Saavedra probably sailed very close to Hawaii, and died in the vicinity of this island, after which his men failed to find a way east and had to turn back to Gilolo in the Moluccas, arriving at the end of 1529. Their reception in the Oceanic islands that they visited, as ever, ranged from friendly to utterly hostile (Landín 1992: 1. 266).

Saavedra's journey was followed by two equally luckless voyages led by Hernando Grijalva (1536–37) and Ruy López de Villalobos (1542–45).[29] The unfortunate Grijalva was commissioned by Cortés to take two ships from Peru, perhaps to assist first Pizarro and then Saavedra, as well as to discover new land and islands in the South Pacific.[30] As no instructions for the voyage have been preserved, it is uncertain what the main objective was, although Landín infers from the size of the expedition that it was more suitable for coastal navigation, which leads him to deduce that Grijalva must have decided of his own accord to proceed westwards (1992: 1. 284–5).

Grijalva's small fleet left Acapulco in 1536, sailing towards Peru in two ships: the *Santiago*, with twenty-two sailors, as well as some soldiers and Indians whose number is nowhere cited, and the pinnace *Trinidad* with seventeen men commanded by Fernando de Alvarado. The *Trinidad* soon returned to Mexico, while the *Santiago*, after arriving in Peru, received orders from Pizarro and left Paita in April 1537, sailing westwards. Grijalva's men, however, seem to have been disgruntled with the choice of route, pointing out the scarcity of supplies. On their way across the Pacific, the fleet saw islands from the Christmas and Kiribati groups, after which Grijalva decided to turn back, but was prevented from doing so by the trade winds. Some of his men indicated their preference to sail towards the Moluccas, but Grijalva refused, which seems to have increased the general discontent on board and one sailor, Miguel Noble, encouraged by others, rose in mutiny, killing Grijalva.

Without their captain, Grijalva's men sailed towards the Moluccas under the command of Esteban de Castilla, stopping on the way at the island of Ganaise, where they were met by a canoe with locals wishing to trade. There, one Spanish sailor killed an islander with his sword and the rest retired, only to meet the islanders and be attacked by them again. All but two Spaniards were killed on the spot, and these two were rescued two years later by the Portuguese Governor of the Moluccas, Antonio de Galvao. As Landín indicates, Grijalva must have been the unluckiest explorer in Oceania for not only did he meet an untimely and treacherous death, but his discoveries in a sea full of islands were nil (1992: 1. 301).

Undeterred by the constant failures, New Spain's viceroy, Antonio de Mendoza, issued instructions for a new voyage to the 'Especiería' in 1542, naming Ruy López de Villalobos as 'captain general'. Mendoza commanded Villalobos to go to Puerto de Navidad, in today's Cihuatlán (Jalisco, México), and take charge of the six ships destined for the voyage. Villalobos was instructed to send back one of the ships with news once a suitable place had been found; to consult his officers on important matters and not to prevent those who wished to stay in the newly-discovered lands from so doing if he were to return (Landín 1992: 2. 320–1). Villalobos also issued instructions for his captains, dated 22 October 1542.

Although Villalobos's voyage ran north of the Equator, only touching briefly in the Marianas and Marshalls, the attempts to return from the Philippines carry some relevance to the exploration of the South Pacific. The six ships – the *Capitana*, *Santiago*, and the *San Jorge*, *San Antonio*, *San Juan de Letrán*, *San Cristóbal* and *San Martín* – were staffed by some 370 to 400 men.[31] Leading an expedition which was probably as ill-fated as those preceding it, Villalobos left Mexico's Puerto de la Navidad on 1 November 1542. On its way, the fleet saw the islands of Revillagigedo, Rongelap atoll, Wotje and Kwajalein in the Marshalls (which he named *Colares*), another island in the Carolines, which Villalobos christened *Los Matalotes*, and *Los Arrecifes* in Palau. He arrived in Mindanao on 2 February 1543.

Villalobos tried to return to New Spain, sending Bernardo de la Torre on board the *San Juan* on 26 August 1544. De la Torre sailed past the Marianas and the Kazan Retto but was unable to continue and had to return. The journey eastwards was attempted again after the ship was repaired, this time commanded by Íñigo Ortiz de Retes. He too was forced to turn back because of the winds, but saw and named New Guinea and other islands north of it. Finally, Villalobos negotiated with the Portuguese the repatriation of the remaining members of the fleet, who had to sail back without him, as he died in Amboina in the Moluccas. Spate assesses the journey as a failure, although 'not the completely sterile failure of Grijalva's men'.[32]

One consequence of this voyage was the previously mentioned expedition of Bernardo de la Torre and his attempt to return to Mexico with the ship *San Juan de Letrán*.[33] There are some hypotheses about his failure to find a way to sail east, both of which took him around the Marianas and then north, to return to Samar (Landín 1992: 2. 368–75). Likewise, a second offshoot of Villalobos's voyage was Ortiz de Retes' journey, which took him to the north coast of New Guinea.[34]

No more Spanish expeditions were launched until 1564 when Miguel López de Legazpi sailed west from the Mexican port of La Navidad with four ships, *San Pedro*, *San Pablo*, *San Juan* and *San Lucas*, as well as a small brigantine. The expedition was organised by the Viceroy of Mexico, Luis de Velasco, and approved by Philip II, who requested the services of Andrés de Urdaneta. Having sailed with Elcano, the mature Urdaneta, who was now an Augustinian friar, was the most experienced navigator available for the voyage. While Philip II indicated that the expedition's target was 'to discover the islands of the west', in fact, as Patrick Williams observes, Philip sought to claim them back for Spain, following Magellan's landing prior to this voyage.

Legazpi's fleet consisted of five ships – the *San Pedro* or *Capitana*, which carried on board Legazpi and Urdaneta, the galleon *San Pablo*, two *pataches* (pinnaces), *San Juan de Letrán* and *San Lucas*, and a small brigantine – in which around 350 men travelled, of whom 150 were sailors and 200 were soldiers. They left on 21 November 1564, sailing past the Marianas, where they made a landfall at Guam, and the Marshalls. One of the ships disappeared during the journey, and the remaining arrived in Ibabao in the Philippines on 13 February 1565. From there, they went to some of the islands, founding San Miguel in Cebu on 8 May 1565. Legazpi remained in Cebu, ordering Urdaneta to return and seek support for the settlement of the archipelago. After encountering the usual difficulties in sailing east, the *San Pedro*, led by Urdaneta, inaugurated the route that would be followed thereafter, sailing north towards the latitude of Japan so as to avoid the trade winds. Urdaneta inferred that the trade winds of the Pacific might move in a vortex as happens in the Atlantic and reasoned that by sailing to the north before heading east, the trade winds would take him back to the west coast of North America. Consequently, Urdaneta steered his ship north to 24° and sailed down to 39° in August, reaching Acapulco in October, having lost forty-four men on the journey.

Following this journey's successful negotiation of the trade winds, the Spaniards settled in the Philippines, with subsequent journeys following the route of the Manila galleon. This trading fleet, which sailed from Acapulco from the first time in 1566, made possible regular trade across the Pacific, transporting gold on the outward journey to the Philippines and spices and merchandise on the return. This two-way commerce continued until 1815, when the Mexican War of Independence (1810–21) and the Napoleonic Wars (1804–15) stopped the galleons permanently.

Two years after Legazpi's momentous journey, the first-ever expedition directed exclusively to the South Pacific departed from the Peruvian coast of Callao. It was led by Álvaro de Mendaña, who would command a further voyage some thirty years later. Mendaña, whose voyages are studied in Chapter 2, dedicated the greatest part of his life to searching for the Southern Continent. First as a young explorer, and then with his wife, Isabel Barreto, and a team of settlers, Mendaña set out from the South American mainland to find the coveted Isles of Solomon. His project was, however, largely unsuccessful, and Mendaña ultimately met his fate in the islands to whose discovery he had dedicated so much time and energy. Along with many of his own people, Mendaña succumbed to malaria in Santa Cruz's Ndeni during the second voyage of the ocean he had explored with zest and devotion.

NOTES

1 Patrick Vinton Kirch observes that 'most (but not all) of its islands were connected to at least some other islands through network after network' (2000: 304).
2 'Strictly speaking, there was no such thing as 'the Pacific' until in 1520–21 Fernao de Magalhãis, better known as Magellan, traversed the huge expanse of waters, which then received its name' (Spate 1979: 1).
3 Serge Tcherkézoff has traced the origin of these 'racial and racist' notions to 1595, culminating in Dumont d'Urville's 'Carte de l'Océanie', explaining the effects of this division in the second chapter of his book, entitled 'Le XIXe siècle: 'L'invention du nom 'Mélanésie'. Des varietés humaines au racisme' (2004: 10, 70–104).
4 Douglas concludes that: 'these labels . . . partly reflected European prejudices about race, skin colour and degree of "civilisation". The inhabitants of the far-flung "Polynesian triangle" did share a relatively recent common origin, which produced marked similarities in language, culture and physical appearance: the term "Polynesia" is therefore appropriate culturally as well as

geographically. "Melanesia", however, is a different matter: the very term proposes skin colour as the main basis for linking hundreds of different cultures with little in common' (1993: 16).

5 'The point', Thomas emphasises, 'is not that the categories are false, but that their persistence is sustained through reiteration and redefinition, rather than on the basis of self-evident human differences' (2000: 134). Thomas analyses the implications of the Melanesian versus Polynesian in one chapter of his book, *In Oceania*, 'Melanesians and Polynesians: Ethnic Typifications Inside and Outside Anthropology' (1997: 132–55).

6 Greene's classification, according to Kirch, 'is not merely a geographic division, but one that consciously encapsulates two major epochs in the history of the Pacific islanders' (2000: 6).

7 The resulting winds 'are sufficiently strong and regular to ensure that the Pacific Islands could not have been settled by unplanned drifters alone; colonising voyages were probably purposeful and well-stocked ... In the western Pacific, especially in Melanesia, winds from a westerly direction occur more commonly during the year; hence perhaps the relative rapidity of the Lapita expansion into Polynesia' (Bellwood 1993: 9).

8 'Urdaneta, Legaspi's chief pilot, and Arellano, one of his captains, independently pioneered the return passage by sailing north of the trade-wind belt into that of constant westerlies which in 42° N brought them to the Californian coast' (Skelton 1958: 187).

9 As Raleigh Skelton remarks, this would allow them to avoid 'the belt of "brave west winds" which in latitudes higher than 25° S were contrary for vessels entering the Pacific by Magellan Strait, they could make their westing with the steady south-east trade winds from Peru or north-east trades from Mexico' (1958: 187).

10 According to Spate, these islands were variously located with differences of as much as 75 degrees (1979: 22).

11 Dava Sobel (1985) sums up Harrison's struggle with the Board of Longitude.

12 Portuguese explorers remained committed to this task in areas west of the Philippines, especially in the Moluccas and coastal India, while Dutch explorers and traders made their way into the South Pacific via Indonesia.

13 Charles's motto, as Earl Rosenthal observes, has been taken to signify his imperial designs, although it had been first created 'in 1516, during his sixteenth year when he was Duke of Burgundy and the King Designate of Spain' (1971: 204).

14 See my summary of Pacific mapping in *Producing the Pacific* (2005: 69–99).

15 The dates in brackets are the regnal periods, while their birth and death dates are, for Charles, 1500–58, for Philip II, 1527–98 and for Philip III, 1578–1621. My main source for the summary of these journeys is Landín (1992: 1. 25ff).

16 Urdaneta may have been preceded by Alfonso de Arellano, who left the Philippines at the same time and arrived earlier in Mexico, although the discovery

has always been attributed to Urdaneta because of the precision of his notes (Landín 1992: 1. 26). In the first volume of his monumental work, Landín deals with the expeditions of Magellan, Gómez de Espinosa, García Jofre de Loaísa, Saavedra and Hernando de Grijalva, while the voyages of Ruy López de Villalobos, Bernardo de la Torre, Ortiz de Retes, Legazpi and Mendaña occupy his second volume. The last volume is dedicated to Quirós's journey, the eighteenth-century voyages to Easter Island and Tahiti sponsored by Viceroy Amat and Mourelle de la Rúa's journey to Vava'u.

17 As Skelton writes, 'Not for the first or last time in the history of discovery, it was a discrepancy between what the venturer expected and what he found that significantly enriched human experience and knowledge. To the world map Magellan added the Pacific ocean, which occupies one third of the earth's surface' (1958: 5).

18 Other sources include the narrative of Francisco de Albo, the original of which is at the *Archivo General de Indias* (Seville), and that of Ginés de Mafra (1542), which is held at the *Biblioteca Nacional de España* (Madrid) and was printed in 1920. Contemporary summaries include those of Maximiliano Transylvanus, Gonzalo Fernández de Oviedo, João de Barros, Antonio de Brito, Fernando Lopes de Castanheda, Francisco López de Gómara, Antonio Galvão and Pedro Mártir de Anglería. For a list of reports and versions of the journey, see Landín (1992: 1. 118–19).

19 'It is conceivable that Magellan's papers were in the *Trinidad* and either seized with her by the Portuguese in November 1522 (and subsequently lost) or destroyed by her commander before his surrender. In his report about the voyage, which was held at Valladolid in October 1522, Elcano stated that he did not write while Magellan was alive' (Skelton 1958: 6).

20 I follow Landín in this identification, though others, such as Skelton and Samuel Morrison, believe the first island, *San Pablo*, to be Pukapuka (1992: 1. 128 n. 1).

21 These islands found their way into maps at the time, including those of Sebastian Münster (1547). They are situated in the Tuamotus, in today's French Polynesia, still bearing the eloquent name of Îles de Désappointement.

22 Landín explores three hypotheses: the first would be Anatahan and the group Saipan-Tinian, the second Saipan and Rota, and the third, which he considers more plausible, Rota and Guam (1992: 1. 131–3).

23 Patrick Williams traces in detail the incorporation of the Philippines into the Philip II's domains in the context of his imperial world view, noting that the islands 'were significant for Philip at a number of levels. Most obviously, they had been named for him; in 1542 the explorer Ruy López de Villalobos had christened the island of Leyte as "Filipina" in honour of Philip, who was then the heir to the thrones of Spain. Over subsequent years the name had come to apply to the whole archipelago of seven thousand islands' (forthcoming).

I am grateful to Williams for allowing me to quote from this manuscript before its publication.
24 Spate provides this comprehensive summary: 'Magellan's voyage, whatever his own initial beliefs, ensured the final destruction of the lingering remnants of the Ptolemaic world: the achievement is writ large on contemporary maps ... No other single voyage has ever added so much to the dimension of the world' (1979: 57).
25 The most important journals from Loaísa's journey are those of Martín de Uriarte, which was published by Fernández de Navarrete (1825–37), and three from Urdaneta, two of which were also transcribed by Navarrete. For sources on this voyage, see Landín (1992: 1. 198–9).
26 Roger Hervé (1982) goes even further than Langdon, assuming the *San Lesmes* to have discovered Australia and New Zealand.
27 According to Landín, the men carried maps and plans made by Magellan (1992: 229). For sources on this voyage, see Landín (1992: 1. 235–7).
28 The objects were mostly mirrors, blankets and clothing, some of which were produced in Mexico (Landín 1992: 1. 232).
29 For sources on Grijalva's voyage, see Landín (1992: 1. 281–2). The most important journal is that of Miguel Noble, who survived the expedition, a copy of which is kept in the *Colección Navarrete* of the *Museo Naval* in Madrid.
30 For sources on this voyage, see Landín (1992: 1. 281–2).
31 The most important journal, that of García de Escalante Alvarado, is kept at the *Archivo General de Indias* (Seville), with a manuscript copy held by the *Real Academia de Historia* (Madrid). None of these accounts has been published other than in Martín Fernández de Navarrete's nineteenth-century collection of copied documents. Navarrete published Fray Jerónimo Santisteban's account, whereas other sources that Navarrete prepared, which he never published, are kept in Volume XV of his collection at the *Museo Naval* (Madrid). For sources on this voyage, see Landín (1992: 2. 325–8).
32 'A great deal had been added, mostly by de la Torre, to knowledge of the Islas de Poniente; Villalobos, who had a taste for toponymy, named Mindanao "Caesarea Karoli" for the Emperor, because of its greatness; the smaller islands to the north he called the "Filipinas", for the prince who became Philip II' (Spate 1979: 98).
33 For sources on the voyage of Bernardo de la Torre, see Landín (1992: 2. 363).
34 For sources on Ortiz de Retes' and Villalobos' journeys, see Landín (1992: 2. 381).

2 Spanish voyages to the Pacific 1567–1606

I Mendaña and the Solomons (1567–68)

In spite of the efforts and discoveries of the journeys outlined in Chapter 1, the fleet led by Álvaro de Mendaña in 1567 can rightly be considered as the first voyage to set out with the specific intention of exploring the South Pacific. Mendaña sailed in order to seek out and chart the mysterious southern land mass, referred to as *Terra Australis Incognita*, which had been hypothesised for centuries before. As is now well known, Mendaña found no Southern Continent, though he discovered and named Santa Isabel, San Cristóbal, Guadalcanal and other islands in the group called the Solomon Islands. These islands only received that name, however, following Mendaña's voyage because his search was associated with that of the Solomonic Ophir, the biblical place where the gold for the construction of the Temple of Solomon had been found, and which had been sought by many explorers.[1]

Mendaña's expedition left El Callao in Peru on 19 November 1567, spent six months in the Solomons and returned to Peru via Mexico on 11 September 1569 (Figure 2.1). Mendaña led a further voyage towards the Solomons in 1595 but was unable to find the islands again. In fact, because of the problem of setting longitude, the Solomons eluded travellers for a further two hundred years. They were only rediscovered after they had already become a mirage in the minds of many who doubted their existence.[2] The nineteenth-century editors of the documents related to their discovery for the Hakluyt Society, Lord Amherst of Hackney and Basil Thomson, class the 'loss' of the Solomons as one of the most puzzling chapters of European exploration.[3]

The Viceroy of Peru, López García de Castro, selected his nephew, the young Mendaña, who was then 26 years old, to lead the expedition to find the Southern Continent and the Islands of Solomon in the South Pacific. For the Viceroy, according to a letter cited by Amancio Landín, one of the reasons for sponsoring the voyage was to provide employment for the

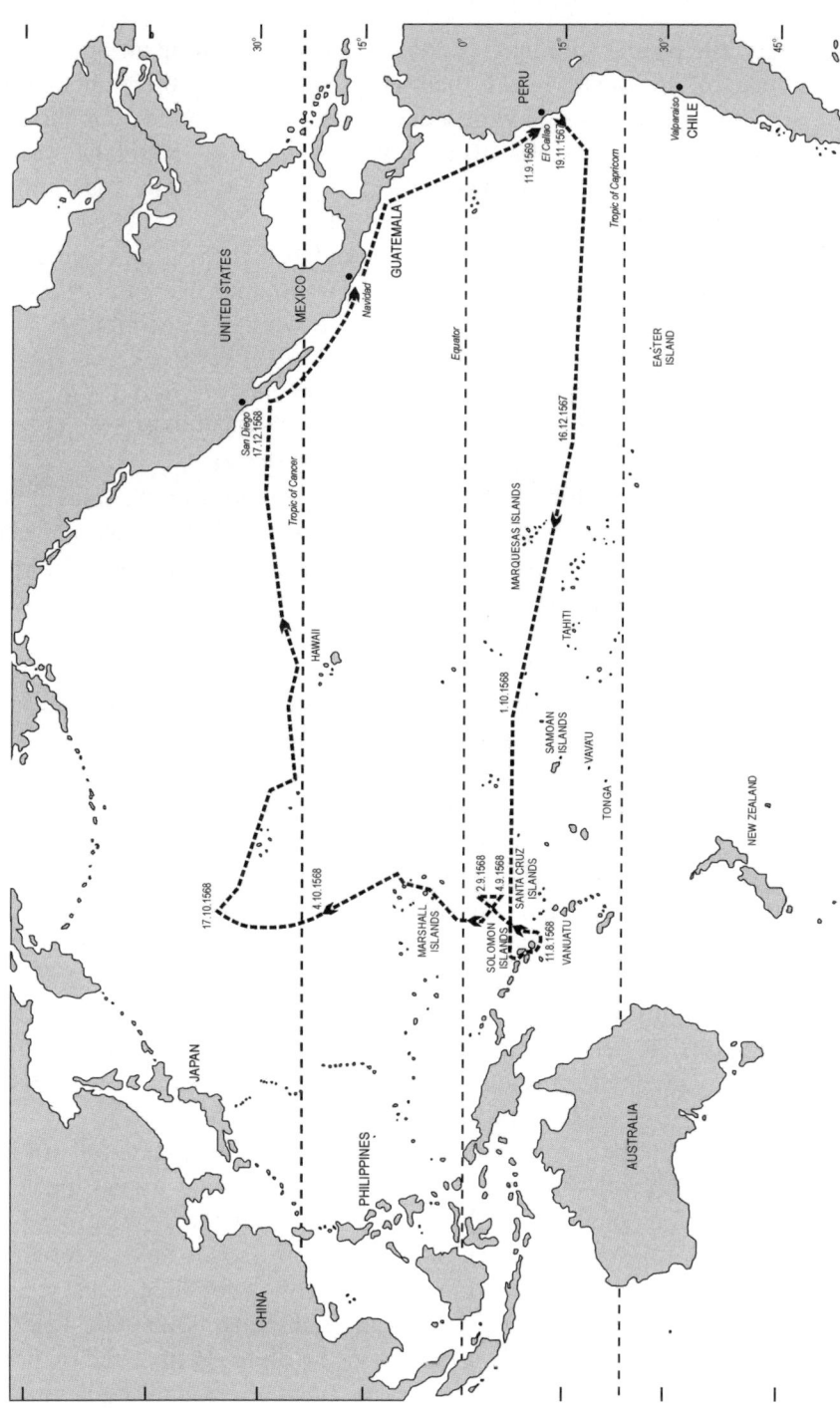

2.1 Itinerary of the first Pacific voyage of Álvaro de Mendaña to the Isles of Solomon (1567–68).

many idle people who lived in Peru, who were awaiting an opportunity to take to the sea and enrich themselves (1945: 27). Of these unemployed men, some 170–80 sailed with Mendaña in two ships: *Todos los Santos* or *Almiranta* and *Los Reyes*, also known as *Capitana*. Mendaña was the captain or governor of the fleet (also referred to as *adelantado*), and the position of camp master (*maese* or *maestre de campo*) was filled by Pedro Ortega, who was originally from the Andalusian town of Guadalcanal, after which the famous Solomonic island was named. Hernán Gallego was the *piloto mayor* (main pilot) of the fleet, while the redoubtable Pedro Sarmiento de Gamboa was captain of the ship *Los Reyes* (*Capitana*).[4] Four Franciscan friars accompanied the expedition that traversed the uncharted southwest Pacific in eighty days, making the first landfall at Santa Isabel in the Solomon group of islands on 9 February 1568.

The contacts with the inhabitants of the Solomons were fraught with misunderstandings, often resulting in tragedy for them, in spite of many sincere attempts to prevent that from happening. There were, however, some cultural exchanges, and we should not minimise the efforts made by sailors, officers, friars and by Mendaña himself to make peace with the Solomonians. Nonetheless, it is obvious from the narratives that even the most considerate among the Spaniards assumed their civilisation to be superior in every aspect of life and their religion to be incontestably the rightful one.

Also important in practical terms, and in light of the consequences, was the dire need for food on the part of the Spaniards, who considered that the islanders ought either to supply or succour them. This was sometimes done by mutual accord or barter but, when that failed, the Spanish sought consent from the friars on board to use other means to take whatever they needed. Thus, when the necessary food was denied, the explorers regularly appropriated some supplies from people who seem to be facing scarcity themselves. To achieve their aims, the Spaniards used various resources, including leaving tokens for the 'trade' or taking canoes or people, including children, as ransom for the required provisions.

Information about this voyage comes from various sources, all of which deal at length with the mutual encounters, giving many interesting details of life in the Solomons at the time. These accounts were gathered and published in Spanish between 1963 and 1973 by Celsus Kelly, in a remarkable archival effort of location and transcription for which later scholars must always be grateful. As a Franciscan friar living in Australia, Kelly was trying to establish his order's history in the South Pacific, and dedicated most of his life to the arduous task of tracing and locating documents spread from archives in Italy, Spain, Peru and the USA. Kelly was successful in finding a good number of extant documents relating to this journey, including Mendaña's long account, which is incomplete.[5]

From Mendaña, we have one short and one long account, both of which were transcribed and edited by Kelly: one addressed to the King of Spain and another to the Governor of Peru. Kelly also edited two narratives from the pilot Hernán Gallego, a further account by Pedro Sarmiento de Gamboa and the longest of them all from the hand of the treasurer of the fleet, Gómez Hernández Catoira.[6] The information in these sources normally echo each others, differing only in length but not in the selection or interpretation of events. Addressed to the Governor of Peru, García de Castro, Catoira's commissioned report is the most detailed and, although syntactically cumbersome in its original Spanish, it is the source mostly quoted in this section, as it follows Mendaña's very closely.

In order to highlight the relationships and exchanges which are the main focus of this book, particular attention is paid to the dealings taking place during the first part of the journey, until the first of the three expeditions of the brigantine departed to explore the islands. Thereafter, as most of the events repeat the pattern established in these initial contacts, they are summarised, only noting some details of relevance to my analysis.

According to all the extant sources, Mendaña's fleet departed from the harbour of El Callao in *Ciudad de los Reyes* (Lima) on 19 November 1567, sailing north-west until they reached the latitude of New Spain (Mexico). The interesting fact that the crew included African slaves as well as Creoles and *mestizos* (that is, of mixed Spanish and Indian blood) is something we find early in the narrative, when a man described by Catoira as a 'mestizo' fell overboard. After one hour of strenuous efforts, the Spaniards managed to rescue him when he was nearly exhausted.

The fleet discovered a small island and, following their religious customs, called it *Jesús*, 'because we discovered it in his name' (Catoira 1965: 32–4).[7] Mendaña ordered a check to see whether the island was inhabited and the sailors tried to get closer but could not reach the shore, when they were approached by seven canoes with approximately seven men in each of them. As they got closer, these 'Indians' returned to the shore, even though, as Mendaña recorded, the Spaniards attempted to attract them back to their ship by making 'signs, calling them with a handkerchief' (Mendaña 1965: 4). The explorers could not find a suitable place to drop anchor and their approach was further hampered by storms in spite of the gestures made by the locals from the land, using fire to help guide the Spanish ships (Catoira 1965: 35).

Those on the *Capitana* lost sight of the other ship, the *Almiranta*, and tried to approach the shore, but the storms prevented them from doing so and the pilots recommended giving up to avoid damaging the ships. Mendaña indicated his wish to reach the shore in order to take possession of the island in the king's name and to provide the crew with fresh water. However, in this matter, Mendaña accepted the pilot's recommendations and they left in search of a more suitable place to anchor (Catoira 1965: 36).

Fifteen days later, on 1 February 1568, the pilot, Hernán Gallego, saw land but, as they approached the shore, the ships encountered dangerous shoals which were christened *Baxos de la Candelaria*, a name which appears up to the eighteenth century in maps, including those of the renowned French cartographer Robert de Vaugoundy. As ever so often with names given by the Spaniards, this one was chosen on account of its religious significance, this time in honour of the Virgin of the Candelaria, whose feast is celebrated the following day (Catoira 1965: 38).[8] Eight days later, the fleet sailed around the island, which appeared from the distance to be a large one, in order to take much-needed wood and water on board (Mendaña 1965: 5). Once again, however, they met with many difficulties and did not manage to find a harbour because of the reefs and the storms. They tried again two days later and, as they neared the coast, they could see crabs, coconuts, and signs of food and water, which delighted the men on board after the long days on the ship. Finally, on 7 February, the Spaniards managed to reach one of the reefs, but it still took two further days before they could land. As, according to Mendaña, they found a 'harbour with no danger whatsoever' following a bright star, the bay was called by the name it still known, *Bahia de la Estrella* ('Bay of the Star') (Mendaña 1965: 5, 11; 1967: 197).

At Estrella's Bay, the Spaniards were received by islanders in canoes, which Catoira described as half-moon shaped. These men carried bows and arrows, as well as local weapons consisting of a stick with a large stone at the end, which the Spaniards called 'macanas' ('truncheons' or 'billy-clubs').[9] Though fully armed, the islanders attempted to 'talk about peace', according to Catoira, whose narrative indicates that the Spanish inferred those intention from gestures. Mendaña's account to the Governor of Peru details this first exchange, indicating how the well-armed Solomonians first approached in their canoes. When asked for the *tauriqui*, Mendaña ordered his men to point to himself to signify that he was their chief, but, as the islanders still refused to board the ship, in order to 'talk peace' Mendaña threw the islanders some red bonnets, which they gave to their chiefs, asking thereafter for more.[10] As ever in these engagements, gesticulation and, more importantly, gifts were used as the first means of communication, in an attempt to set a tone of camaraderie and encourage hospitality.

The invitations to board were only heeded after a bold sailor, of his own will, threw himself overboard and swam to meet the islanders, reaching their canoes and boarding one of them. On seeing this, some climbed up to the ship with apparent fear, although Mendaña tried to soothe it, embracing them and displaying signs of 'love'. While on board, the islanders were offered food, which they ate, and wine, which they did not find to their taste. They were also taught some Spanish words, with all narrators of these events commending their pronunciation, and they imitated the sign of the cross, 'and one of them did it many times' (Catoira 1965: 40).[11] This inaugural scene concluded with the Spaniards teaching the islanders some Christian prayers. In this manner the Spaniards established the pattern to follow in further encounters, in which they displayed the missionary zeal that characterises these journeys.

Throughout these engagements, the demonstrations of mutual friendship and welcoming were ratified and sealed by the Spaniards offering gifts, including food, wine, beads, bonnets and other things, which were all 'well received'. However, these exchanges were not as gratuitous as might appear at first sight, for gift-giving, as Marcel Mauss's pioneering study showed, entails a set of mutual obligations, which need to be followed rigorously.[12] This aspect did not escape either of the parties who, though acknowledging the goodwill that accompanied donations, recognised that these would have to be reciprocated in some way or other.

The initial gift-giving continued until the islanders started taking from the ship items which had not been offered to them, throwing them into their canoes. This annoyed the Spaniards greatly, especially when one of them tried to steal the ship's bell: 'and would have thrown it out if it had not been taken away from him' (Catoira 1965: 40).[13] After this, the explorers sent Juan Manríquez with some soldiers and sailors on the pilot boat ('*batel*') to look for a place to anchor the ship, and some of the islanders went with him while others stayed on the ship. The party could not find a suitable harbour but met with other islanders who appeared to be making inhospitable signs to them, forcing the explorers to give up their enterprise. Nonetheless, as they returned to the boat, the local chief showed sadness at their departure, urging them to return and indicating by gestures that he would give them food and water (Catoira 1965: 40; Mendaña 1967: 196). Once again, misunderstanding seems to have prevailed and the

Spaniards admitted their failure to interpret accurately the signs given by the islanders.

Eventually, the pilot, Gallego, indicated a place where they could take the ship and they discussed whether it would be suitable. As Mendaña trusted Gallego, they landed there and proceeded to give the island the name it still bears *Ysla de Santa Ysabel*, chosen because the Spaniards had left Peru on her saint's day and they felt that she had been a good 'advocate' who had led them safely to the harbour (Catoira 1965: 42; Mendaña 1967: 198). Initially, Isabel's islanders did not seem friendly towards the newcomers, an attitude that was probably determined by the fact that they had already been the victims of various incursions on their land, which normally resulted in loss for them. The newly-arrived Spaniards, according to Matthew Spriggs, followed in the steps of Polynesians, whose voyages and settlement on some Oceanic islands had resulted in mass killings, as well as slavery for many.[14]

At Isabel, the islanders observed the visitors with fear, which probably increased when the Spaniards fired into the air. After landing, Mendaña, helped by some officers and the Franciscan friars, planted a cross before which they all prayed, following which they performed a ceremony of possession that would be repeated in all the remaining islands. In this way, as had been done throughout the Americas, the Spanish ratified to themselves that they were taking control of the island in the name of the king, in accordance with their customary proceedings: 'the General took possession of the land in the name of His Majesty and the necessary procedures were followed' (Catoira 1965: 42). Like Catoira, Mendaña's account relates that, soon after they arrived, the Spaniards went ashore to plant a cross carried by the Franciscan Françisco de Gálvez. Afterwards, Mendaña took possession 'of all that land in the name of Your Majesty, after having prayed and sung the hymn *Vexilla regis prodeunt* (1965: 7). This famous hymn, which was written by Venantius Fortunatus in the sixth century AD, was intoned regularly during these voyages, especially when carrying a banner or a cross.[15]

Spanish performances and rituals continued with the celebration of masses the following day, after which the Spaniards met the chief of the area, whom Catoira refers to as 'Bylebanarra', and who came from a village called Samba.[16] Bile-banarra, who is thereafter referred to by Mendaña as Bile and will be here named likewise, was marked as chief by the regalia that he wore, which the journals describe in some detail. Apart from a painted face, Bile's attire consisted of a headdress of white and coloured feathers and bracelets of bones around his wrists, which revealed hands described as being white as alabaster.[17] Bile brought with him coconuts to offer as a mark of friendship to welcome the newcomers, and Mendaña reciprocated his generosity. The islanders then made signs of peace, imitating those already shown to them by the Spaniards until they heard 'a black man playing a flute' and performed 'a dance never seen before' (Catoira 1965: 43).

As with the gifts of food and trinkets, music was here used as a means of communication and exchange. To this end, the islanders regaled the Spaniards with songs played on cane instruments made of various sizes, which Catoira likened to European organs. The Solomonians also made sounds with shells, which they called '*coflis*', and were used to transport information across the islands. The explorers, in turn, corresponded with performances of their own, playing the trumpet, drum and fife while the soldiers sang accompanied by *vihuelas*. The reciprocity of this exchange was acknowledged by the islanders, who showed surprise and pleasure while dancing to the Spanish tunes (Catoira 1965: 44; Mendaña 1967: 199–200).

Though ignorant of each other's language, communication at this level was made possible by mutual effort and a degree of goodwill. In a similarly friendly, though at times patronising, mood, Catoira commended the islanders' pronunciation, mentioning that both parties could converse about visible things, such as the sky. Mendaña also referred to this fact, praising the 'indios' 'because they pronounce our sounds as clearly as we do', which was corroborated by a local man's clear articulation of a Christian prayer (Catoira 1965: 7; Mendaña 1967: 195).[18] The Spanish missionary inclinations were fuelled by the ease with which the islanders pronounced and memorised religious words, which Catoira compared favourably with Amerindians from Peru, concluding that it would be simple to acquaint them with 'our Catholic Holy Faith' (1965: 43).

The exchange of gifts, trinkets, music and words was complemented by the swapping of names, a custom that signals honour and amity in many Pacific islands. Thus, Mendaña became Bile and vice versa, with both happy with the exchange. However, Bile was not the sole chief on the island and, as the Spaniards heard mass, other islanders came with a different *tauriqui*, Meta, who did not seem to be as well-disposed towards the visitors. Other chiefs, whose relation with each other seems to have been at odds most of the time, are mentioned thereafter, and the Spaniards tried to use their internal division to favour those that they considered their friends, very much as they had done in conquering the great empires of Mexico and Peru.

During the initial days, then, the relationship between Spanish and islanders was cordial, with the indigenous people appearing to have been favourably impressed by Mendaña's generosity and his treatment of them. As time passed and pressure on food supplies mounted, tensions between the two groups gradually increased. This was a pattern that would be repeated and the islanders would shoot arrows when they saw the Spaniards approaching or when they were asked for food. After this, one or more of their numbers might be killed by Spanish guns, the harquebus, while the rest fled to higher land pursued by the Spaniards, who then took food from the islanders' stores.

Until this started to happen, the Spaniards enjoyed a good relationship with the islanders of Santa Isabel, as shown by exchanges of gifts and bartering of goods. In fact, Bile went so far as to offer that Mendaña be carried on his men's shoulders, which Mendaña refused, and the islanders came every day with some food, though they showed a some degree of suspicion toward the newcomers by always going on board armed.

The scarcity of food and the density of the population in these islands were probably the main reasons for the mutual misunderstandings that soon started to occur, with the groups on the island reacting against the foreign presence. Increasingly, as the Spaniards extended their stay, which would amount to three months, some islanders displayed an overtly hostile attitude. Bile attributed this antagonism to other islanders who, he said, wanted to kill the Spaniards and eat them, indicating that he had refused to join in with this. However, as Bile did not return in the days following his statement, the Spaniards assumed that he had joined in the 'treason' planned by the others (Catoira 1965: 45; Mendaña 1967: 201).

Besides the errors or abuse in trading food or gift-giving, the different value systems of the parties involved also infused some engagements, which may be seen as failed exchanges. These included the offer of women and of human flesh by the Solomonians, which caused a degree of friction. The first time women were offered was after the Spanish had asked for, and been refused, water. To their surprise, women were brought to them, whom they overtly rejected, making eloquent gestures, such as spitting on the floor, to make themselves understood. According to all the accounts, the Spanish attitude towards women puzzled the islanders so much that, when the Spaniards retired to urinate, they were followed to see whether they were men because, according to Catoira, the islanders did not know how to judge their attitude (1965: 45).[19]

Relations continued to worsen while the Spaniards remained on the island repairing their boats and awaiting the return of the brigantine, which was sent to explore neighbouring islands three times. When the Spaniards met with Bile's father, an old and respectable man, in their eyes, they noticed some locals shouting to them, urging them to leave their island using the Spanish words 'fuera, fuera' ('Out! Out!') (Mendaña 1967: 203). These words, accompanied by gestures, were repeated on other occasions, showing the indigenous people's incorporation of the knowledge acquired in order to put their message across. On this particular instance, the explorers accepted the command and retired so as not to offend the islanders, but they returned afterwards with Mendaña. By this time, however, everybody had fled from their houses, leaving food supplies behind, which Mendaña ordered his men not to touch.

The crew then held a meeting and Mendaña indicated his wish to send a party inland in order to 'know and understand' the land. They decided to barter for food so as to preserve what little they had on board for the rest of the voyage, and sought the approval of the religious authorities on board. Friar Francisco de Gálvez promptly sanctioned Mendaña's methods because, instead of merely taking the food, Mendaña gave 'graciously' in return. If circumstances were unfavourable for the exchange, Friar Francisco suggested that the Spanish could seize food from the locals but in moderation, so as not to affect them adversely. Furthermore, Friar Francisco urged them to leave payment in exchange, and warned against taking anything else from the Solomonians, explicitly mentioning women and children. With this assertion, Friar Francisco, like the islanders before, identified women with men's property, thus qualifying the previous refusal of the Spaniards to accept them as gifts. Lastly, Friar Francisco indicated that the Spaniards were allowed to counter hostility if they should meet any (Catoira 1965: 47; Mendaña 1967: 204–5).

For the excursion, Mendaña chose Sarmiento de Gamboa, who was by no means among the most peaceful of his crew, to lead a party of twelve men, including the camp master, Ortega. Information about the Spanish expedition travelled through the island by means of the shells or *coflis* which the Solomonians used for communication so that, when the Spaniards asked for water, they were again denied. Sarmiento saw many islanders gathering, who he assumed to be threatening until one man approached and embraced them, calling them brothers. The Spaniards spent the night with the islanders but kept vigil, because they were afraid of a possible betrayal. The next morning, Bile directed the explorers to meet other islanders who, once more, asked them to leave, using the Spanish words 'Afuera! Fuera!' (Catoira 1965: 50; Mendaña 1967: 206).[20]

The explorers walked close to Bile, using him as a defensive shield, because they assumed that, if Bile left them, the islanders would start shooting arrows. Bile tried to run away and, even though initially a soldier prevented him from doing so, he eventually succeeded. The Spaniards still kept with them another local man, whom Catoira identified as a brother of Bile's uncle, Salacay. Nevertheless, the shooting of arrows started and the Spanish first responded with their harquebus, firing in the air. As soon as a soldier was wounded, the Spanish aimed at the crowd and maimed one man, whom Sarmiento promptly finished with his own sword.

When Sarmiento's party arrived back, Mendaña showed his disappointment at the broken ties of friendship that he was working hard to establish. To restore this bond and the goodwill of the islanders, he ordered the release of their prisoner three days later. Before the hostage left, the Spanish gave him presents, showing their friendship with expressive signs. The islanders reciprocated by sending food in return and promising to come back with more. However, they did not, and Catoira assumed that it was because of fear, though it might have been due to the scarcity of provisions on the island (1965: 53).

As Mendaña believed that the King of Spain would like have as much information as possible, he sent Pedro de Ortega with a party of thirty armed soldiers to explore the island, which they did in eight days. Initially, they met a handful of islanders who made signs of peace, walked with and guided them. The Spaniards then found three women who first came out to see them, but who ran away when approached. As they were lodged and fed with coconuts, as well as roots, Ortega gave his hosts some of the items they had carried for the purpose, in exchange, accompanied by demonstrations of amity. Later, the Spanish met other '*naturales*' who offered them sugar cane, while music from the *coflis* could be heard when, unexpectedly, more than one hundred islanders came out to threaten them. Ortega showed restraint, ordering not to shoot, and they continued marching ahead, while the islanders left, shouting as they did so.

When the Spanish party reached the top of the mountain, they found a village with armed people, estimated by Catoira to be as many as five hundred. Some of the islanders approached in order to talk, making peace signs as they walked. Ortega asked to see the *tauriqui*, who came and embraced him, speaking in friendly terms. The explorers requested water because they did not know where it could be found, but they were refused it repeatedly. Ortega threatened them by shooting at a tree, while some soldiers held the *tauriqui* captive as they walked away. They were met by other islanders, one of whom confronted them, and tried to intimidate them with his billy-club. Ortega asked his men not to shoot and they kept on walking, taking another prisoner before nightfall.

The following day, the explorers continued their climb up the mountain, which became so steep that they had to use their hands to make progress. The islanders followed them closely, shooting arrows at those in the rearguard and wounding one man in the leg. To prevent this from happening, one soldier, Gabriel Muñoz, shot four times in the air to frighten off the islanders. While this was happening, one of their prisoners, whom Catoira named Enríquez because he had swapped names with Hernando Enríquez, freed himself, swiftly throwing himself down the precipitous hill. The Spaniards continued their slow advance while the islanders harassed them with arrows and were at times shot at, with two of them subsequently wounded.

On reaching the summit of the mountain, the explorers could not see the end of the island to appreciate its extent. They asked the *tauriqui* who was still their prisoner whether it was an island or a continent, and he clearly indicated that they were on an island.[21] Soon after, this *tauriqui* managed to free himself and escaped during the night. The following morning the Spanish party started to come down but they found it quite difficult, aggravated by the continual attack from the rearguard, which eventually wounded two Spaniards. Once more, the Spanish shot at regular intervals to keep the islanders at bay and also burned some houses on their way so that those who followed had to attend to the fire and would leave them alone.

When the exploring party arrived at a river, the arrows became more persistent and were accompanied by stones, which the islanders pelted at them, while they also bared their buttocks in contempt. The Spanish shot one 'Indian' and displayed the corpse to the remainder so as to scare them off, but to no avail, as the Solomonians continued their volley of arrows. When the Spaniards arrived at what they believed to be Bile's domain, they stopped to eat and saw the locals rush off to guard their houses, fearing that they would also be burnt. They also gave water to the Spaniards, which Catoira judged as being 'more from fear than friendship', even though Ortega called them 'brothers' in their language and tried to show them kindness (1965: 60).

Because the Spanish party had gone to explore the island 'in peace', they did not take food from the local stores, returning to the ship to report what they had seen, which included altars adorned with snakes, lizards, scorpions and creepy-crawlies, which they believed to have been venerated. In relation to these people, the exploring party indicated the differences among them, especially in the colour of their skin and hair, with some classed as 'blond'. Of their own behaviour towards the islanders, the priest who had gone with the party, Friar Juan de Torres, attested to the 'Christianity and order' of the actions undertaken by Ortega (Catoira 1965: 61).

It is at this point in the journey that we find the first references to cannibalism among the Solomonians. As the crew heard mass kneeling down, some canoes arrived and Mendaña started to talk to one 'principal', who complained about Sarmiento having killed some 'Indians' (Catoira 1965: 61–2). To demonstrate his friendship, this chief, Bene, offered Mendaña a 'quarter' of human flesh.[22] Mendaña sent a black man to fetch the flesh, which they saw clearly to have been a human arm with part of the back still attached to it. Because of the size of the arm and hand, the Spaniards thought that it must have belonged to a boy.[23]

To the explorers, the horror of cannibalism was compounded by the fact that the human flesh was offered as a gift to seal friendship and some soldiers voiced the opinion that it should be thrown away. Mendaña, however, wishing to display a stronger rejection and to make the Solomonians understand that he considered eating human flesh an evil act, decided to bury it in full view of everybody. The islanders' humiliation was stressed by Mendaña in his succinct account: 'on seeing that we had belittled their gift, like ashamed or grieved men they threw themselves on their little canoes and with their heads lowered they made for the shore and left' (1965: 10). Similarly, Catoira indicated their attitude to have been one of 'affronted people' (1965: 63). Their affront did not prevent the islanders from lighting a fire, which was believed by those on the ship to be a sign that the human banquet was being consumed, a fact later confirmed by Bile.

The way in which cannibalism is treated in the accounts of this journey shows that it epitomised a dreaded sense of otherness and was treated as a marker of barbarism.[24] The Spanish attitude towards the eating of human flesh attests to a fact that colonialism served an important strategic function. For Europeans, as Peter Hulme has amply illustrated, what was perceived to be offensive behaviour often provided a justification for the domination and enslavement of indigenous peoples.[25] Hulme's insights illuminate the apprehension of cannibalism, which was not so much an empirical category as an historical, ideological and ultimately strategic notion. The parameters used to class cannibals are comparable, Hulme proposes, to Western dualisms such as 'civilised' versus 'primitive' (1986: 83). It is worth remembering, however, that this epistemology was already questioned during the early modern period by some thinkers, the most prominent of whom was Michel de Montaigne who, in his famous essay 'Of cannibals', challenged the 'barbarism' of the supposed 'cannibals'. Montaigne poignantly suggested that 'each man calls barbarism whatever is not his own practice; for indeed it seems we have no other test of truth and reason than the example and pattern of the opinions and customs of the country we live in' (1965: 152).

Fear, as well as prejudice, is inherent in many of the assessments of cannibalism. In the case of the Solomons, this is also revealed later in Catoira's narrative in a further reference that corroborates the amount of guesswork and inference entailed in the assessment of the eating of human flesh. As one 'Indian' touched the leg of a soldier, the Spaniards imagined that he was acting as if in a butcher's shop to test the tenderness of the product on sale: 'there was even one Indian who went so far as to touch the legs of a soldier . . . He must have touched it to check whether he was tender to eat, because it must have been given to him in the distribution they had done among themselves' (Catoira 1965: 103). The Spaniards quickly assumed that there had been already a partition of the possible booty, and that they had been 'distributed' among the islanders for their next meal. In this, they partook in feelings inspired by cannibalism, which include revulsion and 'endless fascination' (Hulme 1986: 81).[26]

In spite of the differences in the way both groups reacted to gifts, such as women or human flesh, or in techniques of warfare, there was a sincere attempt by many Spaniards to understand the locals and to act as go-betweens among the two parties. For example, to repair the strained relation with Bile and his people, a soldier volunteered to talk to the islanders, believing that they would not harm him. Mendaña rejected the option, only to witness how another soldier, of his own will, boarded a boat and departed, disobeying his orders. The Spaniards were worried that this man would be killed by the islanders, but Mendaña did not condemn the gesture, instead reminding his people of the need to take risks when taking part in such expeditions.

This curious, unnamed soldier spent the night with the Solomonians and in the morning the Spaniards fired a volley to call him back. His hosts brought him to the shore unharmed, and he confirmed that he had been well treated, fed and even offered a woman. Regarding this 'gift', the soldier mentioned that the islanders had again reacted with 'admiration' on seeing that he did not want to lie with her, going so far as to show him graphically how to 'use' women (Catoira 1965: 64). After rejecting the woman, the man had spent all night talking to the local people, something that was probably appreciated by the islanders. This soldier's gesture illustrates that, in spite of the obvious difficulties, the early explorers made some considerable effort to accept and value the people that they encountered.

After this event, the signs of goodwill between the Spaniards and Bile's people continued, and their ensuing dialogue allowed the voyagers to gain an understanding of the local feuds between Bile and his enemies, including the chief Meta. Also as an indication of his friendship towards the Spaniards, Bile sent his own nephew to stay on the ship with Mendaña, who made sure that the visitor was received hospitably and was well-treated, dressing and hugging him on arrival. The same treatment was given to three islanders that went with him, and the four of them insisted that they did not want to leave the ship, asking to go with the Spaniards to Castile or Peru as servants. Remarkably, Catoira's journal uses the local and Spanish word for servants, *criados* and *nactonys* (1965: 65), showing a reasonable acquaintance with basic words and social structures of the islanders, as well as a good level of mutual recognition.

Efforts to accept the different culture in its own terms were impeded by unfamiliarity with the language. Mendaña was aware of this and set out to get a competent interpreter, which, in effect, meant 'stealing' a local man. He opted for one from Meta's people in order to spare his friend Bile, after consultation as to what to do to prevent Bile from becoming the target of Meta's revenge. To indicate a possible type of retribution, Mendaña again deployed the fear of cannibalism, suggesting that, after the Spanish left, Meta's men might 'eat Bile's Indians' (Catoira 1965: 66).

The camp master, Ortega, was charged with the duty of fetching someone to act as interpreter and left with thirty-five soldiers and four islanders, whom he disguised, dressing them as Spaniards. On the way, it rained heavily and the group found refuge in a small hut where they lit a fire but could not keep it going because of the rain, spending all night wet. With their food also wet, the explorers were reduced to eating palms, before proceeding on to a different island, where they were surrounded by many people whom they greeted as 'brothers'. The 'Indians' travelling with them confirmed that they were Bile's vassals and the two groups talked, with those from the exploring party indicating that the Spaniards were going to kill Meta, which seemed to please the others (Catoira 1965: 68).[27]

The Spaniards spent a second night very much like the first, with rain preventing them from lighting a fire, and in the morning they ate coconuts with the islanders who, on seeing that they were not harmed and conscious of the Spaniards' hunger, brought them roots to eat. Both parties 'conversed' in friendly terms, but this did not prevent the Spaniards from taking four islanders as hostages to use as interpreters. Although they manacled them, the prisoners untied themselves in the night, but did not succeed in escaping and were taken back to the ship. Three of the kidnapped, according to Mendaña, were Meta's sons and he let two of them go free, while keeping the remaining one with him. Fifteen days later, a brother of this prisoner came to join him and cried sitting next to him, a display that impressed the Spaniards but did not move them enough to release him.[28]

In spite of the sporadic displays of power on the part of the visitors, they paid tribute to some local customs, including folklore, canoe-building, physical nimbleness, and even social deportment. For example, when a party of islanders went to the boat to talk to the Spaniards, one among them was described as 'very gallant' and said to behave with such distinction that the Spaniards wondered how 'barbarians' could be so elegant.[29] Mendaña spoke to this man, who was also imitating European manners and covering his mouth when laughing 'with discretion' (Catoira 1965: 70). These gestures were interpreted by the Spaniards, following their own customs, as signs of distinction. Elegance was easily translated into nobility when they confirmed the bravery of this 'grave' man, who, after looking at the boat for a time in silence, told the Spaniards that, although he was afraid that they would kill him, he still wanted to make friends with them and would bring them food.

Later in the narrative we learn that another islander, an old man, gained praise from the Spaniards when he tried to take them on single-handedly. The Spanish believed that he had done so because they had, regrettably, killed a woman who might have been his wife (Catoira 1965: 136). As on other occasions, here the Spaniards used their own parameters to assess the alien culture, which meant that the local culture was seen in favourable terms precisely by comparison with a Christian view of the domestic world and the adoption of behavioural patterns similar to their own.

A further example of this attitude is given when Mendaña talked to an unnamed man about religion and the king of Spain, using local words to put his meaning across. Mendaña was certainly understood, and the islander's demonstration of his belief in divinity was again classed by Catoira as unlike that of a 'barbarian': 'He then made a sign which was not that of a barbarian; because he stretched his hand up in the air, with the palm facing down, pointing towards heaven' (1965: 71).[30] Although this clearly revealed a man of unique and outstanding character, surpassing the norm of his fellow islanders, such assessments also imply that, even if temporarily, the Spaniards were able to assess other cultures by bypassing the strict divide of 'barbarians' versus 'civilised' peoples.

At this point in their stay, the Spanish fleet prepared to depart and repaired their boats using wood that, according to Catoira, was abundant on the island. Mendaña consulted his people and all agreed to trust the assessment of the pilot, Gallego, who believed that they should not leave until they were certain of the route, which was a difficult task, Gallego added, for they had no maps of the area and no knowledge of the currents and shoals. Sarmiento did not agree with Gallego, being of the opinion that they should continue the voyage because one of the islands they had left behind was part of the sought-after 'large kingdom' of *Terra Australis Incognita* (Catoira 1965: 74). They ultimately agreed to send an expedition to find this large island or continent.

While this discussion was taking place, Bile arrived and we are offered an interesting insight into local knowledge and the abstract conceptualisation of the known world, which for Europeans was embedded in maps. To get their meaning across to Bile, the Spaniards used local words, such as *naclonys* ('servants' or 'vassals'), *gases* ('women') and *solis* ('children'). With their limited repertoire, they told Bile about the existence of the King of Castile and, using 'vna carta de marear' ('a sailing chart'), pointed to a small point, telling him that it was his own island. This surprised Bile, who believed his island to be large in relation to the world around: 'a small island was pointed, telling him that it was his. He was astonished and said that his island was much bigger' (Catoira 1965: 74).

Effective communication did not extend to the Spaniards' understanding of the local kingship system and the degree of authority over its different domains by diverse chiefs. This meant that they often failed in their assessment of the situation and in establishing ties of friendship, as was the case when they reached the lands of a *tauriqui* called Brata. There, the camp master was called by the islanders to get food and, as the Spaniards approached, the islanders started to shoot at them with arrows. Although the camp master made some effort to ease the situation, calling the islanders 'brothers' and urging them to be calm because they would not be harmed, the arrows continued to fly. Thus, the Spaniards resorted to shooting with, we are told, and more than twenty people, including two chiefs, died as a result.[31]

Conflicting messages were, again, exchanged when Bile returned the following day to visit the Spaniards, bringing coconuts, *binahu* and a turtle. Bile did not want to go on board and showed his displeasure at the woodcutting going on. However, he asked for and was given a dish with which to eat because, Catoira wrote, the islanders had neither dishes nor vessels for cooking.[32] After taking his gift, Bile left quite pleased, which was probably the reason why more 'Indians' came on the following days with food, including Bile's brother, Riquia, who was a chief of another area and who slept on board. Like other Solomonians, Riquia displayed his curiosity about the visitors and their customs, indicating his wish to go with the Spaniards to meet the 'King of Castilla' (Catoira 1965: 75; Mendaña 1967: 219–20).

Although focusing almost exclusively on human contact, the narratives of this visit are not wholly devoid of natural description. For example, the birds, spices, fruit and trees are itemised and compared with those of Peru or Castile (Catoira 1965: 75–6; Mendaña 1967: 220–1). In this, Catoira and Mendaña follow closely the paradigm set out by Michel Foucault in *The Order of Things*, regarding the taxonomy of resemblance as, for example, when describing a type of grapefruit as similar to those from Cartagena. Foucault proposes resemblance to have been the hallmark of early modern epistemology, concluding that 'representation ... was posited as a form of repetition: the theatre of life or the mirror of nature'.[33]

Resemblance also played a key role in the physical description of the islanders, thus complementing that of their natural habitat. As frequently in European accounts, skin colour was a prime marker of differentiation among the indigenous peoples encountered, with reference to the degrees of blackness also made in relation to their hair (Catoira 1965: 76; Mendaña 1967: 221). The women, in turn, were assessed in terms of the Spaniards' criteria of beauty and, following the epistemological pattern of resemblance expounded by Foucault, compared favourably with women from Peru. Catoira and Mendaña also observed that the islanders' teeth were completely black and their tongues red, due to their chewing betel. In attesting to this, the position of eye-witnesses was emphasised, while the corroborating testimony of others was likewise acknowledged, which Catoira did explicitly when relating the otherwise unbelievable size of the local bats.[34]

While the Spaniards were preparing to leave and waiting for the brigantine, which had gone to explore the island and stayed away for more than thirty days, Bile stopped his visits. On one occasion, as a Spanish group went up a hill to locate the boat, they noticed Bile running away and they thought that it was because he was afraid that he might be taken onto the boat when they left. His fears were not unfounded, as proved when the brigantine arrived without a single hostage to act as interpreter because those captured had escaped. Mendaña ordered two men to be taken because he did not want to leave without 'lenguas' ('interpreters'). When they seized the men, the visitors sent some gifts to emphasise that, in spite of all appearances, they still wanted to be friends with Bile and his people. Paradoxically, Riquia indicated his wish to go with the Spaniards, but was not allowed. It is interesting to note that these facts are detailed as though both parties fully understood one another, with Catoira going so far as to indicate that the 'natives understood our language very well by now, and we did theirs; so that it seemed that we had grown up together' (Catoira 1965: 79).[35]

In spite of hostilities, as in any social arrangement, the islanders often visited the Spaniards to eat with them. Following hierarchical rules which seem to have been mutually accepted, the 'prencipales' ate with Mendaña, sitting at his table, while the remaining men were given food elsewhere. Catoira saw this as the local adoption of Spanish manners, though the same might also have been the case for the Solomonians. In terms of manners and deportment at the table, Catoira commended the islanders' politeness, indicating that they were very clean and did not dirty their hands, acting as though they had been raised with those manners: 'They are all so clean that they hardly wet their fingers, and they cleaned themselves with politeness, as though they had been brought up in it' (1965: 79).

It is curious, however, to observe that the manners referred to by Catoira had only recently started to become a sign of public distinction throughout some parts of Europe, extending from the upper to the higher-middle social strata. Manners were given increasing importance during an era when social mobility started to become a possibility for many. Indeed, as Norbert Elias's pioneering work showed, the adoption of manners is embedded in the very concept of civilisation and morality, as well as the notion of distinction that the spread and increasing sophistication of social etiquette epitomised.[36] Thus, the same parameters that were used to segregate different social classes in Western Europe were thus employed to classify the cultures encountered in other parts of the globe.

Unfortunately, Mendaña's long journal to the Governor of Peru breaks off at this point, with the last section preserved mentioning that, as the time spent on the island increased while waiting for the brigantine, many sailors and soldiers started to get sick with fever, probably with malaria (1967: 224). Mendaña also included a brief of the brigantine's journey, which very much echoes that of Catoira.[37]

From the remaining sources, a summary of the events on the Solomons from this time on, which also applies to the three voyages of the brigantine, shows a repetitive pattern of events, very much like those related so far. This means that, although there were some efforts to establish a fair exchange, there was also a fair degree of misunderstanding, and often abuse, by the Spaniards. Nevertheless, the visitors were by no means always the winning side in the resulting skirmishes, although their weapons proved superior on more than one occasion.

This was precisely what happened when problems arose due to the scarcity of food and the Spaniards insisted on being provided with pigs and local produce. These demands ended up in fights where the casualties, on average one or two, were invariably among the Solomonians. Following this, the islanders usually retreated to the mountains while the Spaniards appropriated some of their food and either left merchandise as compensation or simply took what they believed to be acceptable.

There was, then, a continual alternation between meetings that the Spaniards described as friendly, in which the islanders came to barter or offer water and food, and other encounters that ended up in fights or, to use Catoira's word, 'guaçauaras'. This pattern was also apparent on the first island that the brigantine encountered after leaving Santa Isabel, which is still known today by the name given to it then, *Ramos*, due to its discovery on Palm Sunday. There, after a brief brawl during which the locals shot arrows and the explorers retaliated with guns, the latter took food from the houses (Mendaña 1967: 226). Similarly, on the next islands, which they called *La Galera* and *Buena Vista*, some initially friendly exchanges turned sour when the islanders understood that the Spaniards were after their food supplies (Catoira 1965: 83).

In Mendaña's brief account, the only details mentioned from the voyage of the brigantine are the places discovered and the names given, indicating also that Ortega had firstly sailed around the island, confirming that it was not the 'continent' that they were looking for, and assessed its dimensions (Mendana 1965: 11–12). Mendaña also declared that Ortega had seen *Ramos*, described as a big island, a smaller island, *La Galera*, and some others named *Buena Vista, San Dimas* and *Isla de Flores*. The biggest island sighted, however, was *Guadalcanal*, which Ortega named after his own Andalusian hometown. Another island, which the Spaniards named as *San Jorge*, was acknowledged by Mendaña to have had an indigenous name: *Borue*. Interestingly, on this island the Spaniards observed some pottery, 'two pots of very thin clay', which, the islanders indicated, had been brought from a 'faraway land', with no further references to these exchanges that were obviously taking place across the Pacific.

Ortega and his party returned and Mendaña considered them lucky to be alive, in view of the many 'fights with the locals' (Mendana 1965: 12). Mendaña decided to leave for a less hostile environment and both ships departed towards *Guadalcanal*, passing the islands of *Ramos* and *Buena Vista*. They anchored in *Guadalcanal* next to a river which they called *Gallego*, and landed to take possession of the island in the name of the King of Spain. Mendaña sent Hernando Enríquez 'to discover in the brigantine', while he ordered Andres Nuñez to go inland with twenty soldiers. Nuñez, we read, had many brawls with the locals, but, like Ortega before him, was fortunate to have no casualties among his men, although he died soon after returning, probably of malaria.[38] After this, Mendaña, with Ortega and twenty-seven men, went up a mountain in order to ascertain the dimensions of the island and, from there, were able to count more than thirty villages. Mendaña also mentioned, as in all the remaining narratives, that the whole island, like those already visited, was thickly populated (1965: 14).[39]

The next day, the Spanish saw the island that they had named *San Dimas*, although Catoira admitted that it had a local name, *Malayta*. The voyagers anchored after a storm and the locals arrived, exchanging gifts as a sign of a friendship which, in Catoira's opinion, was 'faked' (1965: 96–7). After these demonstrations, the Spaniards walked up the hill with Friar Francisco carrying a cross, while his fellow friars intoned the psalm identified by Catoira as '*Bexigilia rexis prodeunt*' (*Vexilla regis prodeunt*). On their descent, they were shot at with arrows and they responded by killing two islanders, while the rest fled.

Scuffles persisted during the following days, when the islanders took down a cross, which the Spanish then restored to its place. In addition, some exchanges of gifts occurred before the explorers took possession of the island on behalf of the King of Spain, this time 'without the locals impeding it' (Catoira 1965: 98). As before, the Spaniards continued to ask for food and, when they were denied, simply took it from the local people, leaving something in exchange.

The local attitude towards the Spaniards' symbolic possession of their land was different for the party that departed on the brigantine thereafter. The Spaniards claimed ownership of and named a harbour of the island of *Ramos*, Puerto Escondido, with Hernando Enríquez using words reminiscent of Columbus's arrival in the Americas, taking 'possession of all that land in the name of Your Majesty and in the name of the General and he followed the necessary procedures'. Unlike in Malaita, however, Enríquez was not so fortunate for the locals tried to obstruct the ceremony (Catoira 1965: 129).

The brigantine's journey lasted from 19 May to 9 June and, during this second voyage, the same pattern of events was repeated (Catoira 1965: 116–49). Initially, the Spanish were either attacked or given food as a token of exchange and thereafter, when they demanded more, the islanders started harassing them and urged them to leave, with their shooting of arrows eventually met by the Spanish harquebus. Sometimes, the explorers requested pigs, and even took canoes to be ransomed in exchange for more pigs. On one occasion, the locals filled pots of water and carried them back to the Spaniards, receiving handkerchiefs, bonnets and beads in exchange for their labour (Catoira 1965: 118–19, 122).

This replication of events and their often tragic outcome was noticed by the Spaniards, who, at one point, were even sorry to see canoes approaching them, predicting what was to follow. Nonetheless, some effort was made to appease the islanders and once, after taking two boys and one man as hostages, the explorers released first one boy and then the man, both laden with gifts so that the others might understand that they would not be harmed so long as they did not initiate hostilities (Catoira 1965: 124–6). Again, at this point in the narrative, Catoira insisted that the Spaniards still made every effort to avoid confrontation: 'we tried to do as little harm as possible, and if we did any it was because of dire need' (1965: 130).

Some level of reciprocity, nevertheless, obtained in exchanges where, as suggested above, the Spaniards did not have the upper hand. For example, there is a curious reference to the Spaniards, while they were on *Ramos*, being tricked while bartering, with the Solomonians trying to pass off stones for gold. As the Spaniards had shown interest in the 'porras' ('stones'), which appeared to be made of gold, an islander gave one to a sailor in exchange for a bonnet. When they found out that it was not in fact gold, the sailors simply ceased bartering (Catoira 1965: 131).

A few days later, we hear again that the explorers took food from the locals but left some behind, as well as items in exchange ('rescate'), because they realised that the islanders were short of supplies (Catoira 1965: 145). The next day, the Solomonians, seeing that the Spaniards were still there, left them a pig without waiting to meet with them. The Spanish party then put their 'rescate' on a stick, which was taken by the islanders later on. In another village, the explorers were met by locals who offered them food, but each person only brought one root, which the Spaniards considered a mocking gesture. However, when they looked in their houses, they saw little food there. As they left, the islanders ran along the beach offering them food, which suggests that they recognised their mutual need. Along the way, the explorers took food from another village that seemed well provided, without the locals obstructing them. They were asked, however, to limit their takings to one pig and not to ask for more, because they had been received in peace, a request that was respected. As an item of 'exchange' for this friendship, the islanders requested that the Spaniards kill Ruabatu, whom they identified as the person responsible for the attacks on the Spaniards (Catoira 1965: 148). As shown in this summary, exchanges were varied and complex, with material goods being normally a prelude to closer relationships, and when hostility, and even murder, could be treated as items of exchange or communication.

After eighteen days away, and having sighted six more islands as densely populated as the previous ones, the brigantine returned with news of the above events and with its people alive on board. However, all were sick with malaria, including the captain. While the brigantine was away for a second time in Guadalcanal, the 'food supplier of the ship' led the most unfortunate party to fetch water. This group, consisting of nine people, including one mulatto, some servants, a Creole from Lima and two slaves, was ambushed as they gathered water, and all but one black man, who managed to run away, were hacked to death. The islanders swiftly mutilated the corpses, chopping off their heads and splitting the brains to eat them (Catoira 1965: 113). Mendaña accounted for this action, noting that the islanders had refused them food on the previous day, and that, with the approval of the Franciscan friars, the Spaniards had simply helped themselves, making them unhappy ('dessabridos') and spurring on their revenge (1965: 14). Ironically, then, Mendaña's account provides a reasonable justification for the violent acts not of his own men, but of the islanders.

In relation to the role played by Africans, such as the survivor of the watering party, Catoira's narrative gives some additional information elsewhere about the important, but largely unknown, role that they played on these voyages. When going about the business of taking food, a fight had started and a black man belonging to Francisco Muñoz was taken by surprise, alone. Catoira praised the courage of this African, who was defending himself vigorously when found by his rescuers, and miraculously went on to survive his many wounds (1965: 110).[40] The Spaniards' attempt to rescue this black man cost some islanders their lives and one of their corpses was hung up on a tree as a visual deterrent to the others.

Frustratingly, however, there are no further details about this black man or other Africans taking part on the voyage. Only with one other incident do we gain an additional insight about the composition and roles of the crew, when we read that the black slaves were washing clothes and cooking (Catoira 1965: 135). Nonetheless, the example above shows that the value of these men was recognised, and not only in economic terms.

After the murder of their watering party, the Spaniards wished to take revenge and, on the following day, Sarmiento led a party that burned houses in various villages leaving, according to Catoira, more than twenty men dead. Meanwhile, the remaining people on Guadalcanal continued to fight and killed one Spaniard in an ambush. In response, the explorers took two prisoners, killed one islander and hacked him to bits, some of which they put on posts for others to see (Catoira 1965: 151). The islanders came to retrieve the head, mourning loudly for this loss.

Because the fever of the malaria-stricken men showed no signs of abating and another man died, the Spaniards left the *Puerto de la Cruz* in Guadalcanal and, as they did so, they observed that the cross that they had planted was still in place. They coasted the island, still repeating the pattern, of 'exchanging' food and skirmishes, while everyone on board grew more sick, day by day. Their plight was worsened by a storm which lasted for ten days while they were on the island of *Santiago*, where they all prayed to the Virgin of Guadalupe in Peru to help them find a safe harbour (Catoira 1965: 154–60).

Eventually, the Spaniards found a secure place, which they named *Puerto de la Visitación*, at the next island, *San Christobal* (Malaita), where they planted the royal banner on the beach and took possession in their customary fashion. They tried to exchange food with the indigenous population but met with hostility and, as Mendaña considered that the island supplies were plentiful, they took what was 'necessary to us' (1965: 16).

From *San Christobal*, the Spanish sent the brigantine on its third and last journey of discovery, with Francisco Muñoz in command of thirty men. They left on 6 July and took twenty-eight days to return, discovering two more islands, which they named *Santa Anna* and *Santa Catalina*, and which were as densely populated as the rest. They had constant fights with the islanders, who wounded two Spaniards and, at the end of the journey, Muñoz took four of them as interpreters. This journey was a repetition of the failed exchanges seen above, in that the Spanish tried to obtain food by ransoming the prisoners they had taken.[41] In this instance, one of the hostages is said to have delighted them with his songs – a gesture that led Catoira to praise the local spirit, writing that it was to be admired that the prisoners did not look sad or cry, even in these adverse circumstances (1965: 167).

Once more, at this point in Catoira's account, we have examples of failed exchanges of women, who were offered as 'gifts' and were refused, to the surprise of the islanders, who again made obvious signs of 'how to use them' (1965: 169). Just as the Spaniards refused this 'present', so did the islanders of *Santa Catalina* rebuff one of the bonnets given to them. Not only did they decline it, throwing it down, but they did so while displaying their buttocks in contempt. By rejecting this gift, the islanders sought to avoid establishing the social ties that gift-giving presupposes and could be reciprocating with their 'failed exchange' of women, which the Spanish had rejected.[42]

The next day, the islanders attacked the Spaniards when they were trying to purchase some hens or pigs, achieving an adverse result when two or three of them were killed. These fights continued and were repeated on the next island, *Santa Anna*, which was said to be called in their own language *Ytapa*. There, the Spaniards were ambushed with the foreseeable consequence of the death of three islanders and the burning of some local houses (Catoira 1965: 173–5). The exploring party arrived back with some wounded men, and Mendaña was disappointed to hear that no new land had been sighted. In the meantime, those waiting for the brigantine had been hearing mass every day on land while being harassed and shot at by the locals, which, alongside the malaria, made them decide to leave once the ships were careened. Before departing, however, Mendaña's sick crew spent ten more days trying to acquire food while being attacked by the islanders, thus having to rely on local rivalries to survive. Mendaña ordered the men to keep together always, but one was killed when he went with another in search for food. Once more, Sarmiento was sent to try and find the culprits and, as he was unsuccessful, he burned some houses (Catoira 1965: 177–81).

Throughout the whole of this voyage, therefore, exchange was seen as a means to seal relations and avoid conflict.[43] Commerce was deployed to this end by both the explorers and the islanders, who used gift-giving and bartering to further their own requirements. Sometimes, however, necessity on both sides dictated the ensuing conflict. There were also occasions when the Spaniards failed to retaliate and the locals taunted them as cowards, triggering the violent response that the officers had initially tried to avoid.[44] Most, if not all, skirmishes were provoked by failed exchange of food, which resulted in the Spaniards' theft and consequent hardship for the islanders. Unfortunately, most conflicts ended with one or more islander dead and others wounded, before fleeing to the hills.

Following the last 'failed exchange', Mendaña consulted with all those on board and they agreed to return to Peru, as too many were sick and they were also running short of ammunition (Catoira 1965: 183–4). They decided to take some more interpreters, as they only had two, and Gabriel Muñoz captured one man, his wife, her sister and their baby (Mendaña 1965: 17; Catoira 1965: 187–90). Although Mendaña wished to release the women, they ultimately decided not to separate the wife and husband. They dressed these women, indicating that one of the friars should keep them locked to prevent them from being harmed, which was only done for two nights, as everyone on board, including 'blacks and servicemen', was quite 'chaste' (Catoira 1965: 191).[45]

The Spaniards finally left the *Puerto de la Visitacion* on 11 August 1568. En route, they faced a hurricane and all prayed, fearing that their end had come, while Mendaña praised one unnamed friar who exhorted them to die like Christians. Although they survived, conditions on the journey gradually worsened because of hunger and the malaria contracted by many, with Mendaña mentioning that every day at least one man was thrown overboard. The only consolation they had, Mendaña wrote, is that he, the captain, encouraged them to die as Christians: 'and the greatest gift they had was to call me to see them die. Not only did I then feel sorry and a great pity for what I was seeing, but even now, and every time I remember how I saw them die, it moves my soul and it breaks my heart' (1965: 23).

Although on the way back to the Americas Mendaña's ship lost sight of the *Almiranta*, they were delighted to see it reach Santiago de Colima (California), from where both ships arrived back in El Callao on 11 September 1569. There, Mendaña informed the relevant authorities of the journey and started preparing a second one to the islands that from then on became known as Islands of Solomon. Nearly thirty years would pass, however, before Mendaña returned to the South Seas in 1595 in search of the Southern Continent, with his new wife, Isabel Barreto, to populate the Solomons with settlers from the Spanish American mainland. This second, and unfortunate, journey would see the death of Mendaña and the demise of his South Seas dreams.

NOTES

1 See my *Performing the Pacific* (2005: 20–1, 34).
2 Lawrence Wroth notes that: 'Though the Solomons continued to be shown upon the maps of that area, there is no record of a visit to them for nearly

two centuries after their discovery, and it was not long before their very existence began to be questioned' (1944: 187).
3 'There is surely nothing in the history of maritime discovery so strange as the story of how the Isles of Solomon were discovered, lost, and found again' (1901: i). Amherst and Thomson details the changing position of the Solomons in maps as follows: 'The Solomon Islands, which were delineated in their approximate position in 1587, now began to find new resting-places in the Chart of the Pacific. In Dudley's *Arcano del Mare* (1646) they are identified with the Marquesas. Delisle, early in the eighteenth century, carried them further westward; Danville suppressed them altogether; Dalrymple, as late as 1790 denied their existence as islands separate from New Britain' (1901: lxxii).
4 'Some authors', according to Kelly, 'relying heavily on Sarmiento sources, either belittle Mendaña's role in the expedition or make him co-discoverer with Sarmiento of the Solomons, and this controversial attribution now finds permanent expression in a plaque, commemorative of the Fourth Centenary of the expedition, erected on the west side of the Dársena overlooking the port of Callao' (1971: 26).
5 This narrative, in its complete form, would have included all the information that appears in the remaining sources about the expeditions carried out by the brigantine on three occasions, as well as the perspective afforded by events on the *Almiranta*.
6 For details of these sources, see the Appendix.
7 A few lines later, Catoira indicated that 'nombre' was also part of the name given to the island, *Nombre de Jesús* (1965: 35). In his brief relation, Mendaña noted that *Nombre de Jesús* was chosen 'because we discovered it near the celebration of the said festivity' (Mendaña 1965: 4), while in his longer account, Gallego attributed the naming to himself, contradicting Mendaña's indication that it was he who chose the name (1967b: 105 and 187 respectively).
8 *Baxos de la Candelaria* were so named, according to Gallego, because they saw them on the vesper of 'la Candelaria' (1967b: 107), with Mendaña also attributing the choice of name to himself (1967: 192; 1965: 5).
9 Samples of these artefacts can be seen in the *Museo Naval* and *Museo de América* in Madrid, although they date from eighteenth-century voyages.
10 In Catoira's account the bonnet is initially a single one. More boats then came, with more *tauriquis* demanding 'bonetes' so that the Spanish threw three or four to them and the islanders gave them to 'sus prencipales' (1965: 39).
11 Mendaña also praised the construction of the local canoes (1967: 194–5).
12 As Mauss notes, 'prestations which are in theory voluntary, disinterested and spontaneous ... are in fact obligatory and interested. The form usually taken is that of the gift generously offered; but the accompanying behaviour is formal pretence and social deception, while the transaction itself is based on obligation and economic self-interest' (1967: 1).

13 On this topic, see also Mendaña's longer account (1967: 195).
14 'As can be seen from oral traditions in the region, the establishment of Polynesian populations on the Outliers was more often than not accompanied by the massacre or enslavement of the previous inhabitants. Perhaps this explains why these new foreigners, light-skinned like the Polynesians, were greeted everywhere they went with such vigorous response except on the two Outliers with which they had contact' (Spriggs 1997: 228).
15 The title given is the first line *Vexilla regis prodeunt*, which continues with 'fulget crucis mysterium, / quo carne carnis conditor / suspensus est patibulo' ('The royal standards are raised / the mystery of the Cross shines / where the creator of all flesh was hung / in the flesh upon the crossbar').
16 Bile is referred to as Bilebanarra in Mendaña's longer account (1967: 198) and the name is given as Bile Ban Arra by Kelly.
17 Mendaña observed that Bile's difference from the rest of the people could be seen in the feathers and the bracelets that he wore, which were made of bone but resembled alabaster (1967: 199). As in other references, Catoira's and Mendaña's accounts to the Governor of Peru are very similar.
18 Catoira noted that on the very first day they were already teaching them the *Padre nuestro* ('Our Father') (1965: 40).
19 Women were treated as merchandise when the islanders in a canoe offered three of them and Mendaña refused them, telling them that 'they could not sell them and to take them away' (Mendaña 1967: 202–3).
20 After this, Mendaña's longer account has eight folios missing, covering the time from 16 February to 18 March (1967: 208 n. 1).
21 This local man represented his geographical knowledge drawing 'a circle on the soil, saying that all inside it was land and all around it, sea' (Catoira 1965: 57–8).
22 Catoira noted that Bene brought with him 'around one hundred and ten Indians', all of whom were armed (1965: 63).
23 In Mendaña's brief account, this flesh was also referred to as a quarter of a boy (1965: 10). Mendaña recounted how Bene asked him in his own language to eat it, and Mendaña answered him also in the local language with the following words: '*teo naleha arra*', which, he added, 'means I do not eat that' (1965: 10).
24 Another marker of barbarism was the role of women. During the second trip of the brigantine, the Spaniards were surprised to see women with lances and perhaps also one of them as leader (Catoira 1965: 141). This event, alongside nudity, sodomy or cannibalism, would be seen by the Spaniards as barbaric, as had been the case in the Americas, where the myth of the Classical Amazons inspired the naming of the river.
25 Indeed, in the Americas, cannibalism proved to be useful as a way of endorsing forced indoctrination for it was 'the radical dualism of the European response to the native Caribbean', which were split between evil cannibals and

friendly natives, that constituted 'the whole intricate web of colonial discourse' (Hulme 1986: 47). On this topic, see also Pagden (1995: 98).

26 Hulme wonders whether the fascination is indeed universal, 'which would lend credence... to a psychoanalytical explanation'. Quoting Freud, Hulme leaves the question unanswered, concluding that our attitude towards cannibalism 'is certainly ambivalent' (1986: 81).

27 The details of the journey were not included in Mendaña's short account.

28 At this meeting on the boat, the islander was asked whether the island had spices, and the Spaniards showed him some which they had on board, as well as gold and pearls (Mendaña 1965: 11). After this, Sarmiento took them back to land.

29 Elsewhere Catoira mentioned that the islanders were too 'sharp' to be 'barbarians' (1965: 72).

30 This man appeared to be happy, never casting a glance at the two islanders who had been taken from Meta's land and were in the stocks. Before leaving, however, he asked Mendaña for them and was refused.

31 Indeed, according to Catoira, over twenty of them, including two 'prencipales', had died (1965: 74).

32 The words that Catoira used suggest that 'nature' was a source of knowledge or, in this case, lack of it: 'it seems that nature has not taught them' (1965: 75).

33 'Up to the end of the sixteenth century, resemblance played a constructive role in the knowledge of Western culture. It was resemblance that largely guided exegesis and the interpretation of texts; it was resemblance that organized the play of symbols, made possible knowledge of things visible and invisible, and controlled the art of representing them' (Foucault 1973: 17).

34 Catoira wrote that unless all on board had not seen these bats he would be thought a liar, a device used to legitimise an account by including others as eye-witnesses. He added that one bat that was killed measured three feet from one wing to the other (1965: 77).

35 From here, Mendaña went on to include the expedition of the brigantine from 7 April to 5 May 1568 and then the return journey (1967: 225–45).

36 Elias traces the 'colonisation' of the bourgeoisie through the manners of the aristocracy, initially in France, and then in Germany (1978: 16–22). Pierre Bourdieu has scrutinised the rise of the idea of taste and distinction, especially with regard to food and its presentation, relating it to the bourgeoisie's aspirations to political and economic power (1984: 177–93).

37 The accounts of the journeys appear in Mendaña (1967: 225–45) and Catoira (1965: 80–95).

38 Nuñez's account of events is related by Catoira (1965: 106–10).

39 Catoira's journal refers to this on several occasions, as, for example, in *Ramos* (1965: 130). Mendaña echoed the surprise at the amount of people, 'which is a thing to marvel at' (1965: 15). This expression of admiration is very much

reminiscent of the hyperbole used by Columbus when he repeated the word 'maravilla' upon arrival in the Americas. Columbus's sense of wonderment has been incisively studied by Stephen Greenblatt in *Marvelous Possessions* (1992), where it is related to the drive to appropriate and possess.

40 A few lines later, Catoira qualified his praise of another slave, who should be given credit for his account of events, even though he was black. His wounds, Catoira posited, proved that, in this case, the African man was not lying (1965: 114).

41 The Spaniards sent one man back after they were given two pigs and asked for more pigs before letting the others go. When the islanders came with two more pigs, a boy was released with gifts of 'chaquira' ('beads') (Catoira 1965: 167–68).

42 According to Robin Torrence, Pacific islanders 'were careful about carrying out exchanges with foreigners because these created social relationships that they did not want' (2000a: 108).

43 Scott Mitchell observes that: 'Given the capacity for the act of exchange to cement social and political bonds, the exchange of foreign goods within indigenous societies could represent far more than the mere dissemination of utilitarian items. Trade provided a means by which conflict between indigenous people and foreigners could be resolved or avoided' (2000: 182).

44 See Catoira (1965: 131). Another instance of the same cycle of events on the brigantine occurred after the Spanish tried to barter for pigs, which they took. As the locals started to arm themselves, the Spaniards retreated so as not to fight, and were harassed with arrows, with the foreseeable result of one islander killed and the rest fleeing (Catoira 1965: 134).

45 Unfortunately, the man, the girl and one of the other boys died in Lima, though they are said to have become 'good Christians' by then (Mendaña 1965: 17).

2

Mendaña and the Santa Cruz (1595)

On his return from the first voyage, Mendaña dedicated the next twenty-six years to canvassing support for a further expedition. On 17 June 1595, after some lengthy preparations, Mendaña set sail for the South Pacific as captain of the ship normally referred to as *Capitana*, but known also as *San Jerónimo*, with Pedro Fernández de Quirós as pilot. Mendaña travelled with his wife, Isabel Barreto, her brothers, Diego and Lorenzo, and some 354 to 378 people, of whom 107 were women, children and servants.[1]

The principal source of information for this voyage is Quirós's journal, or, rather, his narrative filtered through the pen of his secretary, the Golden Age poet Belmonte de Bermúdez.[2] As a consequence of the convergence of these two personalities, the account is not just biased in favour of Quirós, but also indulges in a number of literary embellishments. Extra caution should, therefore, be exercised, probably more than with other voyages, and the reader must rely on an often highly-embroidered representation of events, clearly influenced by narrative devices that may be easily fitted within the baroque paradigm of literary tropes, including conceits and hyperbole.

In this rather wandering journey, Mendaña went in seach of the Solomons in order to colonise and settle them. In addition to his wife and brothers-in-law, Mendaña was accompanied by Isabel's sister-in-law, Mariana de Castro, and two priests. The *Santa Isabel*, also known as the *Almiranta*, was led by Admiral Lope de Vega, who married Mendaña's relation, Mariana de Castro, only a few days before departing.[3] The third ship was the *Galeota* ('galleon') *San Felipe*, which was commanded by Captain Felipe Corzo. The fleet also included a frigate, the *Santa Catalina*, led by Lieutenant Alonso de Leyva (2000: 126).

Instead of finding the Solomons, Mendaña first arrived in and named the *Marquesas de Mendoza* in honour of the Marquis of Cañete, García Hurtado de Mendoza y Manrique (1535–1609), who was Viceroy of Peru from 1590 to 1596 and had overseen the arming of the fleet. From there, Mendaña sailed to the Santa Cruz archipelago where he died of malaria, as did many others throughout the journey. Following Mendaña's last will and testament, his wife, Isabel Barreto, was named Governor and, helped by the skill of Quirós as pilot, after much hardship, hunger and loss of life, she led the remainder of the fleet to the Philippines (Figure 2.2). Barreto commanded the only remaining ship in the fleet, the galleon *San Jerónimo*, which departed with 120 people on board. Of those, another forty died before leaving the Santa Cruz archipelago, probably victims of malaria and fifty more on the way back because of scurvy, hunger and thirst. Only thirty-five to forty arrived in Manila and, of these, a further ten died in local hospitals.

The second ship, the *Almiranta*, was lost before arriving in Santa Cruz, apparently reaching instead Pamua, in the Solomons.[4] Archaeological work led by Roger Greene and Jim Allen in the 1970s showed that the men and women from that ship established a settlement of some months' duration, before disappearing, probably being killed by the islanders.[5] An analysis of the pottery found led Greene to the conclusion that it was not autochthonous to the island but

> an imported product of sixteenth-century Spanish origin for which the 1568 exploration of this coast by Gallego is an inadequate explanation ... the *Almiranta* of Mendaña's expedition, the one galleon headed towards this destination in 1595 when it became separated from the rest, reached the 'Islands of Solomon' discovered twenty seven years before, made a landfall there and founded a settlement of some months' duration. (1973: 27)[6]

According to Quirós's journal, the tragic loss of life on this expedition could be foreseen in the problems that plagued the journey and which started to appear even before the ships departed from Peru: 'the disorder that this journey had were many, and for the attempt that this history tries to achieve, it is compulsory to mention some of them which, in my opinion, have been the cause of the unhappy ending that the voyage had' (Quirós 2000: 116). Quirós (or Bermúdez) remarked that as soon as the camp master, Manrique, boarded the ship, he started arguing with others. The first person to face Manrique's temper was the counter master of the *Capitana*, to whom Manrique tried to teach his own job ('cosas de su oficio'), telling him, according to the narrator, 'words which oblige little but offend much' (2000: 116). While preparing to leave from the Peruvian harbour of Paita, Manrique also proved his quarrelsome bent with the vicar, with Captain Lorenzo Barreto and, finally, also with Quirós (2000: 123–5).

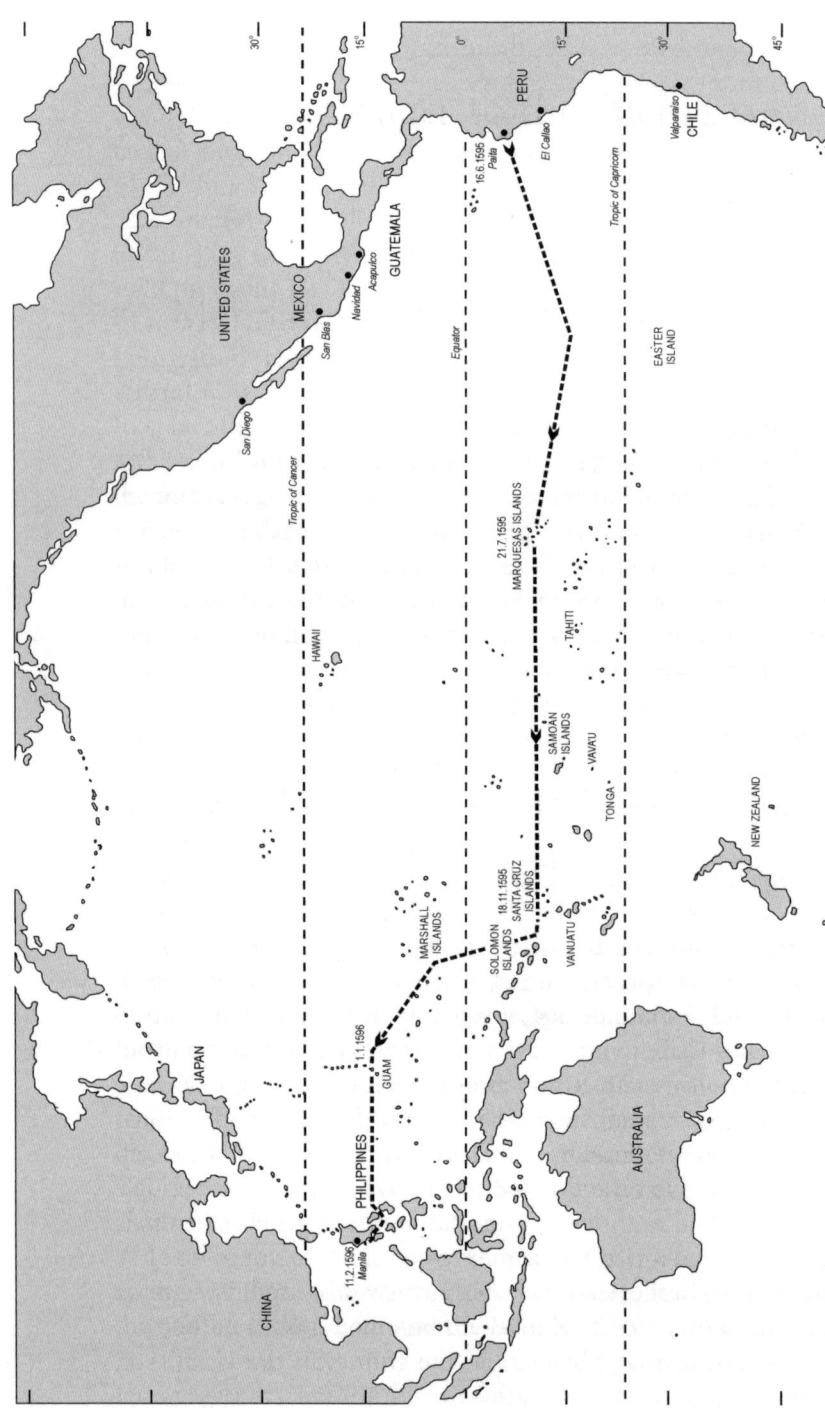

2.2 Itinerary of the voyage of Álvaro de Mendaña and Isabel Barreto to the Isles of Santa Cruz (1595).

After these hardly auspicious beginnings, the fleet left Paita on 16 June and, at the beginning of the voyage, fifteen couples married. They arrived at an island wrongly believed to be the sought-for land, which they called *Magdalena*, 'for being the day before her festivity' (2000: 127). As was customary, the crew sang the psalm *Te Deum* to thank God for their safe delivery and the following day the ubiquitous welcoming canoes appeared, numbering around seventy with 3–10 people in each. Quirós saw that 'around four hundred Indians' who made up the welcoming party were: 'nearly white and with a genteel physique, big, strong, muscled, with good feet and legs, and hands with long fingers. Good eyes, mouth and teeth, as well as the rest of the features. Even their speech was robust'. The islanders were completely naked, with their hair worn 'like women, very long and loose', which made the writer class them as 'gente bárbara y desnuda' ('barbarous and naked people'), although he thanked God for the pleasure given by observing in them his creation: 'it was a pleasure to see them, and there was much to thank their Creator for' (2000: 128).

The poetic licence of the writer was thus given free rein in the depiction of a boy of around ten, whose face seemed to the poet like that of an angel, with hair like a woman. Paradoxically, such angelic appearance gave the narrator more sorrow than he had experienced in his whole life, he indicated in hyperbolic terms, because he knew that the boy would be lost to Western civilisation for eternity: 'I have not had greater pain in my life than seeing that such beautiful creature would remain lost there' (2000: 129).

The 'Indians' brought in their canoes coconuts and a species of walnuts, as well as water, bananas and food wrapped in leaves. They looked intently at everybody on board, laughing overtly at the appearance of the Spanish women. One of the men boldly boarded the ship and Mendaña dressed him up with a shirt and a hat, which the man kept admiring and laughing at, while calling on his friends. Some forty of these came on board, besides whom the Spaniards appeared to be midgets, 'of small size' ('de marca pequeña'). The islanders moved around the ship, touching everything they saw, including the men's colourful clothes. On seeing their surprise, the soldiers demonstrated their common humanity by baring their chests and lowering their hose (2000: 129).

The Spaniards gave the islanders shirts, hats 'and other small items', which they quickly hung from their necks, while dancing and singing. As on the earlier voyage, music and dance were used as a means of communication although, in this case, the dancing islanders started calling others and, in Mendaña's opinion, overstaying their welcome, refusing to leave the ship in spite of being asked to do so. In addition, they did not only touch but also 'with great freedom they stole everything they saw', going so far as to take meat and bacon from the Spanish larders. Mendaña ordered the firing of a volley to scare them off, which it did, making them jump off the ship and swim to their canoes (2000: 130). An old man taunted the Spaniards, making 'fiery signs' with his eyes, while the rest of the islanders threw stones, wounding a soldier as a result. Shooting thus began and the old man was struck in the forehead, falling dead along with seven or eight more. Other islanders were wounded and retreated, only to return with a green branch and 'a white thing' in their hands, which were interpreted as signs of peace since it was also accompanied by the gifts of some coconuts left on the ground (2000: 131).

As noted on the previous voyage, this island was thickly populated and the journal remarked on the fact that it was unknown to the Spaniards, as were the next ones they found, which were called *San Pedro*, *Dominica* and *Santa Cristina*. All are in the archipelago still referred to today as *Las Marquesas de Mendoza*, 'in memory of the Marquis of Cañete' (2000: 133). Unbeknown to anyone on board, the first European contact with Polynesians – a rather 'fatal' one – was taking place.

While searching for a harbour on the island that the Spaniards called *Dominica*, the explorers were again welcomed by many canoes with islanders carrying a green branch and a 'white thing', which was interpreted as intending to befriend the visitors. The explorers could not land, however, owing to the wind, and the next day Mendaña sent the troublesome Manrique with twenty soldiers to find a suitable place. For no apparent reason, according to Quirós, these men shot some islanders, including a father and son, causing the perpetrator to complain that the 'devil' had ordered him to do such a thing. The pilot asked why he had not shot in the air instead and the soldier replied that he had done so in order not to tarnish his reputation as a marksman, to which Quirós commented dryly how such a reputation would serve the man during eternity in hell (2000: 133–4).

The following day, the *maese* was sent again, this time to search for water, as well as a suitable place to use as harbour. Manrique called on the locals to help him get the water, and they agreed, bringing with them coconuts and other fruits. As on the previous voyage, the islanders also offered women to the visitors, who seemed to have enjoyed 'good conversation', as well as a fair amount of fondling. The islanders, however, refused to fetch water and ran away instead with the pots provided, followed by fire from the cannon.

Eventually, the Spaniards managed to land, but not before enduring much hardship, which resulted in complaints from the crew. Once anchored, Mendaña, together with his wife and the majority of the crew, went to the beach where they heard mass for the first time, while the islanders observed them with respect and silent attention, going down on their knees and imitating the gestures of the Spaniards (2000: 135–6). Barreto sat close to a local woman, while attempting to cut a lock of her 'blonde' hair – a gesture that was rejected by the woman, which obliged Barreto to desist.

At this point, Mendaña took possession of the four islands, sowing maize as a part of the ritual: 'The General took possession of all four islands in the name of His Majesty, and he walked on the village, sowed maize before the Indians and had all possible conversation with them before embarking' (2000: 136). While doing this, Mendaña left the camp master behind, and Manrique and his men soon started to fight with the islanders, who threw stones at them, wounded a soldier and ran to the hill, taking with them their women and children.

The Spaniards set up a camp to take on water, while the Marquesans tried to restore ties of friendship with them, according to the journal, because of their awareness of the harm caused by the Spanish weapons 'they tried to make peace and friendship in a way that would be understood, because when the soldiers were walking among their ranches, they would come out to offer them bunches of bananas and other fruits' (2000: 137). Curiously, both parties are said to have achieved a level of closeness, with each islander choosing one Spanish man as special friend. The Marquesans even learned to sing some religious songs and they exchanged with their special friend words referring to the environment, which they repeated in both languages. These signs of mutual camaraderie were, however, marred by intermittent shootings, which on one occasion resulted in the deaths of two islanders.

Quirós believed that Manrique's cruelty manifested itself in the mutilation and display of three 'Indians' corpses, who had been wantonly killed. For Quirós, the threat these locals might have posed was obviously belied by the fact that they had no weapons, unlike the four armed ships that the Spanish possessed. The displayed bodies were retrieved by their fellow islanders in the night, which fuelled Quirós's anger, claiming that the islanders had committed no crime to deserve their ill-treatment at the hands of the explorers (2000: 138–9).

After this unsightly event, the Spaniards got ready to depart and, in spite of the open hostilities witnessed, a local 'Indian, who was a friend of the priest', came to them, making signs of friendship. His loyalty was such, Quirós praised, that when the Spaniards left, this man wanted to go with them, and showed his deep sadness at their departure. Mendaña indicated that he wished to leave around thirty men, some of them married, to settle on the island, but his crew were displeased with this idea and Mendaña abandoned it. The journal lamented that the Spaniards must have killed around 'two hundred Indians' on the Marquesas, and that those deeds ought always to be condemned (2000: 139).[7] For Annie Baert, however, the number of islanders killed given by Quirós is an exaggeration, with the number being something between twenty-five and seventy (c.1999: 178). Whether or not the numbers can be aligned with the extravagant Spanish taste for hyperbole, this first contact between European and Polynesians was certainly an ominous one for the islanders.

Although relationships with the local people are the main focus of Quirós's journal, the natural and cultural environments also receive some attention with, for example, a depiction of *Santa Cristina*, the harbour of which was called by the Spaniards *Madre de Dios* (2000: 140). The narrative makes further reference to the physical features of the land and to the fact that, like the earlier island that the explorers had seen, it was densely populated. The skin colour of the locals and the weapons they used were also remarked upon, as were the women, some of whom were thought to be more beautiful than 'damas de Lima', even though the narrator admitted to having seen none personally (2000: 141). This assessment of women thus followed the epistemological pattern deployed during the previous voyage, entailing description by means of resemblance and assimilation of the newly-encountered peoples to the Europeans' own world, in this instance without Quirós so much as qualifying himself as an eye-witness, which would have been a logical means to corroborate the claim. A similar paradigm obtains in the journal's depiction of the canoes, as well as in those of the carvings of the sacred houses, where food offerings were found. Also included are some generalisations about the supposed character of the people encountered, their appearance, the domestic animals found on the island and fruits and vegetables seen or cultivated (2000: 142–3).

Before leaving this island, the Spaniards raised three crosses, and headed out to sea, arriving on 20 August at a different archipelago, which they called *San Bernardo*, 'because it was his day' (2000: 144–5). The explorers doubted whether these islands would be inhabited and continued sailing until they reached another land mass nine days later, on 29 August, which received the eloquent name of *Isla Solitaria*. At this point the narrative offers a lengthy criticism of Manrique's character and of the attitude of many soldiers who, in the writer's opinion, should have been replaced by more religious 'varones' with kinder personalities (2000: 147). The description of events, rumours and personalities is, however, rather embellished, which invites us to read it, in parts, as a fictional account. In spite of the obvious colouring of events or characters, Quirós's version of events has been used as evidence for this journey and many of its exaggerations have been taken to be a faithful account of the voyage.

The condemnation of Manrique is balanced by the praise lavished on Mendaña's attitude, with the journal mentioning that the admiral did everything in his power to make peace and to set an example. There is an added emphasis on Mendaña's humanitarian side, as seen in his overt sadness when sailing among the islands because of the hardship and the scarcity of water. Furthermore, his resolution to die with the men and women who had accompanied him on this unfortunate voyage is highly commended (2000: 150–1).

After a few more days of navigation, another island was sighted, at which time the *Almiranta* was lost, never to be seen again. All on board lamented the event, especially Mendaña, Mariana de Castro, who was the wife of the ship's admiral, Lope de Vega and an Indian woman who 'cried the death of a soldier who travelled in the ship and was her friend' (2000: 152). As the Spanish approached this island, they were met by a canoe, followed by a fleet of around fifty more. The men shouted from their vessels, waving their hands to call the visitors, who reciprocated. When the canoes reached the ships, the Spanish saw that all on board were men, described as very dark, with their hair and teeth dyed. They were all naked, except for 'parts which they covered with flax cloth', and wore beads, teeth of fish and other artefacts on their arms and around their necks. Their weapons consisted of wooden sticks topped with stones, the type of billy-club called by the Spanish *macanas*, which they used as swords (2000: 154–5).

The explorers tried to speak to these islanders, using the language that they had learnt in the Solomons, which resulted in mutual misunderstanding. In the meantime, the islanders kept staring at the ship but did not dare to board, resorting to shooting arrows which harmed neither the ship nor the people on board. The Spanish riposte consisted of a shoot-out, which killed some and wounded others and, as happened during the earlier voyage to the Solomons, the remaining islanders fled, fearing for their lives, to the nearest mountain. The next day, the explorers sought a place to anchor, which they found in one small bay to the north-west of the island where the 'indios' of a nearby village came out to shoot arrows at them, receiving, in their turn, two volleys. The Spanish continued sailing around the island, stopping for the night at a different harbour from where they could discern dancing and music, which was performed 'as it is their custom, hitting one stick against another and with drums of hollow wood' (2000: 157).

These musical 'Indians', who wore red flowers on their heads and in their nostrils, boarded the ship, leaving their weapons in their canoes. One of them, a man dressed in blue, yellow and red feathers, appeared to the Spaniards to be the leader, and Mendaña received him 'with great love and taking his hand' (2000: 158). This chief, Malope, exchanged names with Mendaña, indicating his satisfaction at being called by the Spaniard's name, and was given a shirt and some trinkets 'of little value' by Mendaña. The Spaniards also provided feathers, beads and bells to the remaining islanders, who put these gifts around their necks, and embraced them, teaching one another signs of peace, such as 'crossing the index fingers'. The islanders asked for metal implements, knives and scissors, showing some curiosity to learn what the Spaniards hid under their clothing.

These friendly encounters lasted four days, during which the islanders came and went from the ships, bestowing food on the Spaniards and taking gifts in exchange. According to the narrative, however, peace did not sit well with many of the soldiers, who 'would prefer to be given the chance to break the peace and to make war' (2000: 160). Thus, when the Spaniards saw fires lit across the island in the night, they inferred that an attack was been prepared. During the following days, as a party was fetching water, a few islanders lay in ambush and shot arrows, wounding three of the soldiers, whom they followed until they were prevented from going further by the sight of the harquebusiers. Mendaña ordered the *maese* to go inland with thirty soldiers, who killed five islanders, while the rest fled to the hills. After this event, the Spaniards retreated, led by Manrique, burning some houses and canoes on their way and carrying three pigs back with them.

At the same time that the Spaniards were withdrawing, Mendaña sent Lorenzo Barreto in the frigate to search for the *Almiranta*, while the *maese* continued his forays into 'Indian' land, killing a further six, who tried to defend themselves courageously. Manrique returned to the ship with seven wounded soldiers and five dead pigs, following which Malope met with Mendaña to complain about the harm caused to him. Malope explained that those who had harmed the Spaniards belonged to a different group from the island and, to prove this, he proposed to go with the Spaniards to exact revenge (2000: 161–2).

At this time, Lorenzo Barreto returned without news about the lost *Almiranta* but having seen three more islands, all heavily populated and with many reefs. The Spaniards moved to a different harbour, where around five hundred armed men threatened them, shooting some arrows. Quirós praised the valour of these men, who fought the visitors until they realised the harm caused by their weapons, seeing some from their ranks dead and others wounded. They carried these dead and wounded men up the mountain, where they disappeared, leaving a trail of blood as they did so. Lorenzo Barreto followed with some soldiers, while the *maese* shouted from the ship that Lorenzo was risking Spanish lives unnecessarily (2000: 164).

The next day Manrique tried to clear some land close to a water fountain 'for the foundation of a village' (2000: 164–5). The married soldiers, however, considered the environment unsuitable for themselves and their wives to live in, disagreeing altogether with the choice of locale, which they found 'sick'. They asked Mendaña to settle instead in one of the already inhabited villages, where the milieu might be more wholesome. By contrast, the unmarried soldiers shared the *maese*'s choice, and soon started felling trees for the foundation of the village, appearing happy with the work undertaken, to the point of forgetting that they had left behind them the wealthy and large 'province' of Peru, 'where no man is poor in hope' (2000: 165). Soon, however, problems resumed when the crew complained about Mendaña's decree that the land, property and people encountered be respected and well treated.

Mendaña named the bay where these events took place *Graciosa*, a name still preserved, and the whole island was given the name of Santa Cruz, by which the archipelago and its main island (Ndeni) are known today. As ever so often, when describing the island, the settlements and housing designs are detailed, as are the canoes, animals and plants in the area, concentrating on a comparison with their likes from Castile or Spain which is very much in line with the paradigm of resemblance already mentioned (2000: 168–72).

Unrest among the soldiers grew, while the pillage of food from the local houses continued, creating discontent among the islanders. Malope's men seemed, however, to be at peace with the Spaniards, and even agreed to help Lorenzo Barreto build some houses. Also, when the vicar raised a cross and some Spanish men went in procession behind him, the islanders tagged along, doing likewise. At this point Mendaña was informed that a document with information against him was being circulated, probably inciting the men to rise in mutiny. Mendaña fell ill, according to the narrative, from the grief that this caused him, though malaria was probably an accessory to Mendaña's sorrows (2000: 174).

In the midst of these 'revoluciones' the church was finished, while some Spaniards tried to provoke the locals, in Quirós's interpretation, to force Mendaña to opt for leaving the island, going so far as to kill two islanders for no reason other than to create conflict (2000: 176). Rumours fuelled dissatisfaction, which extended to criticising Isabel Barreto's attire, with an estimation of how many years of sustenance would be provided by the sale of her dresses. This section of the narrative closes with a biblical comparison, likening the events on board to a Babelian 'tower of confusion' built on ostentation and vanity, very much along the lines of the baroque's *desengaño* (disillusionment): 'foundations of revenge and disordered vanity made up of ambition and greed' (2000: 178–9).

Eventually, everybody's enthusiasm, the vicar's included, faded and nobody wished to remain on the island, with only Quirós regretting that the souls of the islanders would be left to eternal perdition. He judged the Spanish men as having 'little fortitude', further alluding to the fact that even 'provinces' such as Rome, Venice or Seville had 'their beginning' (2000: 183, 185). In this way, Quirós, through the pen of his secretary, placed indigenous peoples at the 'beginning' of time, at once closer to Paradise and further from civilisation. By abandoning 'such enterprise and such land', he wrote, the Spaniards would be judged as 'enemies of God and the King, as well as of their own honour and that of their general' to which others replied that: 'honour must be where the King and the Pope reside, and not among Indians' (2000: 189, 191). Quirós, in turn, answered that they should inform Mendaña if they wanted to leave and, as though it was a consequence of these discussions, the narration informs that the death of the *maese* had already been plotted between Mendaña and Lorenzo Barreto, and entrusted to some soldiers (2000: 196).

The unrest in the Spanish camp continued until one day when Malope invited them to eat. When Quirós saw the scarce food and asked for more, the islanders armed themselves and started shooting, while the Spaniards took Malope with them as hostage (2000: 195). The chief asked his men to provide the Spaniards with food, which they did, also offering to go with the visitors to take food from others on the island. He did so, going with a Spanish soldier and calling on people to give the Spaniards food in some 'pueblos' where they were provided with cane, bananas, coconuts, nuts and fourteen pigs. So much food was given that the Spaniards could not carry it all, although, according to Quirós, the soldiers' greed was still unsatisfied after receiving freely and with goodwill more than enough (2000: 199).

When this party arrived back on board the ship, Isabel Barreto informed Quirós that some soldiers were plotting to kill Malope. Quirós, who is always referred to as 'el piloto', passed this information on to Mendaña, urging him to ensure that no harm was done to Malope, who had been kind and friendly to the Spaniards. We hear next that Isabel woke up the following day with premonitions about the killing of her brothers, and talked to the sick Mendaña, who ordered his men not to harm Malope. Subsequently, the *maese* was stabbed twice by Juan Antonio de la Roca in a scene reminiscent of a revenge tragedy. When the dying Manrique asked to be allowed to confess, he was answered that there was no time, but a 'good woman' came to help him 'die well'. Thus, the journal adds, 'they finished him', leaving Mendaña overcome with sorrow for the dead man, deeply moved by his cruel end (2000: 202).

As is customary when someone dies, a summary of the *maese*'s character and life is given in the narrative, explaining that Manrique had been a good, hard-working soldier, whose main fault had been his inability to keep his mouth shut, 'and I understand that nothing else killed him' (2000: 203). Some disturbances followed his death, with confusion among the conspirators and their victims and another soldier was killed, while some shouted '¡Mueran traidores!' ('Death to the traitors!'), and the women screamed in an effort to defend their husbands (2000: 204). Ultimately, for no apparent reason, the turbulence is said to have subsided, and Mendaña ordered everybody to hear mass.

No sooner had these events been recounted than, out of the blue, in the afternoon they learned from a soldier that Malope had been murdered. Quirós censured the action, praising the dead man and demonising his killer in these terms: 'In this way and so unjustly they killed Malope; and they gave so much evil in exchange for so much good that it seems more like the work of the devil than that of a man' (2000: 207). Those involved in the murder tried to excuse themselves, saying that Malope and his men were plotting treason, but Mendaña ordered the killer and two of his accomplices to be seized and put in the stocks. Lorenzo Barreto detained the 'alférez' ('lieutenant'), while his wife complained, fearing for his fate. Eventually, thanks to the intercession of Isabel Barreto and others, and due to the shortage of healthy men on board, the men were released. In order to show to the islanders that there had been some retribution for the death of Malope, the two heads of the already dead soldiers were shown to them. Nonetheless, poetic justice took its course, and Malope's murderer killed himself passively by refusing to eat and drinking salt water, while being constantly tortured by the accusations of his colleagues. With his death, we are told, there ended the 'tragedy' of the Solomons, where the justice for which Solomon was renowned was sadly missing (2000: 208–11).

In the meantime, the islanders mourned the death of Malope and, the narrative continues, true and deserved punishment came from heaven to everybody. This retribution was meted out in the form of sickness, in all likelihood malaria, from which Father Antonio de Serpa soon died, to the dismay of the vicar. Next, Mendaña passed away, leaving Isabel Barreto as 'governadora' and 'universal heir'. His death was lamented by his wife and others, although some seemed to be pleased. After these two deaths, more ('uno, dos, ó tres') followed daily. In an assessment reminiscent of Lope de Aguirre's desperate quest for El Dorado, we are told that this would be God's retribution for their having provoked His wrath (2000: 213–16).

The islanders sought an opportunity to avenge the harm done to them, and frequently ambushed and shot their arrows at the Spaniards. They caused the explorers little harm, however, though they tried to aim at the body parts that were most vulnerable: the eyes and the legs. When they came to fight the Spaniards in their 'home', Lorenzo Barreto, as a reprisal, sent a soldier in command of a party of twelve to burn their houses. After this took place, some islanders informed the Spaniards that it had been men from other tribes who had injured them, assuring the explorers that they had remained friends and accusing them of breaching the bond of friendship previously established with Malope's murder. Lorenzo asked them to bring food, and they obliged, leading Quirós to conclude that this was indeed nothing but a failed exchange for the islanders, for they received war against the gift of their livelihoods (2000: 219–21).

Lorenzo, who was also quite sick at this point of the journey, sent the frigate once more in search of the *Almiranta*. Having seen no sign of the lost ship on their way, the captain of the frigate grabbed eight boys whom he brought back to the ship. Meanwhile, the sailors asked Isabel to take them away from the islands, as people continued to die on a daily basis. Along with her brother and others, Isabel tried to help the sick on board but, owing to their sheer numbers and the few remaining healthy crew on board, they could not do much. Lorenzo died on 2 November, and was followed by the vicar, who passed away without the comfort of being confessed, with someone reading to him passages from Fray Luis de Granada's *Símbolo de la fe* as consolation.[8] The vicar's death, which left the remaining people bereft of a confessor at the hour of their death, was seen to be also a divine punishment for their evil, which had 'angered God' (2000: 227).

While the explorers remained on the island, they kept sending parties periodically to get food, which they obviously obtained by robbing houses in the villages. The islanders defended themselves and Quirós tried to prevent his colleagues from shooting, other than in the air. Seeing the unfortunate course of events, Isabel Barreto consulted with the pilots and they all agreed to depart once more in search of the *Almiranta* and then head for Manila. They left 'in quest of the island of San Cristobal', where they thought the lost ship might be, indicating that the month spent in Graciosa Bay had cost the lives of forty-seven people, with everyone else sick, 'but happy' to be heading off. Again on leaving, according to the narrative, which uses words reminiscent of a baroque drama, the sailors reviled the place as a 'corner of hell', shouting: '¡Ahí te quedarás, rincon del infierno, que tanto nos has costado!' ('We leave you there, corner of hell, which has cost us so dearly!') (2000: 234).

The journey to Manila was laborious, with the ration reduced to a half pound of cockroach-infested flour and half a pint of 'repugnant and smelly' water (2000: 236). Everybody on board was sick and hungry, with up to four corpses a day thrown overboard. The journey progressed with disagreements on the part of the crew about Barreto's measures until they arrived in the Marianas ('Ladrones'), where they were welcomed by strong men 'of reasonable hue', who called the Spaniards friends and offered them food, including fish, in exchange for iron. Everybody was happy with the exchanges, although it seems that, even in these circumstances, wanton killing was still practised and someone shot two men 'for a piece of the bow of a pipe' (2000: 249).

After more hardship and endless days during which Barreto prayed, believing that they had reached the end of their lives, the remainder of the devastated fleet arrived in the Philippines. Reaching the harbour made everybody rejoice and thank God's mercy: 'because he knows how to give as much grace as he wants to whoever serves him' (2000: 255). There, the sailors bought hens and pigs, paying with money ('reales'), as well as knives and glass beads, which the Filipinos are said to have appreciated more than silver. They remained anchored a few days, exchanging items for food, and eating so much that three or four of the sick men died as a result. Further conflict gathered momentum because Isabel Barreto was in command at this stage, but it was quelled by the pilot who, however, shared this dislike of feminine rule (2000: 258ff.).⁹

The diminished crew led by Barreto left for Manila, arriving in Cavite, two miles south of the capital of the Philippines (2000: 269). Only fifty people remained alive at this point and Barreto is said to have been received as though she were the Queen of Sheba. Like her predecessor, she had just returned from the true Islands of Solomon, from where, it had been believed that the gold for the temple of Jerusalem had been carried (2000: 271). Also reminiscent of popular lore, is the description of the frigate, which did not reach the harbour but is said to have been seen with everybody on board dead. Filled with rotten corpses, the frigate wandered the South Seas, and the myth, which started with these voyages, would be forever tainted with notions of paradise embedded in gold, gore and death.¹⁰

The failure of this voyage's quest for the Solomons, according to Quirós's journal, was due to the difficulties of setting longitude, the interests of individuals and lack of adequate instruments. Thus Quirós closed an account, 'the best I could and knew', of the events, while taking the opportunity on hand to offer his services to continue the search of 'the said lands and others which he suspected and was certain would still be found in those seas' (2000: 287, 288). To do so, Quirós performed a role that strikes his readers as reminiscent of medieval chivalric tradition. According to his own version of events, he sold all that he had to buy a pilgrim's outfit to wear on his way to Rome to canvass support for his next expedition. His interview with the Pope, as well as the numerous Memorials he wrote during the next fifteen or sixteen years of his life, have all been well-documented. The result of his insistent quest was Quirós's last voyage of discovery, in 1605, during which, as in the previous two, Quirós and his crew suffered hardships and discovered different people, sometimes to befriend, sometimes to fight and always to engage in cross-cultural discovery (2000: 308).

NOTES

1 Juan Gil gives the figure of 354 men and women (c.1989: 106), whereas Justo Zaragoza gives 378, 280 of whom could carry weapons (2000: 126). Zaragoza's figures are used by Geoffrey Badger, who estimates 'a total of 378 men, women and children, of whom many expected to become settlers in the new colony' (1996: 34).

2   For sources on this voyage, see the Appendix. All references in this section are to Justo Zaragoza's single-volume edition of this journey until they arrived in the Philippines (2000: 115–253). Zaragoza also includes some events in the Philippines, as well as another description of the islands (2000: 254–308).
3   Lope de Vega, initially appointed as captain of the *Capitana*, was given the title of Admiral, and his ship is referred to as the *Almiranta* after having married Mariana de Castro (2000: 119).
4   Matthew Spriggs has continued the work started by Jim Allen and Roger Greene in that area, concluding that: 'There appear to be no remaining Melanesian accounts of these contacts.' Spriggs suggests that archaeological evidence would tone down 'the somewhat exaggerated Spanish accounts' of this journey (1997: 226).
5   In the *Sumario breve*, Juan de Iturbe, who travelled on the 1605 expedition, wrote that the 'natives of Tarimaco' mentioned the *Almiranta*, indicating that the 'women and children had escaped, but that the rest had been killed'. Surprisingly, Iturbe added that Quirós either did not take this information seriously or willingly ignored his colleagues' plight: 'Quiros was unwilling to take any steps to go to their rescue in spite of being very near – only sixty leagues away' (1966: 2. 275). On this topic, see Spriggs (1997: 238).
6   Archaeological evidence shows that the lost ship beached at Pamua and there 'established what became the second European settlement of short duration in the Oceanic area of the Pacific' (Allen and Greene 1972: 91). Remains of the pottery found in this excavation are held by the Museum of the Solomon Islands in Honiara and at the Otago Museum in Dunedin (New Zealand).
7   A little later in the narrative these deeds are attributed to the lack of mutual understanding (2000: 144). Spate adopts these figures in his summary of this 'first substantial contact between European and Polynesians' (1979: 128).
8   Fray Luis de Granada's *Introducción al Símbolo de la Fe* (*Introduction to the Symbol of Faith*) was published in 1583.
9   The assumptions about Isabel Barreto's rule, as well as the possible biases inherent in her unkind historical portrait, largely rest on Quirós's account. Following centuries of disregard, Barreto figured in a novel by Robert Graves, *The Isles of Unwisdom* (1949). Along similar lines, in another historical novel about this voyage, Pemón Bouzas (2005) has presented Isabel as a beautiful, intelligent and manipulative woman, who knew what she wanted and how to use her beauty to fulfil her ambitions. In *Producing the Pacific* (2005: 44–59), I highlight attitudes and prejudices towards Barreto.
10 The account is completed with a comparison of the Santa Cruz, Solomons and Marquesas.

2

III   Quirós and Vanuatu (1606)

> A new geography – and with it a new cartography and topography which charted the progress of the European empires, and which culminated in Abraham Ortelius's *Theatrum orbis terrarum*, and Georg Braun and Franz Hogenberg's *Civitates orbis terrarum* of 1572–1618 – provided a wholly new and far more immediate image of the 'world' than any that had been available in either antiquity or the Middle Ages. (Pagden 1995: 38)

From Álvaro de Mendaña's first voyage to the Islands of Solomon in 1567 to that of Pedro Fernández Quirós in 1606, certain important changes took place in the development of European geographical knowledge. The revolution that was signposted by the explorations of Christopher Columbus and Ferdinand Magellan took hold not just of people's imaginations but also, and perhaps more importantly, of their actual perception of the universe. Nowhere are the new developments more markedly shown than in the maps and atlases that proliferated at the time. Often based on strategic maps and plans used by travellers or for military purposes, these printed maps were eventually also employed to decorate the houses of the wealthy, as well as to signify dominion and power.

The most famous of these atlases was commissioned by Spain's Philip II and compiled by Abraham Ortelius in his *Theatrum Orbis Terrarum* of 1570. As far as the South Pacific goes, the most interesting feature of Ortelius's world map, entitled *Typus Orbis Terrarum* (Figure 2.3), is the sizeable portion of land named *Terra Australis Incognita*. This enigmatic land mass stimulated the desire to explore, inhabit or Christianise it until well into the eighteenth century. Indeed, this is precisely the zeal which infused the journeys of Mendaña and, especially, those of Quirós, whose name has repeatedly been associated with 'futility'. Such 'futility', according to Lawrence Wroth, was clearly displayed during this second voyage, where his leadership qualities were seen by his subordinates to be wanting.[1]

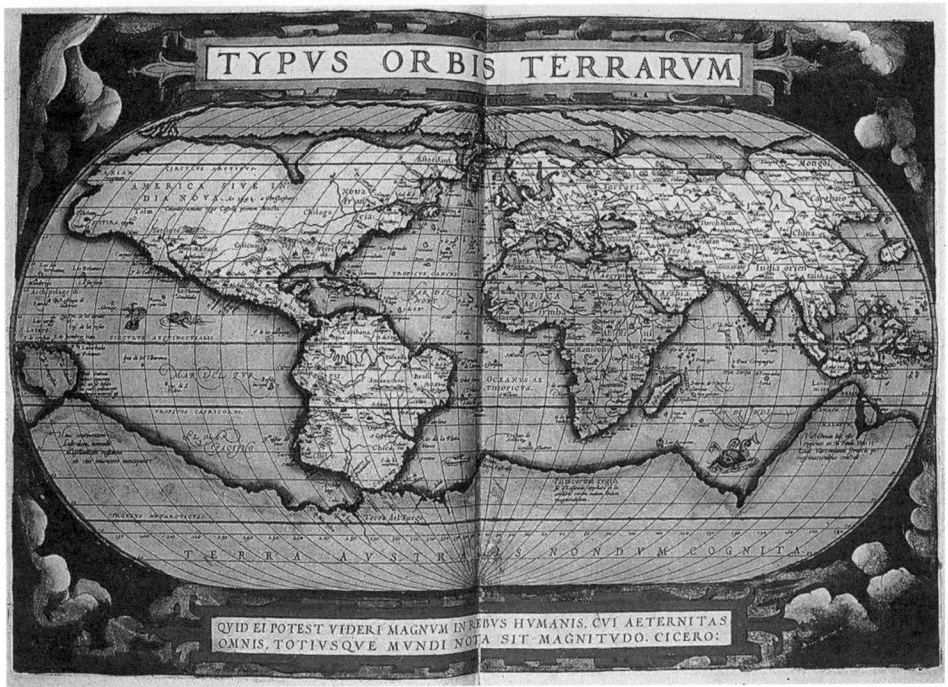

2.3 Abraham Ortelius, 'Typus Orbis Terrarum', from his atlas *Theatrum Orbis Terrarum* (1570), contains a large version of the long-sought *Terra Australis Incognita*.

During this journey to what would be Quirós's *Austrialia del Espíritu Santo*, Quirós faced the constant threat of mutiny.[2] Also, he was unwell and withdrawn, eventually giving up on his enterprise for reasons that still remain puzzling. Quirós's decision to abandon the search for the Solomons, which was probably based on his poor health and the conflict on board, has been unanimously condemned by historians. As John C. Beaglehole has noted, had the ships held course, they would almost certainly have sighted New Zealand, Australia or both.[3] Quirós's ill-fated assessment thus marked the end of his life as explorer.[4] On his return to Madrid in 1607, he tried to have a new expedition entrusted to him for discovery and settlement in the Pacific until, in 1615, he received permission to return to Peru and died on the way to South America in June of the same year.

From the failed expedition led by Mendaña in 1595 and until his death, Quirós had assumed Mendaña's role and dedicated himself with passion to canvassing support for a further expedition.[5] He was finally put in command of the third voyage of South Pacific exploration studied here, which departed from the Peruvian port of El Callao in 1605.⁶ This expedition consisted of two ships, the *Capitana, San Pedro y San Pablo*, and the *Almiranta, San Pedrico*, and a launch, *Los Tres Reyes*. Quirós was in charge of the *San Pedro y San Pablo*, with his declared enemy, Diego de Prado y Tovar, as second in command while Luis Vaez de Torres was captain of the *San Pedrico* and Pedro Bernal de Cermeño of the launch, *Los Tres Reyes*.

Neither the Solomons nor the Santa Cruz archipelago was found on this journey, though Quirós landed in Vanuatu's Santo. Believing it to be part of the Southern Continent, he named it *Austrialia del Espíritu Santo* to honour the monarchy of the Austrian Hapsburgs and pay homage to the southern ('austral') find. From Santo, the fleet divided and Quirós returned to New Spain (Mexico), failing to meet with Luis Vaez de Torres (Figure 2.4). Confused as to the reasons for Quirós's failure to assemble at their agreed rendezvous, Torres led his ship through the strait that today bears his name between the southern coast of New Guinea and the north of Australia, inferring the island status of New Guinea and sighting Australia.

Torres' deed was, however, largely unknown until the eighteenth century, when Alexander Dalrymple found in Manila a letter written by Torres recounting the voyage. Dalrymple published it, and proposed that Torres' name be given to the strait and islands, as they still do today.⁷ Torres has also found modern champions, including Australian scholar Brett Hilder, in the twentieth century who, in a detailed study, laments the silence regarding Torres' achievements, especially when compared with the recognition given to Quirós as a result of his own self-promotion.⁸

Quirós's diary of the journey, as reproduced by Justo Zaragoza in his famous nineteenth-century edition, begins with a brief summary of Quirós's memorials and letters, before narrating the departure of the ship from El Callao and transcribing the instructions given (2000: 317–33). It seems that from the very beginning of the journey Quirós was rather ill and after three days, 'he lacked health, because from Lima his head was in such state that he could neither stand sun nor shade, neither bare nor covered' (2000: 317). Quirós also had some sort of seizure ('pasmo'), but did not die, managing to pass on the relevant instructions to the three ships in his fleet.

In these directives, Quirós remarked on the need to record faithfully all the events, describe the locals, their religion, habitat and the treatment that they ought to be accorded (2000: 322ff.). After noting that the

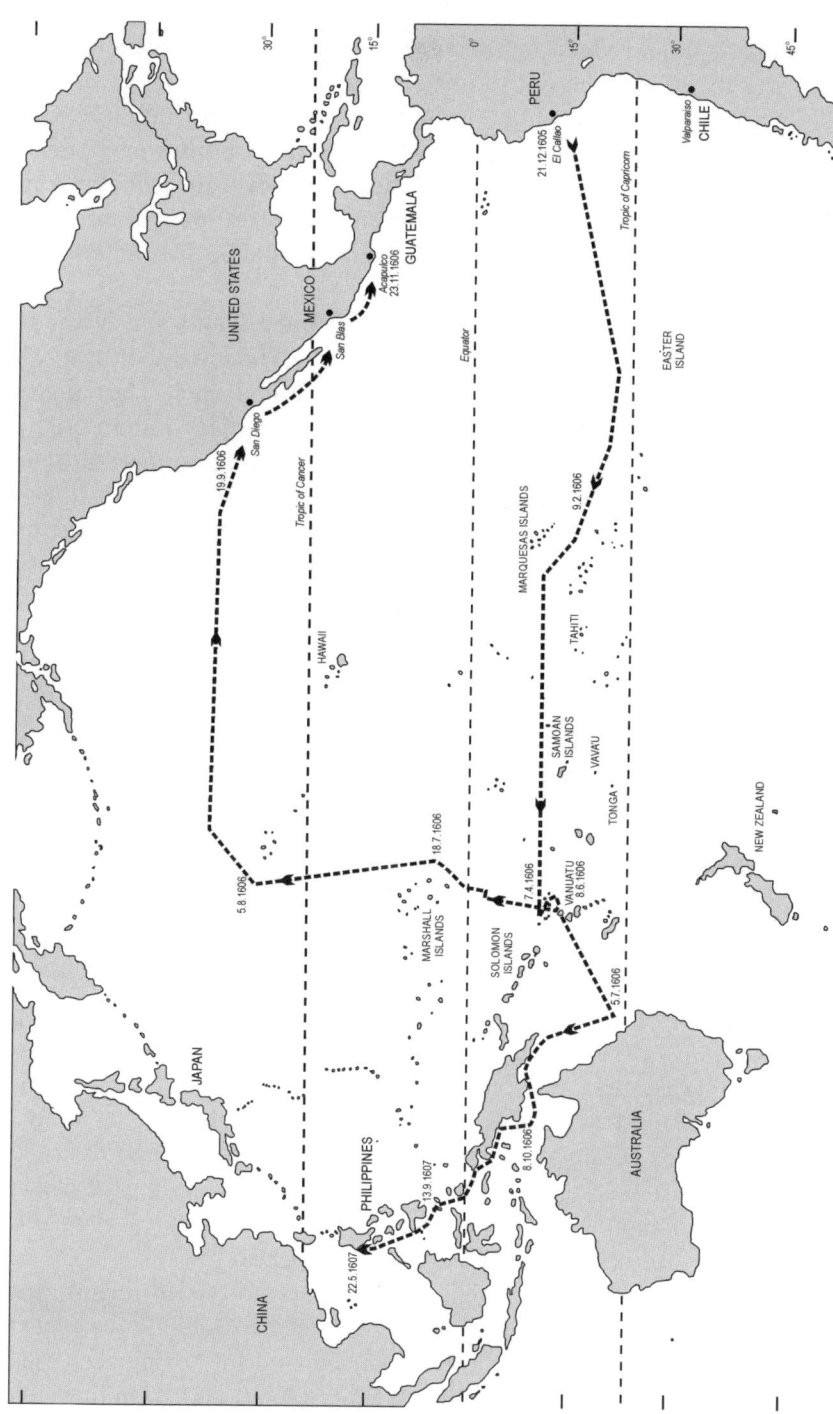

2.4 Itinerary of the voyage of Pedro Fernández de Quirós and Luis Váez de Torres to Vanuatu (1605–6).

Spaniards should always be careful when approaching indigenous peoples, Quirós urged his men not to mistreat any 'Indian . . . nor capture him if it is not to release him fully dressed and caressed'. Furthermore, Quirós also warned against causing harm to their trees, houses or gardens, or breaching peace treaties made with them, and advocated shooting only if and when strictly necessary for self-defence. The treatment of the 'Indians', Quirós added in a rather paternalistic tone, should be 'like fathers to sons' (2000: 331–2).[9]

Quirós's fleet discovered the first uninhabited island, which was given the poetic-sounding name of *Luna-puesta* ('Hidden Moon') at which point the *Almiranta* disappeared, only to be found again. They arrived at a second island, from which they obtained pineapples and an unknown kind of green fruit that they did not eat, continuing on to a third, uninhabited island where they faced a storm (2000: 337). A further five uninhabited islands were seen, with the last of them receiving the name of *San Miguel*, until on 10 February, when the first inhabited island was located.

The sight of smoke, indicating human habitation, was accompanied by the actual detection of people on the beach, which delighted everyone so much that 'their vision was celebrated as though they were angels'. The boats were then sent to meet these islanders, who awaited them with lances, suggesting that they were 'at war'. The Spanish attempted to communicate using gestures, and considered retreating so as not to forfeit the opportunity to make peace. Two bold sailors, however, swam to the shore and the islanders, seeing them land, greeted them three times 'all at once, lowering their heads and arms' (2000: 341–2).[10]

The Spaniards rightly inferred that they were welcomed, ratifying their assumption when the islanders kissed the new arrivals on the cheek, which was interpreted as 'darse la paz' ('exchanging peace'). Another two Spaniards swam to meet with those already on land and, to reciprocate the welcoming gestures, the four gave all that they had on them, which 'the Indians received as tokens of love' (2000: 342). By way of exchange, the Spaniards obtained a palm as symbol of friendship and returned on board to start looking for a place to anchor the ship, sending the two boats in search of an appropriate harbour. This island, which was named *Conversion de San Pablo*, is believed to have been Hao.[11]

The Spanish men who went on the boats proceeded inland, finding what seemed to them burial grounds. In order to 'sanctify the spot', they raised a cross and, on their knees, thanked God for having been the first to hoist their royal flag in 'unknown lands' (2000: 344).[12] On their return, they were met by an old woman, whose age they calculated at around one hundred years old.¹³ They took her on board the ship and the captain rejoiced in her presence, feeding her with meat and soup. The woman ate everything that she was given with overt demonstrations of pleasure, but could not chew the dry biscuit until it was soaked in wine, which she appeared to enjoy too. The Spaniards gave her a mirror and she laughed at her own reflection. These joyful exchanges continued and, when the Spaniards were giving her things 'to dress and take away', four canoes approached the ship.¹⁴ They decided to take the woman to land, so that the local people could witness their peaceful intentions. In spite of these attempts, the islanders on the canoes asked the visitors to leave their island, following which they went with them to see the raised cross and, when told by the Spaniards to kneel before it, dutifully obeyed (2000: 345).

When the Spaniards asked these men about the local chief ('señor') they were directed to a man wearing a head-dress of black feathers. The explorers enquired whether the chief wanted to go to the ship and he agreed to do so, boarding the boats with other islanders. Some, however, jumped off and swam away, apparently out of fear, while he was prevented from leaving and was tied up, which he resisted, making hostile eye gestures, a feature traditionally deployed across the Pacific to scare enemies. Quirós received this man with the same palm that he had been given before as a sign of peace, and regaled him with 'breeches and a shirt of yellow taffeta', a hat, a sheath for a knife and a medal. Embracing him, Quirós indicated that he was free to go, which seemed to appease the man. In the meantime, those Spaniards still on land strove to avoid conflict with the islanders, clarifying that the hostage was being released, something that the islanders had not realised initially because he was dressed in Spanish costume (2000: 347).

In González de Leza's narrative, another event on this island, in which 'el capitan de los indios' gave Sergeant Pedro García a feathered turban, is also mentioned. This interesting item is described in detail because possessing feathers, as well as women's hair, was greatly esteemed by the islanders. Dutifully, Quirós showed appreciation for the precious gift, thereby demonstrating an understanding of the mutual respect required to establish ties of friendship (2000: 627). This means that, regardless of the often-assumed superiority on the part of many visitors, they were aware that a level of esteem for the other culture would be a necessary prelude to a peaceful contact. It also shows that, contrary to expectations, a number of them were prepared to admit openly their position of vulnerability or recognise some indigenous customs or traits as fully human and on a par with theirs.

If at this stage of the voyage there were some problems with the islanders these were certainly made little of by those on board, where, according to Quirós's journal, sailors appeared to be conspiring against their leader and planning to rise up in mutiny. The value of their enterprise and the trust placed on the crew by the Spanish king were arguments deployed by Quirós to persuade the schemers to modify their hostile attitude. To that effect, Quirós also indicated that exploration was a costly affair, stating that 'discoveries cost their creators dearly' and that the men on board ought to 'esteem and be grateful for having had the luck to quest, search and taste the fourth part of the globe' (2000: 350–1).

Quirós's advice notwithstanding, on leaving the island, the problems continued, until the Spaniards saw another island, which they called *San Bernardo*. They landed in search of water but could not find any, seeing only the frame of an old canoe, as well as abundant fish, coconuts and various birds, which indicated the presence of water, according to Quirós, who was at this stage quite unwell. However, the ships continued 'in quest of the island of Santa Cruz' because they were in desperate need, not only of water but also of food supplies (2000: 354).

On the next island which the fleet encountered, they noted smoke and, as they approached the shore, two canoes came to 'reconnoitre them', but did not wait for them. The launch ('zabra') went closer to the beach and was met by 'una flotilla' of ten canoes, in which travelled some tall men 'well made and handsome, and of good colour'. These 'handsome' men sang while rowing in unison, exercising not only their arms but also their vocal cords 'with great skill' (2000: 355). The islanders refused to board the Spanish boat but kept the food and objects that were thrown, and showed their estimation of these items by smelling them without, however, trying anything. González de Leza remarked on this detail, likening the indigenous people to monkeys, 'because all that was given to them they kept, and smelled it as monkeys do, asking for everything they saw'. Nevertheless, González de Leza acknowledged that to marvel at one another is a reciprocal gesture, and that the explorers were equally in awe when watching the cultural displays of the islanders. Much as the islanders 'marvelled at', observing the Spanish ships and people, so too did the Spaniards at the islanders' appearance and disposition, lamenting that such good people would remain in the dark without the light of Christianity: 'to see them so ready and gentle people, feeling sad that they lived in so remote a land and without the light of the baptism' (2000: 634).

Describing the islanders led Quirós to rhapsodise about one of the boys in the canoes who was so 'sweet in smiles and caresses' that he was taken to be a girl and, on first sight, stole the hearts of the hardened men on board (2000: 356). While the Spaniards admired the boy, the islanders started dragging the launch ('zabra') to the shore with ropes so that the captain ordered some shots to be fired to scare them off. The fact that the shots did not frighten the men demonstrated that they had knowledge neither of guns nor of swords, the touch of which wounded some. At this point, an old man challenged the Spanish overtly with incomprehensible shouts, brandishing his lance and threatening them. The Spanish shot in the air to scare him off, but this seems to have had the adverse effect of spurring him on. To avoid causing further harm, those in the launch and boats retreated towards the ships, hindered by the islanders (2000: 358). They decided to go onshore the next day in search of a harbour, so as to obtain supplies of water and wood.

The following morning, many armed 'indios' waited on the beach for the explorers, who tried to reach the shore by boat, capsizing before achieving their aim. As the islanders advanced, they were faced with Spanish harquebus and withdrew, taking with them their local chief, whom they were transporting on poles. Another boy, described as a 'painted angel', came to the Spaniards, appearing to offer himself for anything they might wish. Quirós embraced and dressed him 'with silk breeches and singlet' and, to show his appreciation, the boy climbed up some palm trees to throw down coconuts for the Spaniards, enquiring whether they would like more (2000: 360).

These reciprocal gestures of goodwill encouraged other islanders, who appeared to lower their guard until one soldier, according to Bermúdez, led by 'Satanás', tried to enter a local house. The homeowner effectively defended it with a stick, striking the soldier unconscious, and he was about to do the same with another soldier who came to help the first when others arrived. The 'indio' was then shot and, on seeing his own blood flowing, attacked more fiercely, dying when he ran into a sword held by a sailor called Gallardo. The journal commends the bravery of the deceased man in terms reminiscent of a contemporary play: 'thus fell dead on the ground one that did not deserve death because of his courage in defending his own home' (2000: 360). With this death, however, a precious opportunity to establish some sort of peaceful understanding with the islanders was sadly wasted.

The Spaniards explored the island and noticed some boys and girls accompanied by a woman, described as lusty, gallant: 'a straight, well-built, lusty and very pleasing lady...with a virile disposition'. Virility in women, it is worth remembering, was a term of praise in Spain at the time, often to stress the uniqueness of some females who, like Saint Theresa or Queen Isabel of Castile, were classed as exceptional and beyond their sex. Indeed, as Melveena McKendrick's groundbreaking study shows, the *mujer varonil* who was inspired in those models became a constant feature of the contemporary drama in which Quirós's secretary, Bermúdez, was steeped. This 'virile' woman welcomed the Spaniards and exchanged signs of peace with them, after which they left her, although she seemed to not be scrupulous ('melindrosa') and, the narrative suggests, would have gone with them if they had so wished (2000: 361–2).

The journal also describes the few items that the locals had in their houses, as well as the various implements they used, explaining the skill that the islanders deployed to make needles out of bones in order to sew clothes and sails (2000: 362–3). That the land was planted and the plots marked with a type of peg to delimit boundaries suggested to the Spaniards a developed concept of private property, much as in their own homeland. Such interpretation by means of assimilation with what was known, though common and perhaps unavoidable, led to misunderstandings, some of which had dire consequences.

The Spaniards left the island, which was given the name *Peregrina*, in quest of Santa Cruz and, in spite of the fact that they were on board ship, since it happened to be Easter, festivities were conducted with processions, which must have had a rather short itinerary. The navigation continued without finding land, which fuelled the sailors' unrest, and the men censured Quirós, insulting him with worse words than could 'be said of a Turk' (2000: 365). While the disorder continued, the pilots discussed their estimations of the distance to landfall, eventually resulting in further arguments and in the chief pilot being put in the stocks.

After these events, the explorers arrived on a third inhabited island, where they saw smoke, an indication that pleased them since they thought that they would be able to locate water. They found a suitable harbour and proceeded inland, stumbling on a small village, where some men were fleeing with women, children and their possessions. Around one hundred and fifty remained to face the Spaniards with their weapons, with one of their party advancing, shouting and challenging the visitors. The Spanish shot in the air to scare them off and, on seeing this, all the islanders took to the water except for one man, who moved forward, asking the Spaniards not to shoot while indicating by signs that he would order his men to put down their weapons. The Spaniards agreed to this and reciprocated the gesture (2000: 373).

This man, who was called Tumai, or *Jalique*, meaning chief or *arii*, showed the Spaniards some of their houses, asking them not to harm them. In return for his friendly gesture, Tumai was given clothing of 'orange taffeta', which he appreciated (2000: 374). In fact, Tumai's friendship became quite useful to the Spaniards, not just for his role as go-between, but also for his ability to supply information, especially with regard to the geography of the island and of those in its vicinity.

The Spaniards anchored the ships and went inland with the six Franciscans travelling on the expedition, who were urged by Quirós to go to the village in order to say the first mass in honour of Our Lady of Loreto and in celebration of 'San Pedro' (2000: 375). While they did this, the 'indios' watched and copied the Christians, from which the narrator inferred that it would be 'easy' to convert them and to remedy the inevitable loss of their souls to God and eternity.

The next day, Quirós received Tumai 'with a happy face and embraces' and the *arii* reciprocated, giving Quirós 'peace on the cheek' (2000: 375). Tumai refused to eat the food that was offered but he imitated Quirós when the former kissed the hand of Fray Martín de Munilla and asked Tumai to do likewise. Quirós enquired whether the islanders had seen ships like theirs before, to which Tumai answered in the negative, even though he seemed to know of the events in Santa Cruz during the previous voyage, including the death of Malope. This, the narrator intimated, was given as the reason why his men had run away on seeing the Spaniards.

At this point, Tumai displayed his knowledge of the area, pointing towards some landmarks on the horizon and naming over seventy islands, including a large land mass called *Manicolo*. Tumai, moreover, drew a chart on the soil, using circles of various sizes to indicate the relative sizes of the islands mentioned and for the large land mass 'opened his arms and hands, without closing them again'. To signify distance, Tumai resorted to the sun, estimating days and nights spent on the way. Lastly, Tumai depicted the islands' inhabitants in terms of their skin colour and whether they ate human flesh, which he signalled by biting his own arm and showing aversion. This tirade seemed to drain him and he indicated his desire to retire, being then embraced and given some gifts ('rescate') before his departure (2000: 377).

The geographical information thus gathered from Tumai was confirmed the following day, when Quirós visited him and showed him a map and a compass. Tumai understood the graphic representation of the world that the map represented and, when Quirós asked him the names of the islands, Tumai answered to everybody's satisfaction. In fact, Tumai's information was corroborated by other locals, who were at first surprised to see the representation of their island universe on paper. Like Tumai, however, they soon deduced the conceptual illustration that mapping entailed and supported the information provided by Tumai (2000: 377).

Thanks to Tumai's goodwill, the relationship between Spaniards and islanders remained cordial, and they exchanged food as well as names with mutual trust, shown by the fact that many Spaniards went to the local villages by themselves and never received any harm. Also, the Spaniards left their belongings around the island, including the clothes they washed, and nothing went astray. Tumai also helped them by ordering his men to fetch water and wood, in payment of which these 'indios' asked for, and received, bells and other items, which seems to have pleased them. For the Spaniards, Quirós's journal observes, Tumai proved to be a 'grave', calm and prudent ruler, who always kept his word. This appraisal is corroborated in González de Leza's account, which commends Tumai in the highest terms, indicating that to write the 'excellencies of this chief would be a never-ending task'. González de Leza, however, made Tumai an exception to the rule, suggesting that no other 'barbarian' could be found with the 'reason' that Tumai had (2000: 653).

The island over which Tumai ruled was given the name *Nuestra Señora del Socorro*, although Quirós acknowledged that it was known 'in local language', as Taumaco (2000: 379).[15] Its features are described following the customary procedure of comparing them to similar places in Europe. For example, Tumai's village was labelled *Venecia* because it was surrounded by water. This is followed by description of the houses, the scant furnishings, the canoes and their construction and some of the islands' main products, including roots, fruit, domestic dogs and hens. An inventory of the islanders' physical traits and racial mix completes this section, where the journal conjectures that their features might be the result of intermingling with people from neighbouring islands because of wars: 'this people, it seems, are fond of fighting with Indians from other lands' (2000: 381).

After this, the diary recounts the departure of the explorers, who took with them four locals to serve as interpreters, while Tumai, in bidding farewell to the Spanish, disregarded the plight of these prisoners, probably in order to safeguard his people. Of these local men, one threw himself overboard to swim ashore to another island some three 'leagues' away (2000: 383). A second man did likewise when he saw another island, so that the remaining two were locked away. One of these, however, also managed to free himself and tried to swim ashore when the Spaniards were distracted talking to friendly islanders in another island named after the Saint on whose day it had been discovered, *San Marcos*.[16]

On one of the next islands that they passed, which they named *Lágrimas de San Pedro*, four canoes with islanders, appearing to be friendly, came to meet the Spaniards, inviting them to their land. As those on board the *Almiranta* refused to accept the offer, the 'indios' gave them coconuts and other fruits before returning to the shore. The Spanish sent the boat to reconnoitre the island in order to seek a suitable place to anchor; this was followed by many locals at a short distance, until one of them, who appeared to be asking questions, went on board. The Spaniards eventually assumed that he was challenging them and that he believed himself capable of capturing them all. Consequently, they imprisoned him and took him back to the ship.

When the Spanish party arrived with their prisoner, the captain, Quirós, embraced this man, and asked him questions, which he seemed to understand and be pleased to answer. While this was taking place, another islander who was on the launch managed to break the lock which imprisoned him and threw himself overboard. After four hours trying to swim with a heavy load, he was rescued when he was close to exhaustion. He was given food and wine, before being locked in the stocks, where he spent the night speaking with his fellow countryman, and both of them appeared to be sad (2000: 390).

The next morning, the captain released these two men, making a show of criticising the soldiers who had locked them up. Quirós appointed the barber to shave them and cut their hair and nails, which surprised them because of the ease with which this was done, thanks to the iron scissors. Afterwards, the islanders were dressed with taffeta in a variety of colours and given hats, beads, knives, a mirror and other trifles. When this gift-giving concluded, the men were taken ashore, which clearly surprised them. On their return to their own people, they were received by many islanders, among whom was a woman with a girl in her arms who appeared to the narrator to have been the wife of one of the liberated men.

Since, as a result of these friendly exchanges, there was a degree of mutual trust, the Spaniards asked this woman to let them hold the girl. They passed the baby from one to the other, cuddling her while doing so, an affectionate gesture that seems to have pleased everybody. As a mark of goodwill, the islanders gave the Spaniards two pigs and some strange looking bananas, which, again, associating the unknown with something already identified back home, were likened to aubergines. From other people on the island, the Spanish received coconuts, sweet cane, fruits and water stored in 'cañas' ('canes') (2000: 392). Following this, the explorers retreated to their ships with one wounded man who had been shot with an arrow in the cheek by some islanders. For Quirós, this breach of the peace appears to have attested to the fact that these two groups of islanders were rivals and were jealous of the friendship the Spaniards had achieved with one of them.

The explorers continued their navigation until they sighted another island, which pleased them because it was so large that the land stretched as far as they could see. They called it *La Cardona* in memory of the Duke of Sessa, who had helped Quirós during the many years he had spent organising the fleet.[17] They went out in a boat in search of a harbour and, while sailing round the coast, were approached by many islanders, who were described as tall and dark. These men were armed with bows and shot some arrows at the Spaniards, who continued circling the island and taking note of its different groups of people. When they reached a bay, they put up for the night and were met by two canoes with 'Indians with their bows ready' (2000: 394). González de Leza's narrative relates that this bay, which is drafted in one of Prado's bird's-eye views, was called *San Phelipe y Santiago* because it was discovered on 1 May, which is the feast of those apostles (2000: 670) (see Figure 5.1, page 214). The Spaniards fired a volley into this bay to scare the locals, who fled while the boat returned to the ship with the news that a harbour had been found (2000: 395).

The next day saw some failed attempts to establish mutual trust, with neither party daring to take the initiative. First, the Spaniards tried to get some islanders to come on board so as to give them clothes before releasing them. The locals rejected the offer, asking instead that the Spaniards leave their boats, which was in turn refused by the Spaniards. Yet the 'indios' threw some fruit in the water, which was taken by the visitors, and Quirós sent a party of soldiers inland the following day in an effort to bring some islanders on board to 'secure peace and friendship' (2000: 396). The party spoke to the islanders, who marked a line on the sand, indicating that it should not be crossed, while other islanders surrounded them in the hills nearby. The Spanish shot in the air, in theory to frighten them, although one soldier struck one old man, apparently a 'principal', dead.[18] After this, all the islanders deserted their villages, while, from his ship, Quirós contemplated the panorama with sadness.

Following these events, possession of the island took place, beginning with Quirós creating 'war ministers' and choosing the office holders.[19] This continued with the establishment of the Order of the Knights of the Holy Spirit, 'with the laws and precepts that have to be followed'. Thereafter, Quirós took formal possession in the name of the Holy Trinity, the Roman Pontiff and His Catholic Majesty, Philip II, gave everyone a blue cross to wear on their breast, ordering that, if he were to die, everyone should continue the 'quest, pacification, population and conservation of all these lands that we are discovering and those that must be discovered in times to come' (2000: 398–401).

When everybody was ready to parade with the flags hoisted in the air, Quirós, in a gesture reminiscent of Columbus, knelt and kissed the land, uttering the following poetic words: 'Ah! Land, sought for so long, pretended by so many and so intensely desired by me!' Festivities and rituals followed, while formally raising the flag as sign of possession, this time, in the name of the Holy Trinity and then, the Catholic Church, Saint Francis and his Order, of John of God and his Order, of the Holy Spirit and, last but not least, of His Majesty the King of Spain (2000: 404–9). Three masses were said, with everyone taking communion, and this was followed by a fiesta during which two slaves were freed. However, one chronicler of the events, Juan de Iturbe, in regard to this latest action, ironically pointed out that, though magnanimous in appearance, it was merely an empty gesture for the slaves were returned to their masters afterwards. Iturbe observed that:

> [Quirós] wished to establish an Order and to call it the Order of the Holy Ghost. And so at Whitsun he gave crosses of blue taffeta to all the crew of the fleet, who wore them on their breasts ... even two negro cooks were rewarded by such largesse, great liberality and munificence for their gallantry and courage. Besides, on that day, he granted them their liberty, although they did not belong to him, and what is more they afterwards continued in the self-same state of slavery. (1966: 2. 286)

After these ceremonies, Quirós selected people for a 'cabildo' ('town council'), distributing the offices which they would hold. Next, he ordered the *maese* to go inland, where he found some villages where the islanders, who were 'occupied in their dances', on seeing the Spaniards, fled to the hills, leaving everything behind, including two cooked pigs and other foodstuffs. The expeditionary party ate this food and took back to the ship twelve pigs and eight chickens, commenting that they saw on the way a tree with a trunk so thick that could not be embraced but by fifteen or twenty men (2000: 412–14).

During the following days, Quirós took some men to one 'hacienda' to sow maize, cotton and other legumes and seeds, actions that were, symbolically at that time, an indication that they were assuming possession of the land. Following this, Quirós sent the *maese* with thirty soldiers to reconnoitre, which inspired the islanders once more to arm themselves, although this resistance did not prevent the explorers from taking three young boys, 'the oldest a seven-year-old', and twenty pigs (2000: 415). When the Spaniards went to fetch water the next day, the locals ambushed them to exact revenge but failed and, in their rage, attempted to pull down the church. On seeing this, Quirós sent people to prevent them from harming the building and the islanders retreated beyond a river called by the Spanish *Salvador*.

The launch was next sent to explore this larger river, locating a village 'of four streets, with a square', from which its inhabitants fled on being advised of the arrival of the Spaniards (2000: 417). There, the visitors found fruit, flowers, fish and shellfish wrapped in plantain leaves, while they were overwhelmed by the noise of the drums with which islanders communicated with one another. Nonetheless, the Spaniards returned to their ship without being attacked and repeated these expeditions a few times, with the journal suggesting that some locals may have been killed on occasion, although the soldiers always denied doing so.

While these explorations took place, the Spanish did not forget their religious festivities and continued their customary rituals with the celebration of the Corpus Christi. They staged an elaborate procession in which the religious images of Saint Peter and Saint Paul were paraded (2000: 418–19; González de Leza 694–5). The preparations for the procession included three masses, on the third of which they staged a parade, led by a soldier carrying a heavy cross made of orangewood. This soldier was followed by a lay friar, an array of various groups playing music and other clusters of people carrying the royal banner. All sang hymns, shot volleys in the air and a fourth mass was said. The Taumaco boy, Pedro, who took part in the procession dressed up in taffeta, was very pleased at this events and proud of the cross he bore on his chest, 'lusty, astonished and happy from all he was seeing and his own cross' (2000: 422). Music, dances and 'good conversations' followed these festivities, ultimately marred by the eating of poisonous fish, which prostrated many of the Spaniards with vomiting and heartburn (2000: 422–4).

The narrative at this point depicts the island's features, including the river named by the Spaniards *Jordan*, which, in line with the assimilative etymology described above, was likened to Andalucia's Guadalquivir. The harbour where they had landed received the name *Vera Cruz*, and is said to have been peaceful and populated by tall, burly people that were neither black nor mulatto and who were only partly clothed, a sign of their level of civilisation for the Spaniards. Also, they appeared to be very musical, playing flutes and drums, as well as shells, while their weapons consisted of bows, arrows and 'macanas'. Their religious and burial practices are also accounted for, noting that they had sacred houses with carved figures to which offerings were made. The journal also observes with some surprise that the islanders did not seem to help each other when they met harm, deducing that they lacked solidarity and were 'not hurt by their neighbours' pain'. As usual, the houses and foodstuffs are given attention, highlighting the staple breadfruit, the raising of pigs, hens, birds, fish, and the cultivation of fruit, such as types of bananas and nuts which were unknown to the Spaniards (2000: 425–30).

Among the local crafts, the pottery made with black clay, the stone masonry and the local dressmaking in 'median looms' are mentioned (2000: 431). Some Spaniards also believed they had seen silver which, along with gold, was often used as a good publicity for future voyages of exploration or colonisation. The island's climate was classed as temperate, remarking on the absence of snow in the mountains and on its wholesomeness because nobody was sick during their sojourn. Lastly, Bermúdez compared the island's towns and harbours favourably with the cities of the Americas, including Paita, Callao and Arica in Peru (2000: 432–4).

However pleasant and inviting, the Spaniards decided to leave the island and, as they prepared to do so, many islanders gathered together, playing their instruments and shooting arrows with no effect whatsoever on the visitors. Quirós ordered that the prisoner boys be shown to the islanders in order to ascertain whether their disappearance was the cause of their unrest. Nevertheless, as the boys were dressed up in Spanish clothes, their relatives did not recognise them initially. When they did, some men approached the ship from the water, which led Bermúdez to believe that they were the boys' fathers. These men tried to ransom the children for food, and gave one pig, promising more. The Spaniards, however, believed that the islanders were preparing to ambush them and fired their guns to make them abscond (2000: 436–7).[20]

While this was happening, and on perceiving the sadness of one of the boys, Quirós tried to reassure him, saying that he should be happy to leave 'gentiles' behind to become part of the kingdom of Christendom. In the meantime, the cross that the Spaniards had raised was still in the same place, which the islanders had respectfully hung with branches and flowers. As the Spanish left the harbour, the ships parted, and Quirós's *Capitana* continued on its way, discovering a further island close to those of *Virgen María* and *Belen*, which they suitably 'baptised', following their religious inclination, as *Pilar de Zaragoza* (2000: 438–42).

From this point on, the narrative centres on the failure to find again the Island of Santa Cruz and the many disagreements arising from Quirós's command (2000: 443ff.). Rightly, Quirós inferred that he did not have many friends on board and complained of the lack of courage and loyalty towards the king on the part of his crew. He ordered his officers to sail north-east and some protested, thinking that they should aim for the Philippines. Quirós tried to reach Guam in the *Ladrones* (Marianas) and from there go to Acapulco but, after collecting water from a storm, they arrived in the Mexican port of Navidad on 21 October of 1606 (2000: 446–69).[21]

On the way to Navidad, Quirós wrote his will, where he indicated that it was impossible to settle 'among those so new and tender people' with men described as birds of prey (2000: 455). Quirós explained why he had not punished those who had conspired against him, giving as a possible reason that even though justice is 'an excellent virtue' it is sometimes wiser not to exercise it (2000: 460). By way of conclusion, Quirós wrote about a sailor's escapade from the ship. His adventure serves to close the present voyage, for it exemplifies the questioning of European civilisation that would become more obvious and complex during later voyages.

This anonymous man, steeped in the life of the hermit Saint Anton, kept gazing at one of the islands, which is unnamed in the narrative. One night, it was found that he was missing. After making some enquiries, some people said that they had seen him make a raft and they realised that he had taken with him all his possessions. The sailor had left the Spanish ship and the civilisation it represented in order to live with the 'indios', a desire he had already expressed. Although judged a good Christian, this 'beachcomber', according to the journal, had taken some unnecessary and, perhaps, unwarranted risks, as it would be extremely difficult for him to reach land. Moreover, even if he did, he would face loneliness, nakedness and severe weather, let alone the possibility that he might be eaten by locals (2000: 61–2). Solitude and the harshness of the climate are thus added to the nakedness of body, as well as the abandonment of Spanish civilisation and religion, the renunciation of which surprised his colleagues. The choice to desert one's own culture to become part of another with little or no possibility of return had, however, already been taken by many going to the Americas. Indeed, it foreshadows the centuries to come, when the Pacific became a home for beachcombers, mutineers, writers, artists and others wishing to turn their back on European civilisation.

Drawing towards its conclusion, the journal explains how the Spanish survived their last storm, during which Quirós, who was quite ill in bed, asked the boys they had taken from the islands whether they would like to become Christians. On seeing death at their doorstep, they agreed, becoming Pedro and Pablo respectively, and with Quirós as their godfather. Their belief, probably spurred on by fear for their own lives, appears to have been sincere, as during the storm they prayed fervently, a sight that, in the narrator's opinion, would soften the hardest of hearts (2000: 464–5). Such faith, or at least that of Pablo, was somehow shaken, however, after the untimely death of the aged 'comisario', Fray Martin de Munilla, close to the end of the journey. As Pablo saw that Munilla was buried in the sea with a weight on his feet, he wondered whether, as he had been led to know, all Christians were meant to rise to heaven after death, whereas this supposedly holy man was taken downwards. Some Spaniards tried to explain to him that it was the soul, and not the body, which went to heaven, while they admired his perspicacity (2000: 467).

These two Pacific boys, Pedro and Pablo, also participated in religious ceremonies, as, for example, during All Saints' Day, when they knelt 'each of them with a candle, lighting it all the time that the sacrifice and communion lasted'. Likewise, they joined everyone in religious displays on the way towards Acapulco, when they stopped on the beach of Citala to complete their christening rituals. There, on the day of 'Santa Caterina, mártir', the crew left the ship, following the royal banner to go to the church, taking Pedro and Pablo, 'both dressed in new clothes, to the baptismal pile'. After mass, the vicar anointed the boys with 'oil and chrisma', which they had not been able to receive during the storm, when they had been baptised in haste and without ceremony (2000: 475–6).

The unrest among Quirós's crew did not die down on arrival in Mexico, where many members of his ship tried to 'discredit the journey' and Quirós was forced to justify it (2000: 472ff.). Quirós's validation included an explanation of the legal right of explorers to settle in places other than their home towns, and he simply indicated that they had the same right as in the Americas (2000: 479–82). Quirós was there faced with the account of Luis Vaez de Torres, whose ship, the *Almiranta*, he had failed to meet at their appointed rendezvous. As indicated by Torres in his report, after waiting for Quirós, he had sailed below the southern coast of New Guinea towards the Philippines, discovering the strait that is named after him.[22]

Apart from addressing the various rumours surrounding his inability to lead the journey to a successful conclusion, Quirós dedicated himself from this time onwards to sending multiple petitions to the king, Philip III, seeking sponsorship for a further voyage to the South Pacific. This voyage, however, was not concluded, as Quirós died en route before achieving his aim in 1614. Thus, poetic justice finally met with Quirós, who ended as he had lived, on the way to his promised land. It would take, however, more than one and a half centuries for other Europeans to find Quirós's sought-after land, and for the Spaniards to venture into the Pacific again. During this time, different ways of seeing the world and the peoples inhabiting it developed, leading to the construction of another ocean whose mysteries would have to be dispelled and to which this book now turns.

NOTES

1 'Returning from Peru and thence to Spain, Quirós besieged the king until a royal cedula of 1603 sent him forth once more on a voyage to explore the South Sea for the lands which were believed to extend from the Strait of Magellan to New Guinea. Quiros reached what was much later named the New Hebrides, and thinking that the large island Espíritu Santo was continental land, took possession of the long sought Terra Australis in the name of Spain, naming it, with the Emperor's fief of Austria in mind, Austrialia del Espíritu Santo. Again Quiros and futility seemed to spell the same thing' (Wroth 1944: 175).

2 In the Introduction to *La Austrialia del Espíritu Santo*, Celsus Kelly lists documents and letters attacking Quirós's leadership on this journey. Those writing against Quirós are just about all those who matter: the Viceroy of México, Felipe Corzo, Luis de Castro, Juan de Iturbe, Diego de Prado, Fernando de Castro, Alonso de Sotomayor and Luis Vaez de Torres (1966: 1. 110–11).

3 'So', writes Beaglehole, 'on the pinnacle of glory, Quirós turned his back; and there began that melancholy retreat the truth of which is so hard to disentangle' (1966: 96).

4 'It was a decision that sealed his fate and ended his career as a *descubridor*. He failed to explore La Austrialia and to establish its relation to the Southern Continent, and . . . he had deserted his consorts' (Kelly 1966: 1. 3).

5 In relation to Quirós's long-winded efforts to canvass support from 1595 to 1606, Ian Cameron remarks that: 'The Viceroy of Peru referred Quirós to the

court of Spain; the court of Spain referred him to the Papacy; the Papacy referred him back to Philip III; Philip handed him over to the Council of The Indies, and the Council of The Indies passed him on to the Council of State' (1966: 163).

6 Kelly offers a summary of dispatches and letters dealing with the objectives of the voyage (1966: 1. 6–11). The most important accounts from the voyage are from the pen of Quirós (or his secretary, Belmonte Bermúdez), which is here broadly used, as is the narrative of González de Leza. I list different sources in the Appendix.

7 For Miriam Estensen, the treatment of the letter illustrates 'the preoccupation with secrecy' of the Spanish authorities at the time. The fact that Torres's letter criticises 'the local Spanish administration' is the cause, Estensen believes, why it 'was apparently never answered. It was placed in state archives where neither the Portuguese nor Spain's English and Dutch enemies would ever find it. The price of such secrecy was that Spain never acted upon Torres's discoveries, which could have led to Spanish claims to Australia' (2000: 62–3).

8 'That such great discoveries were made only to be filed away so successfully in the archives that the world has been largely ignorant of them to this day is a very poor reward for Torres and his men, who received neither thanks nor repayment from the Spanish Crown. Quiros, on the other hand, thanks to his genius for exaggeration and propaganda, achieved great renown and lasting fame for his meagre discoveries, which were still inspiring exploration at the time of Cook' (Hilder 1980: 10).

9 Another narrator of this voyage, Fray Martín de Munilla, also uses the comparison of indigenous peoples with 'children', who should also be seen as 'mortal enemies' (1963: 27).

10 González de Leza gives the names of the two men as Francisco Ponce and Miguel Morera, both from the *Capitana* (2000: 621).

11 Landín observes that others identify this island with Anaa (1992: 3. 651 n. 2). Kelly charts the different attributions given to this island by various authors (1966: 1. between 62–3).

12 The Spaniards were not planting just one cross, according to González de Leza's account. After mentioning that they raised 'a tall and well-made cross', González de Leza adds that the Spaniards hoisted crosses just about every day, going so far as to having individuals each raising their own crosses (2000: 624).

13 González de Leza's journal mentions that she had one bad eye (2000: 623).

14 The workmanship of the canoes was praised by González de Leza, who likened them to 'galeotas', which 'could not be better made in Castile' (2000: 623).

15 In González de Leza's account the name given to the island appears as *Nuestra Señora de Loreto* (2000: 648, 658).

16 The next two islands encountered were uninhabited and were also named mostly following religious criteria as *Margaritana, Verjel, Lágrimas de San Pedro, Portales de Belen* and *Isla de la Virgen María* (2000: 387–8).
17 The full name of the seventh Duke of Sessa was Antonio Fernández de Córdoba Folch de Cardona y Anglesola Aragón y Requesens II.
18 In González de Leza's narrative, we learn that this dead man was hung from one foot on a tree, so that the others would see him (2000: 677).
19 See González de Leza (2000: 680–8) and Munilla (1963: 69–73).
20 In fact, González de Leza remarks that even if the islanders had given as much food as there was on the island they would not get their boys back (2000: 698).
21 The last section of González de Leza's narrative deals mostly with the position of the ship, which were calculated with navigational aids such as 'taking the sun' (2000: 702–14).
22 As Oskar Spate posits, 'The significance of [Torres's] voyage was the determination of the insularity of New Guinea and the consequent northern delimiting of any possible Terra Australis, and the opening (though its use was long delayed) of an alternative western passage to and from the Pacific' (1979: 140).

Voyaging and the Pacific 1606–1770s 3

> Whoever considers the progress of science and of commerce, within a few centuries, must confess that mankind are much indebted to those heroes who went in quest of *New Lands*. (Dalrymple 1770: xvii)

As would be expected, navigation techniques improved gradually and significantly from the sixteenth century onwards. This led eventually to the solution of the long-standing problem of longitude and to upgrading in the building of ships. Also, diet and hygiene on board were greatly enhanced during some later eighteenth-century voyages, especially following the lead of James Cook, who included fresh fruit and sauerkraut in the crew's daily meals, with the intention of avoiding scurvy, which had been the scourge of sailors for centuries. However, cockroaches, rats, thirst and hunger were still rampant, as were other discomforts associated with journeys in cramped conditions, often lasting several years.

Before the series of remarkable voyages that took place in the last third of the eighteenth century, the Pacific still remained, by and large, the mysterious Southern Ocean that sixteenth-century voyagers had traversed. Following upon the so-called 'age of discovery', which had been inaugurated and carried out for the most part by Iberian explorers, the number of visitors to the Pacific remained small. In relation to the islands of Oceania, although visits from various Asian ports have been conjectured upon and are certainly possible, only a handful of European ships ventured into its southern waters. Nevertheless, some sections of the Pacific island world, especially those closer to today's Indonesia and the Australian mainland, were investigated in expeditions sponsored by the Dutch East India Company.

Always perceived as motivated first and foremost by advantageous commercial objectives, the Dutch were the first European navigators to explore the northern coast of Australia. They also travelled further into the South Pacific in three remarkable voyages: the circumnavigation led by Isaac Le Maire and Willen Corneliszoon Schouten (1616); the voyage of Abel Tasman (1642) during which New Zealand was first sighted and visited; and the discovery of Easter Island by Jacob Roggeveen (1722).

These voyages fuelled, and were fuelled by, other voyages and the publications about them released in the last part of the sixteenth century, among which the account of Jan Huyghen van Linschoten's voyages stands out.[1] These journeys led to the creation of the Dutch East India Company (VOC) in 1602, which administered the Dutch colonial territories and grew to become a large enterprise both in terms of its fleet and manpower, ousting the English and Portuguese from Indonesia before heading into the Pacific and tracing the, then, unknown coast of Australia. The name New Holland, which was given to Australia by the Dutch at the time, appeared subsequently on many maps well into the eighteenth century.

The important voyage of Le Maire and Schouten was not, however, part of the Dutch East Indian Company's design. Although he was a founder of the company, Le Maire had broken away from it and was trying to trying to find an alternative route to the Spice Islands in order to challenge the company's monopoly with his own Australia Company. Until he and Schouten found the southernmost route to round the South American mainland, in 1616, it was thought that the only possible way was via Magellan's strait. Schouten and Le Maire sailed on board the *Eendracht* and the *Hoorn* from Holland in June 1615, reaching Port Desire in Patagonia, where they faced the same difficulties experienced by Magellan's fleet. There, the *Hoorn* caught fire and was lost, while its sailors joined the crew of *Eendracht*. At this point, Le Maire directed the ship beyond Magellan's strait to the strait that today bears his own name, Le Maire, christening the cape after the lost ship, *Horn*. From there, they sailed to the Island of Juan Fernández, and on to today's Pukapuka, which they named Honden, and landing afterwards in the northern islands of the Tongan archipelago before reaching the Moluccas via the northern coast of New Guinea.

Following upon Le Maire's and Schouten's voyage, the Governor of the Dutch East India company, Antoonij van Diemen, sent Mattijs Quast and Abel Janszoon Tasman in 1639 to look for the 'islands of gold and silver', thought to be in the South Pacific. These men sailed for about five months, greatly adding to the knowledge of the Pacific, but failing to find the Southern Continent. Tasman led another expedition in 1642 in search of *Terra Australis Incognita* in two ships, the *Heemskerck* and the *Zeehaen*, with Frans Jacobszoon Visscher as pilot. In November of that year, Tasman sighted the island that would be named after him, Tasmania, which he christened Van Diemen's Land after his sponsor. Tasman then sailed eastward and sighted New Zealand in December. When he saw Maori canoes approach, Tasman sent seven men in a boat, four of whom were immediately killed in what became known as Murderers' Bay, and which is today called by the more appealing name, Golden Bay. Sailing north, Tasman discovered Tongatapu, which he named Amsterdam Island, as well as other islands of the Tongan group. There, the locals were kinder towards the visitors than the Maori, and Tasman exchanged iron tools and nails for a large amount of food, including pigs, chickens, fruit and coconuts. Tasman returned to Batavia (today's Jakarta), calling at the Fiji Islands, Ontong Java and New Ireland on his way.

After this journey, the most important incursion of the Dutch into the Pacific was that of Jacob Roggeveen to Easter Island in 1722.[2] Seeking the so-called 'Davis Land', Roggeveen landed on Rapa-Nui or Easter Island on 5 April 1722. Realising that the island might not be the one that had been sighted by the buccaneer Edward Davis in 1687, Roggeveen gave it the name it bears today, Easter Island, or Paasch Eylandt in Dutch, to commemorate the holy day on which it was seen. Although Roggeveen's visit to the island was brief, it gave us the first description of the famous effigies on the island.

From Roggeveen's voyage onwards, the British presence started to be felt in the Pacific, in spite of the fact that navigation difficulties remained a daunting handicap to charting the ocean's waters and islands throughout the greatest part of the century. Added to the trade winds mentioned in relation to earlier voyages, the main difficulty in navigating the Pacific was the so-called 'problem of longitude'. This 'problem' was of such magnitude that, in England, a board was created in 1714, with the expressed intention of solving it. Based in London, the Board of Longitude offered the substantial reward of £20,000 to whoever could find an effective way to set longitude. After several unsuccessful attempts, John Harrison's chronometer was found to work accurately, and his creator was given the coveted prize money.[3] Harrison's chronometer, which was set to Greenwich Mean Time, enabled navigators to calculate their position anywhere in the world by comparing the local time with that at Greenwich. These precise time measurements had an effect on James Cook's second voyage, in 1772, in which, 'Cook . . . carried on board chronometers, one of which was a copy of John Harrison's masterpiece, his fourth marine timekeeper of 1759 . . . Equipped with chronometers and improved sextants, future navigators were able to find longitude with a precision sufficient for all practical purposes' (Williams 1966: 168).

Alongside the improved navigational techniques of the eighteenth century, Pacific exploration was greatly stimulated by the maps and books published about the area, which acted as active incentives to further discovery.[4] Fictional and non-fictional accounts started to be issued in quick succession, especially in Britain, following the publication of William Dampier's account, *A New Voyage Round the World* (1697), and Daniel Defoe's *Robinson Crusoe* (1719). Whether factual or fictional, books were a great stimulus for the era of Pacific exploration that ensued, with one of the most important being Charles de Brosses's *Histoire des Navigations aux Terres Australes* (Paris, 1756). In this sizeable volume, illustrated with the best maps of the time, also of French origin, he summed up the important voyages that preceded those of the eighteenth century.[5] As well as mentioning the main voyages looked at in the first part of this book, de Brosses itemised other journeys led by Dutch or Portuguese explorers. Brosses' influential account was soon followed in England by John Callender's version of the same voyages, entitled *Terra Australis Cognita* (Edinburgh, 1766–68). In fact, it could be said that these books 'participated' in the rivalry between France and England, playing an important role in the charting and appropriation of the Pacific (Williams 1966: 6).

To a lesser degree, Spain also took part in the British and French rivalry regarding the Pacific not only through its involvement with France after the War of Succession but also, and more especially, because of what it perceived as its historical claim to the area. As Spain was, during some of this time, an ally of France, it was the British who were seen to challenge its dominance in the Pacific, at least in the eyes of the Bourbon King, Charles III.[6] This challenge became overtly expressed after the voyage of Commodore George Anson (1740–44), as Skelton posits:

> The British 'siege' of Spain's *mare clausum* in the Pacific opened with authorized raids on the Spanish trade routes and ports, culminating in the spectacular voyage of Anson in 1740–4. It was more systematically developed, in the second half of the century, by projects for establishing trading stations in the East Indies, by political manœuvring for the naval bases necessary to the exploration of the Pacific from the east, and by a series of expeditions. (1958: 229)

The expeditions that Skelton refers to were launched from the Viceroyalty of Peru because of fear of a British invasion, which was felt within Spain and even more so in the South American colonies bordering the

Pacific. The Spanish rulers, and their Spanish American representatives, believed that the British voyages that started to gather momentum in the second half of the eighteenth century were a direct menace both to the South American mainland and to the area which had been, to borrow Spate's term, a 'Spanish lake'. Spain's claim to the Pacific, which had followed upon Balboa's discovery of the ocean in 1513, had made the South Seas a Spanish *mare clausum* for over two centuries, where only pirates attempting to seize the Manila galleon dared to enter.

The Spanish assumption that the Pacific was part of its empire was, however, ignored at a time when Spanish rulers had lost most of their standing in world power. Indeed, Spain was, at this time, using most of its scarce resources in the maintenance of its American empire, which was showing signs of increasing unrest greatly spurred on by the discontent of its Creole population and the war of independence in the United States.

After Anson's, the most important British voyage was that of Commodore John Byron on the *Dolphin* in 1764, which was promoted by the British Admiralty following the end of the Seven Years War with France in 1763. This expedition, which inaugurated the British chain of discoveries, returned to England with a sizeable booty of goods taken from the Spanish galleons. Also, and perhaps more importantly, it carried back a great deal of geographical information from charts seized from the Spaniards, and the success of the voyage served to fuel the desire to continue exploring and plundering the ocean. The effect of the journey was immediately felt across Europe because accounts of its achievements were swiftly published.[7]

Byron's voyage was followed by the exploration of Samuel Wallis in the *Dolphin* and Philip Carteret in the *Swallow* (1766–68), as well as those of Louis Antoine de Bougainville from France in the *Boudeuse* and the *Etoile* (1766–69). Following instructions to search for *Terra Australis*, Captain Wallis led a circumnavigation in which he failed to find that continent but discovered Tahiti and named it King George Island in honour of George III. Wallis's ship had no scientists on it, which was, according to Marshall and Williams, 'a sure sign that the Admiralty was more interested in new lands than in new peoples, in tangible returns for British trade than in scholarly investigation' (1982: 264).

By way of contrast, Bougainville 'was truly a man of the Enlightenment, a friend of Brosses, well-read in Montesquieu, Voltaire, Rousseau and Buffon' (Marshall and Williams 1982: 265).[8] Bougainville's mission was to encourage French settlement in the Mauvines, Spanish resistance to the British and to search for *Terra Australis* so as to claim its possession.

In April 1768, Bougainville reached Tahiti, which he named Nouvelle Cythère, and immediately claimed the island for France. Bougainville admired the island and its peoples, especially the women, and compared the Tahitians favourably with the inhabitants of Vanuatu, whom he saw as ugly, malformed and plagued by leprosy.

The myth of the 'noble savage' and of sexual freedom associated with the Pacific were greatly stimulated in Europe following the accounts of Wallis's and Bougainville's voyages, which wrongly assumed communal property of land and, to a great extent, of women. Thereafter, 'Tahiti was to become to Europe the symbol of the beauty and romance of the Pacific islands', although there was certainly nothing romantic about 'the diseases introduced by European seamen' (Williams 1966: 162). In spite of the fact that many of the myths about the Society Islands and its noble inhabitants were soon dispelled, they were so deeply ingrained in the European consciousness that they have remained alive to varying degrees until the present day.

The voyages which effectively removed many geographical and ethnographic fantasies from the European imagination were those led by Captain James Cook, whose expeditions finally laid to rest the belief in the Southern Continent and confirmed the discoveries of Bering in the Arctic. Cook also solved the remaining problems attached to the geography of the Pacific, mapping Eastern Australia and most of New Zealand, which were still thought by many of his contemporaries to be linked as part of the Southern Continent.

During his first voyage (1768–71), Cook, accompanied by the scientific team of Joseph Banks and Daniel Solander, arrived in Tahiti and in the Society Islands, where he restored the British claim to the islands.[9] Cook also led a second voyage in search of the Southern Continent, on which he took with him as scientists the father and son team, Johan and George Forster (1772–75). On this voyage, Cook arrived in New Zealand and went to Tahiti again, observing that the abundance of food supplies noted on the previous voyage had all but disappeared. This was the case partly because of the foreign ships that had visited the island and partly because the locals were involved in bitter, internal wars. Also, the Tahitians had been the victims of a plague of influenza brought about by foreigners, probably by the Spaniards who first visited the island in 1772 and then remained on the island for a year in 1774–75. During this second voyage, Cook was instructed to chart and explore all lands encountered and carried with him a copy of Harrison's chronometer. From this time onwards, navigation was rendered easier by the determination of longitude, facilitated by the accurate measurement of time.

Thus, throughout the 1760s and 1770s, British explorers, with help from French from other European powers, gradually shaped Europe's knowledge of most island groups of the South Pacific. The Spanish contributions to charting the area were directed firstly to Easter Island in 1770 and then to Tahiti and Tonga, where the last expedition of discovery, also spurred on by Spain's rivalry with Britain, landed in 1780. That year, Governor Basco y Vargas authorised the navigation led by Francisco Mourelle de la Rúa, who, on board the *Princesa*, departed with José Vázquez as pilot, and arrived in the Vava'u group of the Tongan archipelago.

It was, therefore, competition between France and England that led to what Marshall and Williams call a 'Pacific craze' taking place from the middle of the eighteenth century onwards, during which time the area was thoroughly explored, mapped and, perhaps more importantly, recorded in books that offered detailed descriptions of the land and peoples encountered.[10] The navigators and scientists who undertook such adventurous voyages became a different type of hero, interested as much in travel and discovery as in observing different peoples. This curiosity, meant to be dispassionate and objective, reached its most powerful expression in the detached observation of Cook as seen, for example, in his sober assessment of cannibalism and human sacrifice.[11] The same approach can be seen in most of the journals produced at this time, which consciously used a style of writing that sought to convey objectivity. Although dependent on the level of education of the writers, the journals tried to avoid figures of speech, hyperboles or language that would display a literary bent and might associate them with fiction, instead of fact, as Barbara Stafford remarks.[12]

The time lapse of more than two centuries since the beginning of Pacific exploration to the eighteenth-century voyages thus witnessed the end of Spanish dominance not just in the old, but also in the new, world. Nevertheless, there was no complete break between the 'old' and 'new' models of exploration and colonisation. Nor were all developments in time measurable in terms of progress, meaning advance towards a supposedly more perfected type of humanity. In fact, historical events do not always adhere to the evolutionary narrative that we often impose on the past or have transported to the understanding of other cultures. Instead, space and time are largely constructed out of present perspectives and prejudices, as Johannes Fabian has convincingly argued.[13]

One of the most prevalent assumptions inherited from the Enlightenment is a belief in a path 'forward', leading towards progress and perfection under the guidance of civilising practices grouped as 'Western'. This teleological interpretation involves the presentation of indigenous peoples on a relational scale of personal and social development that is not value-free, as the division between Melanesia and Polynesia shows. Furthermore, it also homogenises the West, offering a simplistic view that can distort a complex pattern of events or thought processes.

That the Enlightenment suddenly brought a completely different (or greatly 'improved') view of the world and its peoples from that of previous eras is a cataclysmic premise that might not stand close scrutiny. This is not to suggest that there were no changes, or that they were not important, but that, as they relate to exploration, there is a level of continuity in the transformations taking place, which can be treated within the broad parameters of the control of other worlds in economic and cultural terms. These continuities, as well as shifts, are apparent in the interests of governments and explorers, and can be appreciated in the encounters between Spanish voyagers and indigenous peoples of the Pacific in the 'enlightened' voyages of the time. Whereas it is obvious that many unconventional interests, as well as a broader understanding of the globe, dominated the later voyages, one can also appreciate stability in, for example, the presumed economic, cultural and religious superiority of Europeans.

The early colonisation in the Americas had a very strong religious and civilising dimension, which sought to incorporate the peoples encountered into the Spanish cultural community, albeit lower down the existing social order.[14] The Spanish model was one in which urbanism, civility and religion went hand in hand, and in which indigenous peoples, *mestizos*, Creoles and peninsular Spaniards would share language, religion and cultural values, as John Elliott observes.[15] The socio-political pattern set was, however, convoluted and bureaucratic in the extreme, with reduced economic benefits for both those living in the metropolis and, at times, even for the Creole population. As time went on, the contradictions of the Spanish paradigm grew when the peripheral Creole communities confronted the demands and prejudices of the metropolis. Gradually, therefore, the Spanish religious and cultural prototype of colonisation became highly irrelevant for those taking the lead in exploration and conquest after the sixteenth and seventeenth centuries, especially the British who, with the French and in competition with them, would set the trend thereafter.

The thoughts and practices associated with the Enlightenment, which started in France and then spread throughout western Europe, gathered momentum from the second half of the eighteenth century, infusing the Spanish attitude towards its colonies, as well as its voyages into the Pacific.[16] Within the parameters of its intellectual and political current, science and reason acquired what anthropologist James Boon calls a 'rarefied objectivity' (1982: 30). This objectivity was thought to be attainable by looking in a detached manner upon a universe, the rules of which could be subject to observation and analyses, as it were, from above.[17]

A dominant belief taking hold of intellectuals throughout the latter part of the eighteenth century was that the world ought to be observed carefully in its minutiae and that this observation would reveal the hidden rules that underpinned it. Interestingly, the same tenets that applied to the observation of nature were extended to geography and non-European cultures, all visible from the gaze that Mary Louise Pratt has incisively labelled the 'imperial eye'. This 'imperial eye' cast its gaze upon a world which might be apprehended in a panorama-like view and could be subsequently possessed and controlled by human forces. The typical, masculine observer, whom Pratt has labelled 'seeing-man', would be a paradigmatic explorer-cum-scientist white male whose personal gaze presented the world from a point of view that was assumed to be universal.[18]

Empirical observation and the attempt to portray fairly and objectively other cultures did not mean that the accounts produced did not contain prejudices, often comparable to those of earlier centuries.[19] For example, the enlightened view of empire and colonisation was part of a comprehension of humanity's evolution that was inextricably linked with notions of progress, capitalism, mercantilism and individualism. Alongside the totalitarianism implied in the supposedly empirical observation inherent in scientific exploration, the alleged altruism of enlightened science has been effectively challenged in recent times (Boon 1982: 37). Nonetheless, belief in the hypothetical disinterest of scientific voyaging and description is far from being fully eroded from the general consciousness.[20]

During the eighteenth century many voyagers, prominent among them Captain James Cook, fit (and perhaps would have fitted themselves) within the 'Enlightenment project'.[21] This project took on the task of supplanting religious or mythical beliefs with reason and scientific observation in order to enable society to progress by 'advancing' – a movement contrasted with the 'backward' look entrenched in religious adherence.[22] However, although these enlightened individuals might see themselves as rejecting myth and its concomitant beliefs or superstitions, it does not follow that they did, or that they did so in an objective manner. For example, rationalism did not entail, for the most part, a rejection of many Christian assumptions; nor did it mean questioning the superiority of Christianity and of European thought over and above the remaining systems of belief on earth.

The European expansion culminating in these voyages was the catalyst for the development of ideas that included a 'chain of universal being' that embraced the plant and animal worlds.[23] This was an evolutionary scale where humans were placed alongside a continuum that specified development on a temporal and spatial scale.[24] Needless to say, the process of ordering the cultures encountered was performed by those who thought of themselves as being at the top of the scale, namely, European white men, which inflected the ensuing gradation with hierarchies of, among other parameters, gender, class, religion and ethnicity. However, in a world which had acquired broader dimensions, the accommodation of alien cultures was neither easily nor uniformly done.

A reaction against some of these European assumptions can be appreciated in the rise of primitivist movements, which used knowledge of the cultures encountered to censure their own societies.[25] For these thinkers, 'primitive' cultures inhabited a universe that was less evolved and that, precisely because of that very 'backwardness', was freer, happier and even more humane. The materialism of the primitivists' own societies was highlighted by comparison with more egalitarian communities ruled by a strong sense of solidarity among its members. Thus, the myth of the 'noble savage', which took such a strong hold in the Pacific, especially in relation to Tahiti, was, if not born, at least widely disseminated.

The notion of the 'noble savage', as it pertains to the Pacific, has been traced by Marshall and Williams to some of the mythical views espoused by Pedro Fernández de Quirós. Other Pacific explorers, however, saw the place in a completely different light, which contrasted sharply with Quirós's 'terrestrial paradise'. For the Dutch, for example, the Pacific stood at the opposite end of the spectrum, a fact partly determined by the unwarranted killing of four members of Abel Tasman's crew on arrival in New Zealand in 1642. Nonetheless, the myth of the 'noble savage', which was first outlined in writing by Michel de Montaigne, proved more resilient than many believed. Indeed, the image of paradise attached to the Pacific remained in the minds of many even after the news of human sacrifice, cannibalism or the killing of James Cook and Marion du Fresne became widely known.[26]

The growth and spread of publications about the Pacific and the desire to believe in an ideal place on earth fuelled the notion of the 'noble savage' during the eighteenth century.[27] Also related to these shifts is the development of scientific interests that are associated with a type of individualistic and philanthropic design, and which gradually countermanded other considerations. These theories notwithstanding, when venturing into the Pacific, Europeans had neither tools to deal with and classify the peoples they encountered, nor any knowledge of their languages. In spite of the contradictions in relation to noble or less-than-noble savages, it is fair to concede that many enlightened thinkers and explorers made a sincere attempt to interpret other cultures in their own terms.

Regardless of its shortcomings, the Enlightenment entailed a remarkable intellectual effort that is worth highlighting. For example, even if the general assumption in Christianity's superiority prevailed, some important areas of Western Europe were keen to challenge religious fanaticism and the wars that it had inspired. This Europe, as John Pocock remarks, struggled to separate the nationalistic fervour underwritten by religion and to view itself as increasingly united by commerce.[28] By the era Pocock refers to as 'the age of encounter', the view of empire that took hold of Europe was one dominated by trade and commerce, as against one traced along religious lines, as in earlier centuries.

The time where gold and God (perhaps in that order), determined travel and exploration was all but fading away, with commerce gradually taking preference. This was the case initially for the Netherlands, followed by England and, later on, for France and even Spain.[29] Charles III of Spain, who reigned between 1759 and 1788, worked closely with notable and less notable ministers clearly steeped in French revolutionary ideology and appreciated the differences between the past empire and his own project (Pagden 1995: 194). Indeed, it was during this epoch that Spain underwent a centralising impulse comparable to that which had taken place in the sixteenth century and, under its Bourbon rulers, tightened the commercial rules to be followed in its colonies. This, as Peter Bakewell observes, has led historians to see the latter part of the eighteenth century, as the only time when 'Spain's American territories became true colonies in a modern sense of the terms: overseas possessions whose own interests were subservient to those of the metropolis' (1991: 79).[30] These differences are apparent in the voyages that Charles III sponsored, whose leaders embraced the theories of scientific observation, even if Christianisation remained in the minds and deeds of many.

Commercial and scientific aspirations were undoubtedly reflected in the way the expeditions to the South Pacific from colonial Latin American were mounted and in the composition of the voyagers on the ships. The changes in the perception of the world and the way travellers and explorers approached it are noticeable with the inclusion of scientists. For the first time, key scientists, such as Joseph Banks, Daniel Solander, Johan Reinhold Forster and George Forster (among the English) or Tadeo Haenke and Luis Née (among the Spanish), were among the those included. With these scientists travelled artists, whose work included the making of maps, bird's-eye views and artistic representations of the world encountered, as outlined below.

Although developments in art and science have always been embedded in relations of power, during the eighteenth century it became increasingly difficult to disentangle them from the imperial enterprise.[31] In this regard, Cook's and Bougainville's voyages established a model that would be followed thereafter. In the Spanish journeys described, draughtsmen accompanied the expeditions to Easter Island and Tahiti that were more or less contemporaneous with those of Cook, while the journey led by Alessandro Malaspina closer to the end of the century mirrored quite closely Cook's journey, with the inclusion of botanists and artists.

The intricate connection between art, science and power that was at the centre of these voyages is apparent in both the journals and coastal views produced.[32] In fact, the extent to which power underlines these eighteenth-century products can be clearly appreciated in ideas about landscape that originated at that time. Denis Cosgrove's now-classic formulation of landscape as a European 'way of seeing' the universe and the various peoples within it is pertinent in this regard, for representations of indigenous landscapes can reveal a relationship of power inherent in observation and description.[33] The strategic, the informative and the decorative in scientific and artistic productions thus merge, so that their use or function becomes hard to separate or define. In this context, the notion of landscape, as W. J. T. Mitchell categorically puts it, is nothing but 'the dreamwork of imperialism' (1994: 10).

Besides reinforcing the concept of an alien or paradisiacal landscape, eighteenth-century voyagers engaged in exchanges that are related in a reciprocal cause-and-effect negotiation to the way in which the individual was apprehended. The changing relationships between the way individuals saw themselves primarily as possessors of private property have a bearing on the way these voyages were led, as well as on the contacts with indigenous peoples. Some differences between the sixteenth- and eighteenth-century voyages can be appreciated in the approach to artefacts and their possession, which is exemplified in the development of museum collections and cabinets of curiosities.

The relationship between collecting and the notion of the self is illuminated by Crawford B. Macpherson's account of the 'possessive individualism' (1962). From the seventeenth century onwards, there emerged a notion of the self that associated the individual with ownership of private property. This individual's zeal to purchase, accumulate and display infused the creation of cabinets of curiosities, or *Wunderkamer*, eventually leading to the birth of the museum.[34] In fact, the first museums arose from just such collections, and it was only after the French Revolution that the notion of a 'public' museum as a temple in which to admire imperial possessions started to spread.[35] England embraced and furthered this collective trend during the eighteenth and nineteenth centuries and museums there started to acquire ethnographic materials that included items from the South Pacific (Marshall and Williams 1982: 58). In Spain, the 1770s saw the emergence of the *Real Gabinete de Historia Natural* from the acquisition of the library and collection of artefacts belonging to the Creole, Pedro Franco Dávila, who became its first director.[36] It was to this *Gabinete* that many of the artefacts and journals from the expeditions to the Pacific were taken, and from which they arrived at their destinations in contemporary museums, such as the *Museo de América* or *Museo Naval*.

Some artefacts from the eighteenth-century Spanish voyages discussed in this book are preserved at the *Museo de América* in Madrid because the Pacific was normally treated as an 'outpost' of the Spanish American mainland by the metropolis. Other important items are now housed in the *Museo Naval* in Madrid. A single object, probably one of the most beautifully-ever crafted artefacts in the Society Islands, is kept at the *Museo Nacional de Antropología* in Madrid. This is, without doubt, the most remarkable gift ever given by the Tahitians: the famous *umete* of Máximo Rodríguez (Figure 3.1). The journey of the *umete* and its place today are very much emblematic of the voyages studied here, and provide an eloquent summary of the ideas outlined in this introduction to the eighteenth-century Spanish voyages to the Pacific.

The *umete*, the function of which remains unknown, was a large oval bowl made of black dolerite in Maurua (now Maupiti) for the chief of Raiatea, and it was sent by him to the Tahitian *arii*, Tu, as a precious gift. Máximo asked Tu for it in order to present it to the king of Spain, and, because of his special standing among Tahitians, it was given to him. After receiving the *umete*, Máximo had to enlist the help of four men, who

3.1 *Umete*. This large ceremonial bowl was given to Máximo Rodríguez for the Spanish king. It was made *c*.1770 in Taputapuatea.

transported it towards the place where the mission in Tautira had been established. At some point, however, the *umete* was stolen but, after some enquiries, was recovered by Máximo, who guarded it all night, looking after it carefully until it reached Tautira. On leaving the Tahitian mission, the *umete* was taken onto the ship *El Aguila*, captained by Cayetano de Lángara, to Peru, where it arrived in 1776. In Peru, it went to Viceroy Amat, who was meant to take it to the king in Spain. As Amat was getting ready to be replaced in the Viceroyalty, the *umete* remained forgotten in his palace. No further references to it appear in correspondence thereafter until Máximo noted in a letter twelve years later, in 1788, that it had not been properly cared for, complaining that it was used by the viceroy's butler for washing clothes.

In another letter, Viceroy Theodor De Croix, who was Amat's successor, indicated that, because Máximo had obtained the *umete* after pleading with Tu, it was a valuable object that should be deposited in the *Gabinete de Historia Natural*.[37] Currently not on display, the *umete* lies in a corner of the *Museo Nacional de Antropología* in Madrid, after returning briefly to the South Pacific for an exhibition at the Auckland Art Gallery, entitled 'The Two Worlds of Omai' in 1977 (Figure 3.2).[38] While in Auckland, three reproductions of the *umete* were made: two for local museums and one

3.2 'The Two Worlds of Omai'. Máximo's *umete* is framed by Sir Joshua Reynolds's portrait of Omai at the Auckland Art Gallery (1977).

for Tahiti. Needless to say, some Tahitians have expressed their wishes that the *umete* be returned to them (Mellén 1992: 29).

Consequently, an elaborate artefact that was already valued by Máximo and the Tahitians in the eighteenth century, the *umete*, seems to have fallen into oblivion until the last decades of the twentieth century. Spurred on by the decolonising movements and the indigenous 'renaissance' taking place in many islands of the Pacific after the 1950s, the *umete* made a temporary return to be admired by the descendants of its makers. Like other artefacts, the *umete* attests to the colonial past that is traced in the remainder of this book, for, very much like the voyages and engagements discussed, the *umete* has been recovering a position that denotes its importance. The *umete* remains not just a valuable artefact but one that bears witness to the interesting exchanges taking place between Spaniards and Pacific Islanders. Among those exchanges, which are the focus of Chapter 4, those held between Máximo and the Tahitians stand out, as the ties of friendship that Máximo was able to establish were deeper than any we know of in the South Pacific until then. This study of the encounters between Máximo and other eighteenth-century Spanish voyagers and the indigenous populations of the South Pacific attempts to illuminate social and ethnic relations that, by and large, reveal a high degree of mutual curiosity and a desire to understand others.

NOTES

1 Van Linschoten (1563–1611), a Dutch Protestant, lived in Seville for a number of years and trained there as a merchant. He also worked for Portugal before going to the East Indies and is thought to have copied Portuguese nautical maps, which effectively meant that the East Indies could be reached by the English and the Dutch. Material related to van Linschoten's voyages was published by The Hakluyt Society in 1885.
2 Roggeveen's journals were edited by Andrew Sharp in 1970.
3 A coherent summary of Harrison's trials is given by Dava Sobel.
4 Skelton remarks that 'Dampier's *New Voyage round the World* – a best-seller from its publication in 1697 – had kindled his countrymen's interest in the Pacific' (1958: 228). Williams assesses this interest, and the role played by books in these words: 'The extension of European trade and power overseas during the eighteenth century was accompanied by a surge of interest at home in the distant lands visited by the explorers, traders and missionaries. Travel books ... became one of the most popular forms of literature' (1966: 101).

5 The main voyages included by Brosses are those of Magellan (1519), Mendaña (1567), Mendaña and Quirós (1595), Quirós and Torres (1606), Tasman (1639 and 1642) and Roggeveen (1722).
6 Charles III, who was born in 1716 and died in 1788, was King of Spain between 1759 and 1788, where four out of the five voyages looked at below took place. The last journey, Malaspina's, which started in 1789 and ended in 1794, was also organised during his rule.
7 'It was a sign of growing European interest in the Pacific that although an authorized account of the voyage had to wait for Hawkesworth's collection in 1773, an unofficial, anonymous narrative published in 1767 was translated into French, Italian, Spanish and German before the end of the decade' (Marshall and Williams 1982: 264).
8 'In publication, if not in exploration', according to Marshall and Williams, 'the French forestalled the English; for brief accounts of uncertain accuracy but lively public appeal were printed before the end of 1769, and in 1771 appeared Bougainville's own account, which was translated into English in 1772' (1982: 265).
9 Two Tahitians who left with this expedition died in Java, while a third, Omai reached England in 1774, and became a celebrity for his social charm and ability to adapt to the culture there (Marshall and Williams 1982: 283).
10 'Between the ending of the Seven Years War in 1763 and the outbreak of the French revolutionary wars thirty years later, Britain and France in particular experienced a 'Pacific craze'... Expeditions set off into the unknown, to return three years later laden with specimens from the South Seas, eager to publish descriptions, maps and views of the wondrous places visited and the peoples seen' (Marshall and Williams 1982: 258–9).
11 On Cook's attitude towards cannibalism and the contrast with that of his contemporaries, including Joseph Banks, see Salmond, who also details Cook's cool observance of the practices surrounding human sacrifice (2003: 128, 136–7, 141–5, and 358–61).
12 'A further consequence of the scientific... travel description is its favoring of a plain, rhetorically unornamented, and seemingly artless style... The struggle to find an innocent mode of literary and visual expression... is discussed in the preface to every notable relation of a voyage of discovery published between the middle of the eighteenth century and the middle of the nineteenth' (1984: 28).
13 'Neither political Space nor political Time are natural resources. They are ideologically construed instruments of power' (1983: 144).
14 Indeed, as Peter Bakewell observes, the word 'incorporation' was used 'instead of "conquest" to describe Spain's domination of the New World peoples and territories', which, Bakewell adds, was designed 'to extend true religion over the globe, and to bring newly discovered peoples into the universal community of the church' (1991: 76).

15 'If Spanish America far outshone British America in the coherence and sophistication of its cultural life at the turn of the seventeenth and eighteenth centuries, there were good reasons for this. Spanish America, unlike British America, had created an urban civilization, in which civic elites, largely Jesuit-educated and with time on their hands, spoke a common religious and cultural language that spanned the continent' (2006: 248). Elliott compares the British and Spanish imperial views in a chapter entitled 'Empire and Identity' (Elliott 2006: 219–51).

16 In relation to France's role in the development and spread of Enlightenment ideas, Mary Pedley posits that: 'No century has been as touched by the science, culture, and language of France as the eighteenth. French influence weighed heavily in every cultural domain from the fine arts to the sciences' (1992: 11).

17 One objective of this 'scientific gaze' was the apprehension of the landscape which, as Matthew Edney incisively observes, is also a creation of the viewer, for, in order 'to see and to record', one cannot but effect 'an ontological imposition on the world', which 'is considered external to the viewer' (1987: 54).

18 Instead, Pratt reminds us that he was nothing if not a 'traveller which deploys an imperious and imperial way of perceiving and viewing from above, offering a visual topography from heights which suggest a masculine and imperial possession of landscape and peoples' (1992: 7).

19 As Pratt observes, many expeditions purposely meant to be scientific, including those of Cook, 'went under secret orders to look out for commercial opportunities and threats' (1992: 34).

20 'The modern moral, cultural and political worlds we currently inhabit are all, in the first instance, the creation of the Enlightenment, and the Enlightenment was, perhaps more than has been recognized, the product of a world which was in the process of ridding itself of its first . . . imperial legacy' (Pagden 1995: 200).

21 Barbara Stafford uses insights provided by Cook and La Pérouse to argue that these men felt their travels not to be self-interested: 'The enjoyment and evident relish mirrored in these narratives is based on the idea that the scientific traveler is usefully, not trivially, engaged' (1984: 25).

22 The value accorded to science is summed up by Smith when he affirms that: 'At the heart of the change lay the improved status accorded to science. During the second half of the eighteenth century the biological sciences, led by botany, which were once the preserve of dedicated savants and their noble patrons, began to acquire a large lay public' (1992: 30).

23 This gradation included the vegetal and animal worlds, as shown in Smith's quotation from Linnaeus' proposed classification of all plants, which states that 'all living things, plants, animals, and even mankind themselves, form one "chain of universal Being", from the beginning to the end of the world'

(Qtd. Smith 1960: 5). The Swedish naturalist Carl von Linné (1707–78) is normally known as Carolus Linnaeus and recognised as the founder of the modern taxonomy of plants and living beings.

24 'It was indeed widely held both by naturalists and writers that Cook's scientists, aided by his seamen, would gradually complete the picture of the universe as a vast ordered chain of being which had been partially known to man from earliest times. But this ancient preconception came into conflict gradually with another preconception possessing antecedents quite as venerable as the chain of being. The ancients had claimed that things in the Antipodes were different from things in the northern hemisphere' (Smith 1960: 34).

25 'The discovery of the New World ... had stimulated discussion on how "civilized" man (that is, usually, European man) had developed from "savage" ancestors. It was a debate affected by the distant explorations, scientific discoveries and intellectual movements of the post-Renaissance era, and was accompanied by wistful queries as to whether the early stages of mankind's existence were not in some ways more acceptable than the current state' (Marshall and Williams 1982: 258).

26 Also questioning the myth of the noble savage in Tahiti are some of the sources for the voyages looked at below as, for example, Juan Pantoja's account of the second Spanish journey to Tahiti. Among other things, Pantoja remarked on the Tahitian custom of gouging out the eyes of their prisoners and eating them (1992: 168). Common property among Tahitians was another myth eventually dispelled.

27 'Although the idea of the "noble savage" can be traced back at least to Montaigne's writings, it was during the eighteenth century that it became a cult' (Williams 1966: 102).

28 Europe, as Pocock puts it, 'remembered itself as having very lately escaped from an age of wars of religion ... [it] saw itself as having overcome these dangers ... first, by the reorganization of "Europe" as a republic or confederation of civilized sovereign states, held together by the ties of commerce, capable of settled government over societies increasingly commercial, and capable of regulating the wars that still occurred by the advanced military and financial technology, which warfare, and civil society in general, acquired in an age of commerce' (2000: 27).

29 Pagden observes that the French, whose imperialism had initially been informed by Catholicism, eventually, 'shifted their ultimate objectives from the cultivation of souls to the cultivation of land and the opportunities for trade ... By the second half of the eighteenth century all three empires, even that of Castile, came to be seen by their respective mother countries as predominantly commercial enterprises' (1995: 37, 73).

30 In fact, Bakewell goes so far as to label the last years of the reign of Ferdinand VI (1746–59) and those of Charles III (1759–88), as 'a second reconquest of Spanish America', which he contrasts with the long period from 1600 to 1750,

in which the empire underwent a continuous process of decentralisation (1991: 76–9).

31 'During the eighteenth century, too, art in the service of travel, like science and power, its masters and employers, began to institutionalise itself. It came increasingly to be realised that drawing was required for the more direct pursuit of scientific knowledge and imperial power' (Smith 1992: 28).

32 This premise will be investigated in Chapter 5.

33 'The landscape idea represents a way of seeing – a way in which some Europeans have represented to themselves and to others the world about them and their relationships with it, and through which they have commented on social relations' (Cosgrove 1998: 1). 'Way of seeing' is a famous phrase used prominently by John Berger (1972) in his now-classic study of Western art.

34 Steven Mullaney defines the 'wonder-cabinet' as 'a form of collection peculiar to the late Renaissance, characterized primarily by its encyclopaedic appetite for the marvellous or the strange and by an exceptionally brief historical career'. Mullaney traces its origin to Vienna in 1550 and pinpoints its demise around one hundred years later (1983: 40).

35 Carol Duncan has traced the evolution of the art museum from 'the Princely Gallery'. The Louvre became the first public museum, a trend that was followed by most Western nations during the nineteenth century (1999: 304).

36 The *Real Gabinete de Historia Natural* opened to the public in 1776, with a collection of curious and rare ethnographic and archaeological artefacts, as well as books and paintings, from all over the world.

37 On the journey undertaken by the *umete*, see Mellén (Rodríguez 1992: 26–7).

38 The catalogue of this exhibition gives preferential treatment to the *umete*. On this exhibition, see Denys Trussell's 'The Two Worlds of Omai'. The *umete* was placed in the room before Sir Joshua Reynolds's portrait of Omai's portrait. This portrait, first shown at the Royal Academy of Arts in 1776, is one of the most expensive paintings ever sold in the United Kingdom, being purchased by the Tate Gallery in 2001 for £10,508,612 thanks to an anonymous donation of £12.5m.

Spanish voyages to the Pacific 1770–94   4

González and Easter Island (1770)   I

Spurred on by what was perceived to be an intrusion of French and, especially, British interests in Spain's *mare clausum*, Viceroy Amat of Peru sponsored four voyages to the South Pacific during the eighteenth century. Following George Anson's and John Byron's voyages, Amat informed the Spanish king, Charles III, that the safety of Chile and Peru depended on the control of Easter Island and other places where foreign forces could establish settlements in the Pacific. Amat's fears, at least in relation to Byron's journey, were probably accurate, as Bolton Glanvill Corney confirms. According to the instructions, Byron's voyage of 1764–66 was meant to survey the Falkland Islands and to 'take possession of them in the name of the King of Great Britain' (1908: xxi). Byron did precisely that, although he was not aware that he had been preceded a few months before by Louis de Bougainville, who had claimed the islands for the King of France. As France had been paid by Spain to leave the Isles Mauvines or Falkland, the Spanish Viceroyalty perceived the strongest threat to their claims over Atlantic or Pacific islands to come from the British.[1] Consequently, on Amat's recommendation, Charles III issued orders urging the visible presence of explorers, settlers and, more particularly, missionaries on the Pacific islands, with the specific mention of Easter Island and Tahiti.

The earliest of the eighteenth-century Spanish voyages of Pacific exploration, which was directed to the Isle of David or Davis, took place in 1770. Rapa-Nui or Easter Island was then referred to as Davis after buccaneer Edward Davis, who reported seeing it in 1687.[2] Although his claim is unproven, this was the very first time in that the island is recorded as having been sighted by Europeans, although the first discoverers of the island were the Polynesian travellers, whose last wave of migration took them to Hawaii, Easter Island and New Zealand, more than one thousand years ago.[3] Subsequent to Davis, Easter Island was explored in 1722 by Jacob Roggeveen, who named it Paasch (Easter) Island to mark the time when it was sighted – a name still used today alongside the indigenous Rapa Nui. Roggeveen's expedition was welcomed by the islanders, though, for unknown reasons, some of them were killed during this brief visit.[4]

The Spanish voyage was designed to explore Easter Island and adjacent ones, take possession, report on their inhabitants and their habitat, and return to the South American mainland, with a view to future voyages. The extant sources recounting this brief voyage have been gathered and edited in Spanish by Francisco Mellén Blanco (1986), presenting a thorough picture of the journey. Most of these journals had been made available in English by Bolton Corney, who edited the accounts and various dispatches related to the voyage for the Hakluyt Society in 1908. Corney translated three journals: one by the commander of the expedition, Felipe González de Haedo, a second, longer version by the pilot, Juan de Hervé, who also drew charts and travelled to Tahiti thereafter, and the third and most complete report signed by the first pilot of the *Santa Rosalía*, Francisco Antonio de Aguera Infanzón.[5]

The Spanish expedition left Callao on 10 October 1770, with González on the galleon *San Lorenzo*, where Hervé was pilot, and Antonio Domonte de Zúñiga in command of the frigate *Santa Rosalía*, piloted by Aguera. The fleet arrived at Rapa Nui on 15 November and took official possession of the island five days later, naming it San Carlos in honour of the Spanish king, Carlos III (Hervé 1908: 117). The Spaniards surveyed the island, drafted charts of its main features and harbours and left on 21 November in search of other inhabited places. No more islands, however, were found, and the expedition arrived back in the port of Chiloé, an island off the coast of Chile, on 14 December 1770 (Figure 4.1).

As the voyage was brief and there was no interpreter on board, contacts with the locals were, although interesting, rather limited in scope and depth. The procedures followed, however, were similar to those deployed during ensuing voyages to Tahiti, and provide a precedent for later cross-cultural engagements. For example, in tone with the instructions given in eighteenth-century voyages, but with an added emphasis, Viceroy Amat urged the officers to ensure that the locals were treated with kindness and to avoid all unnecessary conflict with them in order to strengthen commercial and social links (Landín 1992: 3. 732). For all we know, these instructions were dutifully adhered to.

The information from Aguera's journal starts with sailing directions until, on 14 November, the Spaniards sighted Easter Island where the smoke seen suggested that it was inhabited, even though they saw nobody on the beaches. The following day, the Spanish observed people on a hill,

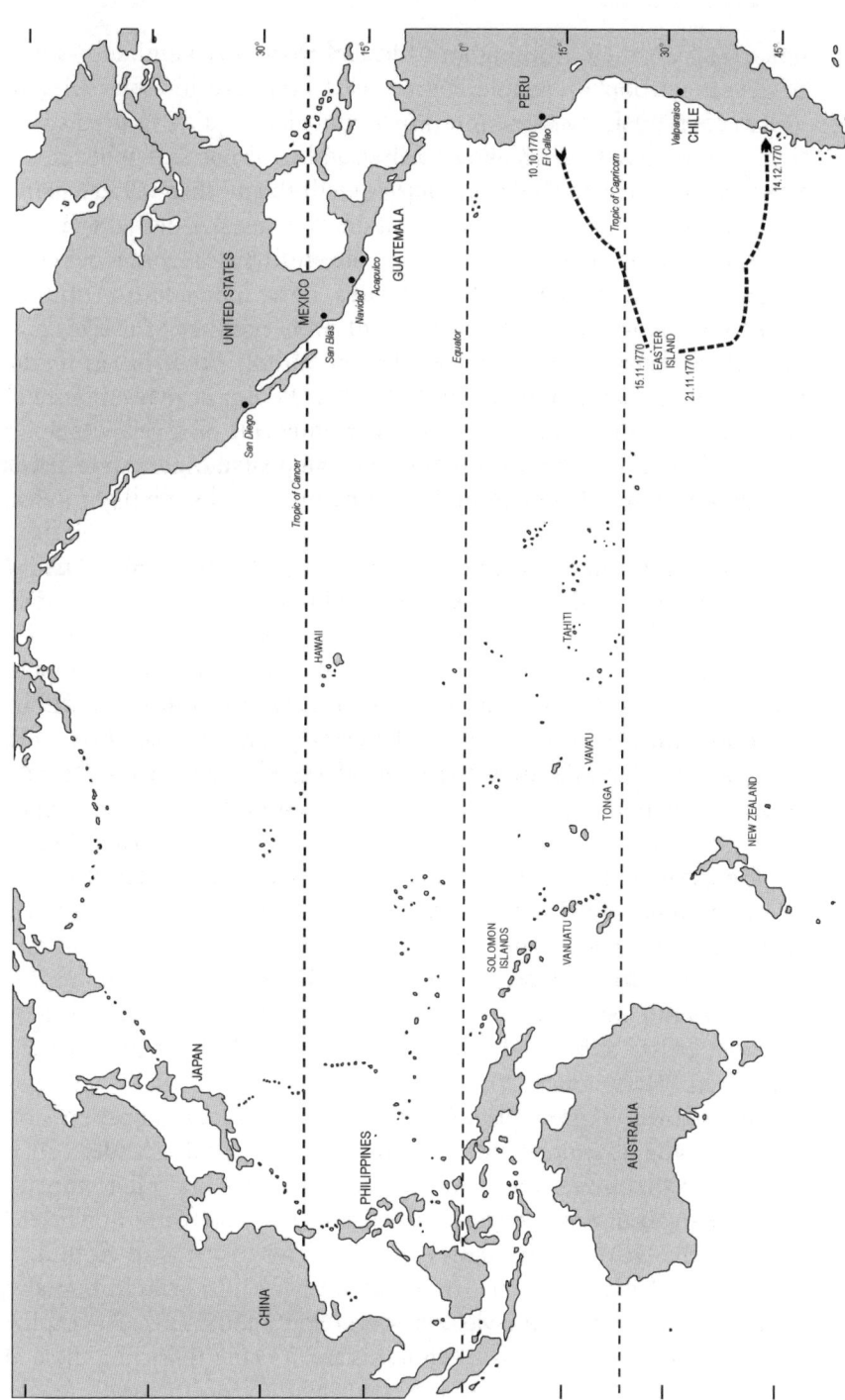

4.1 Itinerary of the voyage of Felipe González de Haedo to Easter Island (1770).

remarking on their clothing and the fact that they were unarmed: 'We observed a troop of people composed of eighteen persons who were walking briskly along the summit of a high ridge ... We noticed some of them clothed in garments like a *poncho* or cloak, coloured' (1908: 91).[6] The Spaniards lowered the boat with twelve soldiers and three officers in a bay which seemed suitable for the purpose and the vessel departed while those remaining in the ship took soundings, observed by many islanders on the beach. The next day, according to Aguera, more indigenous people gathered to watch them: '[We] saw a considerable number of natives posted on the heights, who collected nearer to the middle of the bay as we sailed towards it, so that by the time we let go there must have been more than 800 people, divided in batches, all wearing cloaks of a yellow colour or white' (1908: 93). The islanders' appearance and manners were friendly, and the absence of weapons and their joyful demonstrations of welcome to the new arrivals corroborated this peaceful attitude.

When the Spaniards anchored and moored, some islanders swam to approach them, while others remained on the beach 'shouting with delight and giving other signs, all intended to make us aware of their docility and of their desire to come on board or to see us on shore' (Aguera 1908: 93). Following these demonstrations of friendship, the ship's two launches went to explore all the 'circuit of the island' and were met by islanders, exchanging gifts with one of them, as Hervé recalled: 'While acting as a beacon ... three of the natives swam off, [their bodies] painted in various colours, and keeping near the boat, shouting constantly, until one of them came at last so close as to present me with a morsel of yam: I gave him some biscuit and tobacco, all of which he accepted' (1908: 120). These exchanges continued when the ship arrived, at which point some islanders jumped on board, showing happiness: 'with much agility, shouting all the while and exhibiting much gayness of spirit. They ran about freely from [stern] to stern, and full of mirth, climbing about the rigging like sailormen' (Hervé 1908: 120).

The Spanish started playing instruments and, as happened on the voyage to the Solomons led by Mendaña in 1567, the islanders obliged, dancing to the music: 'Our people] played the *coxa* and fife to them, and they began to dance, evincing great pleasure.'[7] Following this brief but warm exchange, the Spaniards gave the islanders items of clothing and adornment, 'ribbons, shirts, trousers, seamen's jumpers and small gilt metal crosses', which were well received (Hervé 1908: 120). The exploring party also shared their food with the islanders and, following these amicable exchanges, the Spaniards went for a stroll, not before hearing the officers' emphatic request that they should not harm the islanders or their fields. They passed a group of islanders who took them to see what Hervé described as a 'large house' and sang and danced in honour of their visitors. The reconnaissance party continued their observations and walked further into the island, noticing gardens and plantations of sugar-cane, sweet potatoes, yams, white pumpkin and a type of yellow root, probably turmeric, which the islanders chewed and used to dye their bodies (Hervé 1908: 123). The peaceful exchanges were attributed by Hervé to the commands given regarding the maintenance of order: 'we made back to our launches to stay the night, without our peaceful relations with the natives having been in any way disturbed, which may be attributed to the order which the officer gave our men not to give them any offence, backed by the threat of a flogging, without which our marines and seamen would have destroyed these poor wretches' plantations' (1908: 123–4). In this cordial tone, the party continued its reconnaissance for two more days, returning to the ship on 19 November.

While they were away, Aguera observed the famous monuments on Easter Island, the 'statues or images of the idols which the natives worship', which the Spanish had thought originally to be shrubs, and that he likened to columns: 'they are of stone and of such a height and corpulence that they look like great thick columns'. The monuments had a concave structure in which the islanders kept the bones of the deceased, 'from which it may be inferred that they serve at once for idols and funeral pyres' (1908: 93). Also remarked upon is the difficult construction of these 'superb' sculptures on account of the access to their location. The islanders' skill at being able to raise such monuments without machines is certainly wondered at and commended in Aguera's narrative: 'That a people lacking machinery and materials for constructing any should be able to raise the crown or headpiece on to a statue of such height causes wonder, and I even think that the stone of which the statues are made is not a product of the island, in which iron, hemp, and stout timber are absolutely unknown' (1908: 94). After this depiction, Aguera's journal lists the measurements of the monuments, also mentioning that they were called *Moay* and that they were venerated by the islanders who showed offence when visitors approached them. Following this, the manufacture of one of these idols, which is associated with Judas, is itemised:

> They have another effigy or idol clothed and portable which is about four yards in length: it is properly speaking the figure of a Judas, stuffed with straw or dried grass. It has arms and legs, and the head has coarsely figured

eyes, nostrils, and mouth: it is adorned with a black fringe of hair made of rushes, which hangs half-way down the back. On certain days they carry this idol to the place where they gather together, and judging by the demonstrations some of them made, we understood it to be the one dedicated to enjoyment, and they name it *Copeca*. (1908: 95).[8]

At this point, some gift-giving took place, when locals went on board and were given presents, consisting of items of clothing and other 'trinkets'. Altogether, the islanders appeared to the visitors to be begging with bothersome insistence because they were 'very poor and lowly people, whose possessions help to make them so importunate in begging that they become really too annoying' (Aguera 1908: 95). No ornaments were worn, and neither metal, nor clothes or hardware were seen on the island, which suggested to the Spaniards that the Easter Islanders had not exchanged goods with visitors until then.

As with earlier voyages, the physical description of the people paid special attention to their colour, said to be 'between white, swarthy, and reddish'. Overall, their appearance was seen to be 'thoroughly pleasing', with their height and proportion of limbs being praised. Their stature was commended as being tall, strong and well proportioned, with the added bonus of having no visible disability. Such features, nonetheless, were interpreted not purely to satisfy the Spaniards' curiosity, but with a practical objective in mind, in this case, the islanders' possible conversion to Christianity and their 'domestication': 'I believe from their docility and intelligence, that it would be easy to domesticate them and to convert them to any religion which might be put before them' (Aguera 1908: 96). In this way, indigenous men were incorporated into existing hierarchies in terms associated with women, such as 'docility' and 'domestic'.

Although respectful, the relationships established during this journey were slightly patronising and rather superficial, showing a degree of detachment on the part of the Spaniards, which very much accords with the enlightened notions of 'objective' observation. Nonetheless, the islanders were pitied on account of their sheer poverty, in spite of which they showed a willingness to exchange with the Spaniards what little they had. For example, only two days after the Spanish landed on the island a large number of islanders, both men and women, boarded the ship with bananas and chickens, which they presented along with their poor clothing: 'readily offered the wretched scraps of clothing and other goods they had about them, until reduced to a miserable loin-cloth of fibre or cotton or some such stuff, with a diadem or crown or plume of cock's feathers or dried sea-weed'. The same clothing was worn by the women, who, to distinguish themselves, covered their head with palm leaves. Both men and women begged continuously, but also offered all they had, including, in the case of women, their sexual services. The fact that this aroused no jealousy among the islanders led Aguera to conclude that the women might have been held in common and that older men were in charge, because they seemed to have taken the lead in offering the women. As in all remaining sources on this voyage, the scarcity of women, who were probably kept hidden from sight, is remarked upon in Aguera's journal (1908: 97–8).

The islanders' relationship with property receives much attention, with it being noted that, although they appropriated for themselves all that they could lay their hands on, they just as easily gave anything that they were asked for. What they did with the property, however, puzzled the Spaniards, as nothing received was seen again, which suggested to them that everything was communal property: 'It appears as if among themselves their goods are held in common, and I believe they conceal as much as they can get possession of below the ground, for we never saw afterwards any of the things we gave them' (Aguera 1908: 99). As happened with Europeans in Tahiti, Aguera assumed that the notion of private property was inherent to the more advanced civilisations of Europe, and that it had not developed among 'primitives', such as the Easter Islanders.

The Spaniards, according to Aguera, made every effort to treat the Easter Islanders 'with every consideration', and, in order to do so 'gave them whatever they asked for' (1908: 99). Hervé's journal corroborates this lavish gift-giving, emphasising that rules were observed and that harsh punishment would be meted out to those who broke them: 'The officer, Don Cayetano de Lángara, issued orders to our people that no one, under pain of a severe flogging, should accept any article from the islanders without giving some equivalent in return, or something of greater value than that which they received, since it was known there was a disposition to exchange articles; and such in fact was put into practice' (1908: 122).

The enlightened paradigm of detached observation was also deployed when referring to the local use of bodily dyes, which the men used, especially the 'principal men, or those in authority', who applied herbs to obtain a bright red hue (Aguera 1908: 98). With regard to another area of importance to the Spaniards, religion, the explorers inferred that the Easter Islanders must have had some sort of 'ministers or priests for their idols' because they offered some apparently holy men blankets and food, while treating them with obvious signs of 'veneration' (Aguera 1908:

99–100). Also, the islanders' language was commended on account of their accurate pronunciation of Spanish words.[9]

The assumed superiority of those describing over those being described is confirmed when we read that, even though the Spaniards had no reason to guess at the islanders' courage or lack of it, the fact that they had no weapons led him to deduce that the Easter Islanders were 'pusilanimes' ('faint-hearted') (Aguera 1908: 99). To corroborate this, the Spaniards tried to see whether the men knew how to use a bow and arrow by giving one to a man who put it on his head, doing likewise with a knife and a cutlass, which he thought of as ornaments too.

The few days the Spaniards spent on the island were thus filled with the routine visits from the islanders and the survey of the territory. Views were taken 'in order to construct as accurate a chart of it as possible, and one that might serve as a guide and record for the future' (Aguera 1908: 100). The launches navigating the island found no wild or domestic animals, and saw little cultivation beyond some plantations of yucca, yams, sweet potatoes and banana trees, with no trees capable of providing planks 'so much as six inches in width'. Because of this absence of shelter, the islanders' habitat consisted mostly of underground caves with narrow entrances through which people gained access by entering feet first. Those higher up the social ladder, the 'more polished or powerful persons', lived in huts thatched with reeds (Aguera 1908: 101–2). The scarcity of resources on the island made these people unlike Europeans, in that they ate and drank little, refusing even to ingest any liquor.

On the day prior to departure, the Spaniards took possession of the island, raising crosses to signify the event. To that end, some 250 armed men, including soldiers and sailors, went ashore, under the command of Alberto Olaondo to reconnoitre the terrain, call the attention of the locals, and raise one cross on each of three different hills on the eastern side of the island (Aguera 1908: 103). Throughout these events, the Spaniards showed no fear of the islanders, a confidence which proved to be well-grounded, as they did not encounter any opposition from the many gathered to observe these procedures, who showed joy and pleasure at the events. As on the earlier voyages, the Spaniards went in procession, carrying the crosses with the help of the islanders, who sang and danced as they went. All circuited the bay, with difficulty, owing to the terrain, and arrived in the afternoon 'at the place at which the crosses were to be set up, and this was concluded with full rejoicings, after the benediction and adoration of the holy images, by the whole concourse of people, on seeing which the natives went through the same ceremony' (Aguera 1908: 104).

Once the crosses were planted, the Spanish flag was raised and the captain of the frigate, Don Joseph Bustillo, took possession of the island in the customary way, in the name of the king of Spain. The ritual was followed by the usual protocol with some of the islanders, assumed to be chiefs, signing a document to 'corroborate the seriousness of the act'. Following some cheers, three volleys were fired with muskets to which the ships replied with a total of twenty-one guns to ratify the formality of the event. The ritual was completed on returning to the boat when 'officers in succession thereupon offered their felicitations and congratulations to the Commodore, who then fixed the following day for their departure from the bay, in consequence of his mission there being now happily concluded' (Aguera 1908: 105).

According to plan, the Spaniards left the next day, armed with a deficient chart produced by the Dutchman Gerard Van Keulen, probably one printed around 1683.[10] Following some difficulties with a 'cable' or mooring tie, they sailed on, arriving back in the Chilean port of Chiloe on 15 December, 'after twenty-four days of navigation from the island of San Carlos we discovered, and sixty-seven from our departure from the Callao' (Aguera 1908: 108).

Aguera's narrative of the voyage concludes with a brief 'dictionary' (1908: 109–10), while Hervé completed his with a summary of the features and the number of people on the island, which he estimated to be 'from about nine hundred to a thousand souls: and of these very few indeed are women – I do not believe they amount to seventy – and but few boys' (1908: 127). To these characteristics, Hervé added the ubiquitous references to the islanders' skin and hair colour, comparing them with Amerindians and, therefore, classing them as being closer to the European mark, using the enlightened evolutionary hierarchy. Thus, according to him, Easter Islanders 'in no way resemble the Indians of the South American continent; and if they wore clothing like ourselves they might very well pass for Europeans' (1908: 127). Like Aguera, therefore, Hervé's narrative remains within the parameters established in the hierarchy of observers and the observed. And, very much like the voyage to Tahiti discussed in the next section, this paradigm consolidates the hegemonic relationship that obtained in most eighteenth-century journeys, and which was the hallmark of ethnography and travelogues well into the twentieth century.

NOTES

1 Corney found all the relevant documents showing the concern of colonial officers in Spanish America about England's exploration of the South Pacific.
2 Although, as Corney remarks, Davis's discovery is doubtful, it was widely accepted as truthful, having been quoted in Dampier's *New Voyage and Description* (1908: xvii, xx).
3 Patrick Kirch indicates that 'the process of expansion out of the Ancestral Polynesian homeland' involved three separate processes taking place from around the beginning of the first millennium until 600–800, when the easternmost areas of the Pacific would have been reached' (2000: 245).
4 In Dalrymple's version of the journal (1996: 85–110), *Roggewein Dutch Voyages*, Roggeveen is quoted as saying that: 'Unfortunately the discharge we had made killed several ... which chagrined us much' (1996: 92).
5 Of these sources, which are listed in the Appendix, the important journal of González de Haedo is sadly lost today. Quotations in this section are to Corney's translations, which have been compared with the originals, and Mellén's edition.
6 Corney's eighteen people are transcribed by Mellén as twenty-eight (1986: 281).
7 Corney reads 'coxa', meaning 'thing' for 'caxa', meaning 'box' (1908: 120).
8 In this case, Corney renders 'loxuria', which is the Spanish term not for 'luxury' but for 'lechery', as 'entertainment', giving the name of the idol as 'Copeca'.
9 Aguera likened the islanders' pronunciation to Arabic and to the 'Lazaron' dialect of Naples. The words that the islanders were taught to learn or repeat related either to the Spanish royalty or to the Christian religion (1908: 99).
10 Aguera referred to this Dutch mapmaker as Wam Keullen (1986: 288).

4

Boenechea and Tahiti (1772)

At around the time that the expedition to Easter Island returned to Lima – towards the end of 1770 – Viceroy Amat was informed of James Cook's first voyage to Tahiti and of the British intention to settle the island. Consequently, Amat changed his initial plans to concentrate on exploring Easter Island during a second voyage to the Pacific and included Tahiti in the journey planned. To that effect, he ordered the *Santa María Magdalena*, also known as *Águila*, or *El Águila*, to be equipped under the command of Domingo Boenechea, with Lieutenant Tomás Gayangos as second in command. The first pilot of the vessel was Juan Antonio de Hervé, who had gone to Easter Island on the earlier voyage and drafted bird's-eye views. Two Franciscan friars accompanied the expedition, the Catalan José Amich, who was also a pilot, and the Italian Juan Bonamó.

This second voyage to the South Pacific departed from El Callao en route to Easter Island on 26 September 1772. After leaving the harbour, Boenechea met with his officers and, following the customary procedure, opened Viceroy Amat's sealed instructions for the voyage. These secret orders commanded them to sail to Tahiti and *San Carlos* (Easter Island), giving them the choice of where to go first. The officers decided to sail towards Tahiti and to proceed on to Easter Island after a brief stop-over in Valparaíso (Chile), to inform the Viceroy about the expedition.

The three accounts of this voyage bear witness to a fair degree of cultural syncretism which can be appreciated in the encounters with indigenous peoples, especially in the recognition and value of certain local customs. One of the accounts is an unsigned journal which has been attributed to the *alférez de navío* ('ship's lieutenant'), Raimundo Bonacorsi, and is widely used in this section.[1] The remaining two accounts were written by the commander, Domingo de Boenechea, and the last one by Friar José Amich, both of which are also unsigned.[2]

According to these sources, the journey passed various Oceanic islands before reaching its destination (Figure 4.2). After deciding to head for Tahiti, the Spaniards discovered and named a number of islands on some of which they saw armed people waiting for them, whereas in others they were pleased to note signs of friendship. Nonetheless, they could not land on any of them on account of the reefs or currents, although they initiated some exchanges in, for example, Mehetia, which they called *San Cristóbal* because it had a hill that reminded the Spaniards of the *Cerro de San Cristóbal* in Lima. There, the Spanish sent a boat which circumnavigated the island, receiving gifts of fruit from its inhabitants, who came out to meet them in their canoes to trade their local products, including fish and 'several curiosities which they exchanged for knives, shirts and charms' (Amich 1925: 54–5). Bonacorsi noticed two naked locals who, carrying coconuts, came to meet the Spaniards to barter the fruit in exchange for any small bagatelle ('qualquiera friolera'). However, it was not just any 'bagatelle' that the indigenous people wanted but any form of iron, especially nails. When invited to board, the islanders were reluctant to accept the offer, and did not offer further gifts when they ran out of coconuts to barter (1772: 111v). Again here, the reciprocity of duties entailed in gift-giving as a means of social communication is highlighted as being understood and strictly adhered to by the islanders. Besides these exchanges, one of the islanders mentioned Tahiti, which pleased the Spaniards, as did the fact that he went on board the ship and displayed a good deal of local knowledge that the Spaniards were able to incorporate into their limited understanding of those distant places.

Around eight canoes with two or three islanders on each returned for the 'same commerce' early the following morning. This time, however, many boarded the ship, observing everything with curiosity but not as much admiration as the explorers expected. While this was taking place, a Spanish party went ashore on a boat in order to find a possible landing spot for the ship, calculating the depth of the water and drawing a plan. Unfortunately, they found nowhere suitable for the ship and had difficulty obtaining water in spite of the help from many islanders of 'both sexes and all ages', who tried to guide them (Bonacorsi 1772: 112).

Although these can certainly be qualified as 'sightings' rather than 'visits', some customs, as well as their habitat and housing design, are recorded in the journals. Thus, on *Todos Santos* (Anaa), we read about two men wearing shell necklaces, a woman fishing and palms used for thatching the roof. Although all the Spanish efforts to communicate with the islanders, using as interpreters the Peruvian Indians they had taken

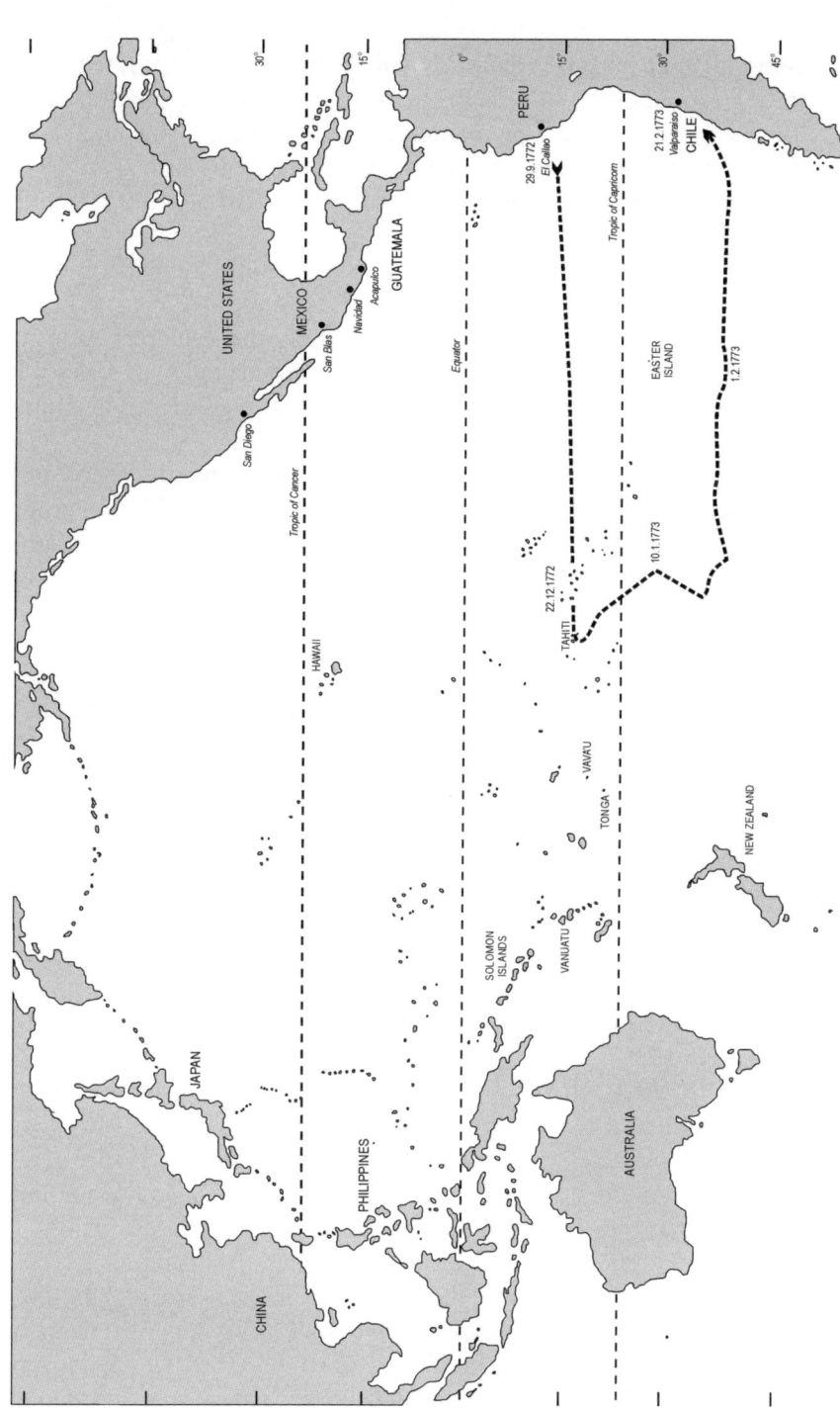

4.2 Itinerary of the first voyage of Domingo de Boenechea to Tahiti (1771–72).

along for that purpose, obviously failed, the islanders appeared to them to be peaceful (1772: 110v).[3] On their way, however, the Spanish saw two 'rancherias' surrounded by planted maize and, once inside one of them, they noticed a human jaw, as well as other ornaments such as baskets and rugs made with palm.[4] They also detected a bench or headrest carved from a single piece of wood, the workmanship of which was highly praised by Bonacorsi (1772: 113). In relation to flora and fauna, comparison with the known species provided a model in which to fit the unknown, as in earlier voyages. Nevertheless, as befitted their time, the explorers were more prepared to deal with novelty and class it alongside different scales, which they did in the case of flora, using the classification designed by Linnaeus to encompass all species on earth.

Bonacorsi's journal next details some indigenous rituals observed when the Spaniards approached what appeared to be the local burial grounds. The enclosure was fenced with sticks and it was clear that the islanders did not want the visitors near the site. The Spaniards dutifully respected their wishes. The exchange of food taking place was, again, reciprocal, and Bonacorsi observed that the islanders did not find all Spanish food to their taste, enjoying only biscuits and bacon (1772: 113v–14). The visitors also took the time to teach their hosts how to plant some of the seeds they had on board, of which they left some samples. Amich's journal refers to this in greater detail than Bonacorsi's, adding that the islanders 'were taught how to prepare the earth to sow, giving them seeds of maize, wheat, pumpkin, melon, watermelon, sweet potatoes, potatoes and garlic and they paid much attention to the way our people did this' (1925: 57). This practice of teaching indigenous peoples to cultivate the land or raise animals was very much in line with eighteenth-century voyages of exploration. Cook, for example, took animals with him, a feature which, for Bernard Smith, demonstrates the 'role of philanthropist of the Enlightenment'.[5]

As with plants, the islanders' culture was, for the Spaniards, one that should be channelled into 'proper' cultivation. This attitude was extended to religious practices which meant that, in spite of the observance of burial practices, Bonacorsi, seeing that the islanders had no religious images deduced that they adored neither animated nor 'supposed' beings (1772: 114v). Having thus assessed the islanders' mores, the Spaniards established the same type of exchange at their destination, the island of Tahiti, which was identified for them by a Mehetian islander travelling with them. After four days spent attempting, but failing, to land, as there was no favourable wind, an 'Indian' came on board and gave the Spanish some plantains and coconuts in exchange for knives and other gadgets. As usual, the Spaniards were met by many canoes carrying unarmed men, a peaceful attitude that was corroborated by the Mehetian islander, who also reassured the Tahitians that the Spaniards were 'affable'. In physical terms, these islanders seemed to Bonacorsi to be of the 'same quality', only even burlier and stronger than those met before (1772: 116–19v).

Once in Tahiti, the captain, Domingo de Boenechea, gathered the officers to inform them of the instructions regarding the treatment of the islanders who, he said, ought to be addressed with due consideration and respect for their property, even if they appeared to be ignorant people 'without culture or upbringing'. Boenechea also warned them against committing any 'infamy' with their women (Amich 1925: 36).[6] It was the commander's responsibility to impose an 'affable and benign' code of conduct towards the islanders 'without intimidating them with that rustic severity under whose zeal true cowardice often hides' (Amich 1925: 40).[7] Amat added that the main objective of the journey would be to bring about the indigenous people's acceptance of Christianity and to ignore matters that might not be of any relevance to that end. Whether or not the punishment for breaking the rules had an effect on their upholding, his instructions seem to have been taken to heart by commander and crew, and Corney believes that they were followed to the letter.[8]

Amat's zeal not to mistreat the locals fits within the model followed by some eighteenth-century expeditions, prominent among which are those led by Cook, who was noticeably imbued with the humane spirit of the Enlightenment. There are, however, some telling differences between Spanish and British explorers, especially concerning the treatment accorded to women. Unlike the Spaniards, Cook was not remiss in letting his crew establish relations with local women in order to keep them loyal, because he realised that what his men mostly wanted was to have sexual intercourse with women.[9] One outcome of the relations between the English sailors and the local women, according to the Spaniards, was evident in the hue of some local children.[10] By contrast, the Spaniards were strictly required to avoid contact with women, and were instructed to show due regard to the women that they met. The objective of this restraint was not to give 'bad example' and to avoid the jealousy of the islanders (Amich 1925: 44).[11] Sadly for the Tahitians, another consequence of their sexual activity with Europeans was the swift spread of venereal diseases.

Besides their behaviour towards women, the Spaniards were also directed to show restraint and fairness in their commercial activities and to spread the Catholic religion. Indeed, commerce and religion mixed in some of their actions, as seen when Bonacorsi affirmed that they wanted to found a settlement so as to 'attract' the locals to Catholicism and to trade with them: 'to attract the moods and wills of the indigenous peoples ... so that they may embrace commerce with Spaniards and the Catholic religion' (1772: 101v). As often happened throughout the eighteenth century, commerce appears as one of the main aims of the journey and is associated here with Christianising the local inhabitants, an aim that is confirmed by the fact that the ship carried two missionary friars, whose multilingual abilities are highlighted (1772: 103).

As far as contact with the islanders is concerned, throughout this journey relations seem to have been largely respectful, even if somewhat distant, especially by comparison with the one that followed. Many of the references in the journals recognise the presence of the local inhabitants, as well as of other European explorers, acknowledging the cross-cultural tone of the encounters between the different parties. From these accounts we learn that the English voyages were well known to the Spaniards, corroborated by the reference to the island using the name given by the English, King George (Bonacorsi 1772: 101v).

In Tahiti, the Spanish frigate landed in Vaiurua, named *Puerto de Santa María Magdalena* by Boenechea, from which a party departed on a boat to survey and chart the island and its harbours. Among the party on this boat, which was commanded by Gayangos, were the Franciscan friar, Amich, as well as the second pilot, Ramón Rosales. Everywhere that this group went, they were well received, with overt and warm displays of friendship. This was especially the case in the domains of the *arii* Tu, who was one of the principal chiefs of the island and whose role would be all-important in the next journey.

The Tahitians felt confident enough to sleep on board the ship and the *arii* with three of his men did so in Taiarapu. Again, the Tahitians were treated 'affably' and responded in kind, offering to help the Spaniards enter the harbour by acting as pilots ('prácticos'). While the Spanish party went about its business of surveying and charting, they were always 'graciously' surrounded by Tahitians. At the same time as they were involved in these chores, they bartered with locals 'of all sexes and ages', trading fruits, coconuts, rugs and even birds, in exchange for axes, knives, nails and other metallic instruments. The following engagement is worth quoting at length, for it highlights the reciprocity of these exchanges, as well as the degree of mutual respect, as seen in Bonacorsi's appreciation of the Tahitians' honesty and loyalty:

It is not easy to give the right sum of all the Indians, who from the time we beached, came in their canoes on board and around us, of both sexes and all ages. Some came at dawn, but the majority and the 'principales' after the sun was high. And all brought something to barter with our people: some, from the time they were approaching, were showing beautiful branches of bananas, coconuts and other fruits which abound on the island; others carried birds, which our people esteemed much; others blankets or cloth of different quality which they make from the bark of trees; others rugs; others shells and snails. In sum, everyone brought what their own industry afforded them to give in exchange for what they lack. What they fancied most were knives (which they call *tipi*), axes, which they call *toy*, nails, and anything made of iron, with which they made hooks and implements to work wood. The chiefs esteemed any piece of cloth, either white or in colour, but, when they started seeing good cloth and shirts, they started to raise the price of their merchandise, and were not pleased with anything other than the finest cloth and shirt, calling everything umbrellas. For the sale of their merchandise, even the boys are clever and astute but, at the same time, are quite loyal and not treacherous in the least, so that if any among us was not satisfied with the product bought, they would be given back whatever they had paid for. (1772: 122v–3v)

The praise of the Tahitians' supposed fairness lavished here is, however, qualified in the next sentence, when we learn that they were also seen to be somewhat distrustful and greedy. These tendencies were checked, the journal adds, by their fear of weapons and the fact that the Spaniards had showered gifts and demonstrations of friendship on them, with the role of the Mehetian islander as go-between highlighted here (1772: 124v).

The friendly exchanges between Spaniards and Tahitians were furthered by mutual displays of friendship, with the Tahitians using the word *taio*, meaning close friend, along with public demonstrations of affection. The Tahitians were eager for these manifestations to be reciprocated and sought to be embraced by their chosen *taio*, with whom they exchanged names (Bonacorsi 1772: 128). Sadly, however, exchanges were not limited to goods or names but were also extended to viruses, and many Tahitians, lacking immunity to European diseases, started to die from an epidemic of influenza. They attributed their deaths to the arrival of the Spaniards, adding that there had been another ship previously which had caused them some harm (Bonacorsi 1772: 124). Besides viruses, the Tahitians were afraid that the Spaniards might hurt them when they left and, therefore, they asked the Spaniards repeatedly when they were planning to go, overtly showing their concern that the occasion might be ominous for them.

While moored, Boenechea appointed Lieutenant Gayangos to command an expedition on the launch to find out how best to circumnavigate the island. Friar Amich and the Second Master, Ramón Rosales, accompanied Gayangos, together with the launch's crew. Boenechea's and Amich's journals incorporate accounts of the journey, including important information about contacts with Tahitians, most of which were friendly and contained exchanges of knowledge and food items to cement their relationship.

The launch left on 5 December and coasted the island, meeting islanders in Taharoa who presented them with food, including bananas, coconuts and other fruits, which Amich's editor wrongly transcribes as 'curos' instead of *euros*, indicating that they made bread with it (1925: 65). The *arii*, 'Pagairiro' (Pahiriro), on receiving a present of, among other things, knives and a mirror, invited the Spaniards to rest in his house. There, Amich and Gayangos noticed a house with only women, a fact that remains a common feature in Polynesian societies. From there, the launch landed on an atoll which was one and a half miles away – 'Oidia' (Hitiaa), which they called *San Nicolás* – and were met by a multitude of canoes laden with bananas, coconuts and fruit. As the journey around the coast continued, this welcoming pattern was repeated when three Spanish men jumped ashore and 'un indio de los principales', Teinui, invited them to his house. Teinui was given 'some bagatelles of those that were carried to that end and he remained well pleased' and offered to guide them in their circumnavigation around the island. The exchanges to seal the mutual friendship continued and Gayangos greeted Teinui's father, O Reti, with the standard gift of an axe and a knife, receiving fish in abundance in exchange, not only from the *arii*'s canoe, but also from those surrounding them. Teinui explained his motives in wanting to accompany the Spaniards to his father, who seemed pleased with the explanation, making signs that he would like to join the voyagers too.

Continuing their journey to the west of the island the explorers met with the main *arii* of Tahiti, 'Heri Etu' (Tu), who was regaled with food, including a roasted hen and fresh bread. Tu responded in Polynesian fashion, speaking at length and inviting Gayangos to join him on land, which Gayangos did and, following local custom, was carried on the shoulders of an islander while many people went to observe the scene. Gayangos was then able to appreciate and describe some of the customs that still obtain in the Pacific, as when he sat with Tu among three women and four men, all of whom greeted him as friend, calling him *taio*, to which he corresponded, using the same word. The customary exchanges of gifts followed, this time with blankets placed on Gayangos's shoulders, to which he reciprocated with 'bujerías' ('small merchandise') that the women appreciated, especially the mirrors. However, the continuous exchange of gifts meant that the Spaniard eventually ran out of goods to give or barter, and he was unable to respond to the gift of a blanket from the *arii*'s sister, handing her a handkerchief. Seeing the handkerchief, Tu also asked for one, and Gayangos gave him the one in his hand, suggesting that it was the last one that he had (Amich 1925: 69–70).

The circumnavigation continued with another interesting exchange, this time with canoes from the domains of Potatau, who provided the Spaniards with fish, seeking hooks in exchange. There, the explorers were able to ascertain not only the islanders' knowledge of metals, but also their skills. This happened when Potatau complained of the size of the hooks and he was also granted some nails, which, he indicated, would be used to make hooks. When asked how he had obtained the iron to learn such workmanship, Potatau made signs to suggest that a ship had been there before, which was also explained how he became acquainted with the function of bullets (Amich 1925: 74).

On completing the narrative of these excursions, Amich added a brief description of the island, singling out what he perceived to be its principal features (1925: 77–90). These included the harbours and the settlements, which he judged as not being 'pueblos' ('villages') but only scattered houses with thatched roofs placed on the seashore. Amich also related the size and quality of habitat to the number of people on the island, which he estimated to be over 8,000, ruled by ten to twelve chiefs, with Tu above them all. As with political hierarchy, assessing the degree of development in urban and housing patterns was a way of categorising the level of civilisation of the peoples encountered, as had happened in the Americas.

Amich's journal concludes with a detailed depiction of the islanders' physiques and body ornaments, including size, colour, tattoos, and women's hair and earrings. His religious status did not prevent Amich from assessing Tahitian women, who he did not compare to women in Spain or Latin America, as previous writers had done, but simply considered them less favourably than the men. Besides their physical features, women were also appraised with regard to their daily occupations and their important role in bartering, which would probably indicate to the Spaniards some similarity with women in their homeland. Foodstuffs and ways of cooking were also described, as this was also used as an indicator of civilisation for Europeans. Another marker of class or level of development which would be used at home was the evaluation of 'vices', including drunkenness, lechery and polygamy. Amich balanced the islanders' having no 'inclination to drunkenness' against their 'lasciviousness', while noting that they were monogamous and did not seem to be jealous, as shown by their offering women to foreigners (1925: 82–3).

Lastly, Amich classed the character of the islanders as peaceful and happy, qualities which they demonstrated with outward manifestations, such as playing the flute. Above all, the Tahitians' navigational skills were highly commended, as was the construction of canoes (1925: 81). With regard to perceived negative characteristics, Amich, like every other European at the time, stressed their propensity to steal. Nevertheless, his interpretation of the mores and habitat of the islanders was obviously hindered by unfamiliarity with the Tahitian language and customs, which he recognised overtly with regards to the islanders' belief system. In relation to this, Amich clarified that, although the explorers did not see temples, there seemed to be some form of worship which he dismissed as 'idolatry' (1925: 84).

Similar to Amich's, Bonacorsi's brief description of events ends with a geographical survey of the island, dutifully 'demonstrated' on the 'extracto pleno' made, indicating the situation, dimensions and harbours of the island (1772: 124–5v). This final section includes observations on the type of soil and on the environment of the harbour of *Santa Maria Magdalena*; the type of places where people lived; how they cooked; their domestic animals, plants and, importantly for the European classification of peoples, the chiefdom system. On this, Bonacorsi reported that while the chiefs of the island ate so much as to be malformed, commoners did not eat pigs or chickens and even went hungry, maintaining themselves mostly with fish and raw seafood (1772: 127v–8).

Among the Tahitian customs which surprised Europeans and that were always mentioned in journals were the sophisticated taboos surrounding the production, cooking and consumption of food. That the men ate in a different house from the women and that they were seen to gulp food was noted by Bonacorsi, who also remarked that the houses where men ate were unlike the larger, oval meeting houses and also unlike the 'ranches' of the 'heris' and 'principales', which were located apart. All the houses had scant furnishings, among which Bonacorsi highlighted the wooden stools and pillows, which were often elaborately carved (1772: 128–9).

As always, there is the mention of the Tahitian habit of stealing, in spite of the fact that the hosts always appeared to be friendly towards the Spaniards. The myth of Polynesian 'free love' also receives attention, although it is qualified by the assertion that the great majority of Tahitians had only one wife. Applying a European assumption, Bonacorsi's narrative infers that the men could 'repudiate' the women, but did not consider whether the reverse also applied. Lastly, as regards religious customs the visitors had not observed any particular 'cult' but noted that the Tahitians sacrificed a pig every six months to their god, and buried them. With a degree of honesty, Bonacorsi, like Amich, acknowledged his limitations as an interpreter of the local 'superstitions' due to his inability to understand the language and culture of the land (1772: 129–30v).

Completing his description, Bonacorsi emphasised the strained relationship which the Tahitians' had with their neighbours, especially the Mooreans, with whom fights seem to have been continuous. In relation to the level of hostility, the Tahitians noticed that the Spaniards had no 'sticks' ('palos'), meaning guns, like those used by their previous visitors against them (1772: 131v). They also showed a good deal of interest towards the habits of the foreigners, as when they told Bonacorsi that they had noticed how the captain of the foreign ship ate with a two-pronged fork. On this note, Bonacorsi finished his account of life on the island with a favourable note about its wholesome climate.

The Spaniards left the island on 20 December, heading towards Moorea in order to check whether there were English settlers on the island, which they called *Santo Domingo* (1772: 133v–4). On arrival in Peru's harbour of El Callao, we read about the four Tahitians who had gone with them, who are also mentioned by Amich, although neither author wrote down the islanders' names in their narratives, concentrating instead on their ages, and the fact that the youngest had been granted his father's permission to go with the Spaniards (Amich 1925: 85). These Tahitians, of whom more is described below, exemplify a level of indigenous inquisitiveness that clearly matched that of enlightened travellers from Europe. Their integration in the colonial life of Spanish America also illustrates the cross-cultural dimension of these voyages, which is neatly embedded in the names that they they adopted. Besides their Tahitian name, they acquired a Christian one, coining a composite that is wholly suitable to denote cultural engagement: 'Pauiti, and here Thomas ... Tipitipia and here Joseph ... Osehellao and here Francisco ... Getuani here is called Manuel' (Bonacorsi 1772: 136). As shown in section III, the two surviving Tahitians, Pautu and Tetuanui, proved to be at home in both cultures and, even though they returned to their way of life in Tahiti, they showed some nostalgia for the places and people encountered in Lima.

Sadly, however, one of the four Tahitians did not reach his destination, dying in Valparaíso, where the fleet had called after leaving Callao in order to take on provisions en route for Easter Island. Tipitipia died there of influenza, having been baptised and given the name José. On 2 April, the Spaniards sailed towards San Carlos (Easter Island) but, when they were close to the island, they realised that they were taking in water and changed their course back to El Callao, where they finally arrived on 31 May 1773. On arriving in Lima, the explorers were taken to see Amat, to whom they presented their journals and charts. There, Heiao, the second of the four Tahitian who had left with them, died of smallpox, after receiving the name Francisco José Amat at his baptism. In spite of these sad deaths, the two surviving Tahitians made the most of their visit, and were hosted at the Palace of the Viceroy in Lima, being christened at Lima's cathedral a few months later, on 11 October, when Pautu became Tomás and Tetuanui adopted the name Manuel. While in Lima, these Tahitians learned Spanish language, helped by Máximo Rodríguez, who was to become an interpreter in the second voyage to Tahiti. Thus, their tutor, Máximo, taught Spanish to the Tahitians while he learned Tahitian from them. This knowledge would help Máximo to become perhaps the first ever ethnographer and without doubt the most interesting and worldly-wise character among Spanish voyagers of all times.

NOTES

1 All translations of Bonacorsi's journal in this chapter are mine.
2 The account is written by Amich until the Spanish arrived in Tahiti, when it became a collaboration between Gayangos and Amich. Both, however, are referred throughout this section as Amich, and translations are mine.
3 Although it would seem to us a far-fetched a proposition as when Columbus took a multilingual Jew on his first voyage, people of Pacific islands removed thousand of miles from one another speak languages which are closely related. Cook used a Tahitian when in New Zealand and was delighted with his usefulness as interpreter there.
4 In the following voyage, Máximo Rodríguez enquired about the lower jaws seen as decoration in some houses and was told that they were war trophies (1992: 139).
5 Smith also notes that 'livestock was to be distributed to the natives, either as gifts to appropriate chieftains or in the process of trade', which means that Europeans disregarded the existing patterns of social relations among the islanders, following a hierarchical design that was very much along the lines they imagined (1992: 206).
6 Amat's instructions as Corney notes, 'speak sufficiently for themselves'. Corney also observes that the instructions denote Amat's particular concern

to ensure 'the fair and honourable treatment of any native races that might be met with' (1913: xxv).
7 Amat instructed that the same care be taken when going inland, warning that those who mistreated the islanders 'with word or deed' would suffer 'severely' and would be made to 'experiment all the rigor of the law'. Also, everyone going onshore had to be licensed to do so and they had to go in groups (1925: 40–1).
8 'It is pleasing to know ... that the relations between the Spaniards and the islanders were never marred by harsh treatment or vulgarity during the whole of their intercourse; and that there were no instances of bloodshed or the abuse of firearms such as sullied the records of more than one visit to Tahiti (and Easter Island) on the part of the explorers of other nationalities about the corresponding period' (Corney 1913: xxv–xxvi).
9 Smith remarks that: 'what Cook's young sailors wanted even more than they wanted fresh food was the bodies of the native women, and it was the one universal product most often offered, most readily available' (1992: 209).
10 In the second Spanish voyage to Tahiti, the Franciscan friars referred to as the padres, commented on the effects of the English presence on the island in the skin colour of children, including a baby who the Spaniards called 'un Inglesito' (1925: 105).
11 'Whatever the intentions of the Spaniards ... they seemed to have taken great pains to ingratiate themselves with the inhabitants; who, upon every occasion, mentioned them with the strongest expressions of esteem and veneration' (Corney 1913: xxvi).

4

III Máximo and the padres in Tahiti (1774–75)

Of the four Tahitians who left with the Spaniards on the first voyage to Tahiti, only two, Pautu and Tetuanui, survived to reach Lima. These young men, who received the Spanish names of Tomás and Manuel, returned home on the third eighteenth-century Spanish expedition to the South Pacific – a voyage that, unlike the previous two to Tahiti and Easter Island, was not prepared as one of reconnaissance. It was designed, instead, with the objective of establishing a mission, with two Franciscan friars: the Catalan Jerónimo Clota and the Extremaduran Narciso González, referred to as 'the padres', following Bolton Corney's lead. Both these friars were left on the island with Máximo Rodríguez, who would serve as an interpreter, and a sailor, Francisco Pérez, whose was to help the friars with their domestic duties, and who is seldom referred to by his name in the journals.

On this 'mission', the Spaniards took with them tools, seeds and cattle to assist them in settling the island. Also, the officers carried with them Amat's famous Questionnaire ('Interrogatorio'), with 100 enquiries about various topics, and a dictionary compiled by Máximo, and possibly Juan Hervé, with the help of Pautu and Tetuanui.[1] Domingo de Boenechea was once more put in command of the expedition and on board the *Águila*, which was escorted by a frigate ('paquebote'), the *San Miguel*, known as *Júpiter*, owned and commanded by José Andía y Varela, who was also its pilot. Amat intended to start the process of conversion of the Tahitians and to discover some neighbouring islands mentioned by Pautu and Tetuanui while in Lima. However, as soon as they arrived on Tahiti, Pautu and Tetuanui returned to their homes and way of living and were, therefore, of no help in securing the Christian conversions.

Following Amat's orders, the fleet left on 20 September 1774 and the two ships parted company on 5 October, meeting again in Tahiti. According to Francisco Mellén Blanco, they discovered some sixteen islands not previously seen by Europeans: thirteen by Boenechea, two by Andía y Varela and one by Gayangos, who succeeded Boenechea in command of the expedition after the former's death in Tahiti in January 1775 (Figure 4.3).[2] Also taking place during this voyage, and perhaps one of the most significant actions performed by Boenechea just before his death, was the ceremonial signing of the Convention of Tautira, which was drafted, and performed, to indicate Spanish possession of the island.

On 5 January 1775, Boenechea, with the padres, as well as various officers from the *Águila* who were commanded by Gayangos, met in Tautira with the main *arii* of Tahiti. Máximo Rodríguez acted as interpreter at this gathering, in which the *arii* are said to have recognised Spanish sovereignty on the island, which, the Spaniards asserted, secured the putative defence of its inhabitants by the Spanish king and his forces. In exchange, the islanders supposedly agreed to be subjects of the Spanish monarch, to whom they were meant to show deference and loyalty. The notary ('contador') of the frigate, Pedro Freire de Andrade, ratified the deed of this covenant, which is kept at the Archive of the Indies in Seville.[3] This document, however, is not signed, unlike a similar deed drafted five years earlier on Easter Island, which has the signatures or marks of three local chiefs and those of the Spanish officers. In fact, it is worth noting that Máximo does not even mention this treaty at all in his detailed account of events on the island.

Máximo's journal, however, goes into great detail about the time spent on the island by the two friars, the sailor and himself, and his narrative is the main source for this section. Other accounts of this voyage used here are those of the commanders, Boenechea and Gayangos, Andía y Varela, the padres, and that of the pilot Juan Pantoja.[4] Besides Pantoja's account, all these narratives were translated and published in English by Bolton Corney for the Hakluyt Society in the early twentieth century (1913–18). As with the previous voyages to Easter Island and Tahiti, Corney carried out a remarkably intense and successful archival and editorial exercise, finding, transcribing and translating not just the main sources for the voyage but also many letters and despatches. In fact, he even located and identified the *umete* mentioned above, which was given to Máximo by the *arii* Tu.

Among the accounts of this voyage, Máximo's is the most inspiring from the point of view of reciprocal engagements, although Andía y Varela and Pantoja also offer many remarkable insights into Tahitian life and exchanges between the parties. Wholly conversant in Tahitian as a result of having been there on the previous voyage and of tutoring the two Tahitians in Lima, Máximo is probably one of the most interesting

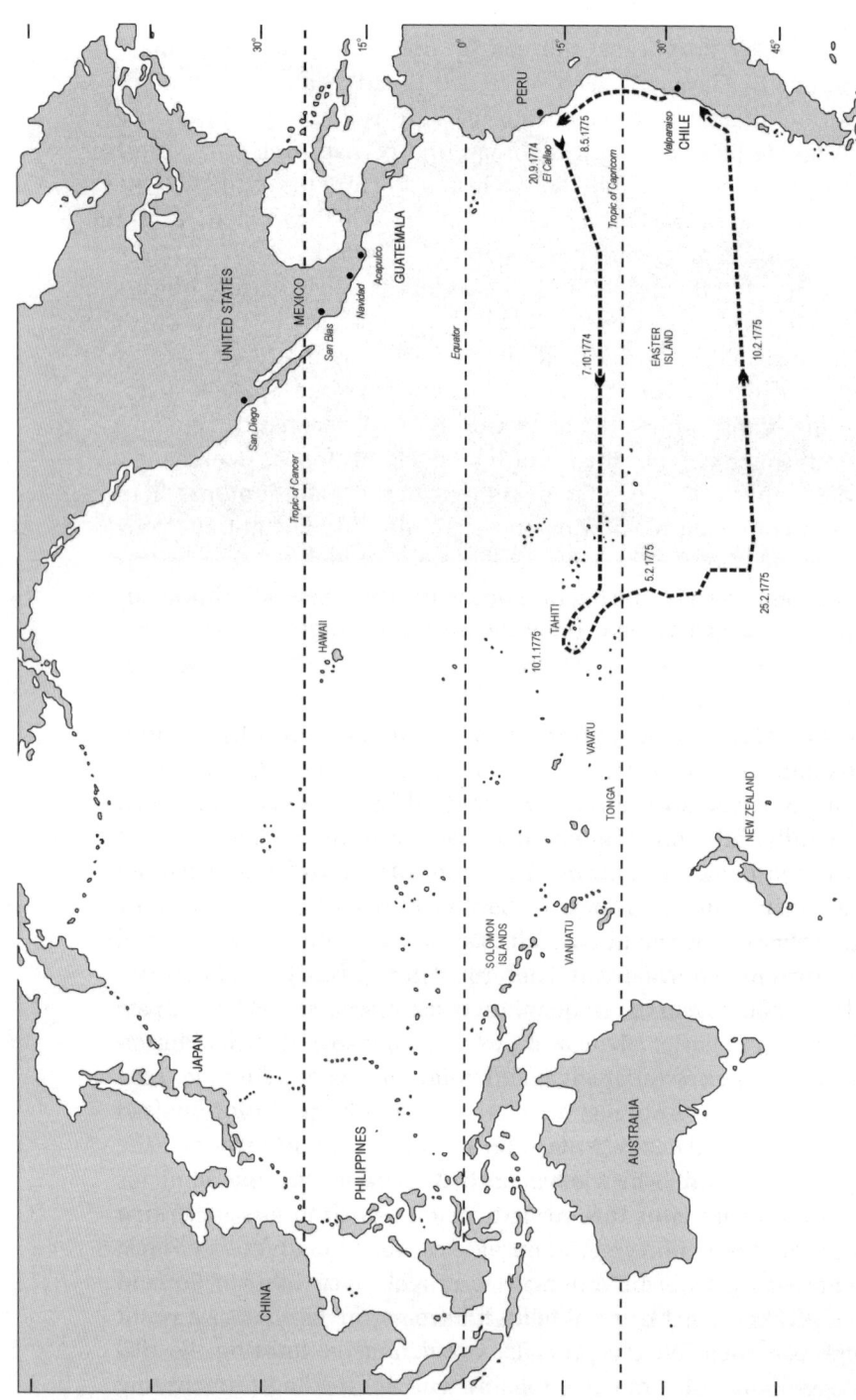

4.3 Itinerary of the voyage of Boenechea and Tomás Gayangos to Tahiti to establish a mission on the island (1774–75).

characters to have entered the Pacific at this time. In fact, Máximo, who was a young, lower-class Peruvian most likely of mixed ethnic background, acted as the perfect 'go-between', and his experiences mirror those of many people whose descendants inhabit the Pacific today.

Untainted by the official rhetoric of many journals, Máximo's narrative sheds a unique light on the cultural encounters between the indigenous peoples of the Pacific and Europeans who followed the first explorers. Throughout his journal, Máximo appears to have become increasingly distant from the friars he was meant to serve and to have adapted well to his new way of life away from the customs of his country of origin, Spanish Peru. However, he always remained an outsider, a participant observer, and this is revealed by his forthright comments and unseemly air of superiority when commenting on the local 'superstitions'. Nonetheless, his straightforwardness gradually endears him to his readers.

Other narratives produced during this 'mission', such as Pantoja's or Andía y Varela's, also show a sincere effort to understand the Tahitian 'others' on their own terms, and are marred only by some assumptions of superiority in terms of religious beliefs or scientific progress. For eighteenth-century explorers, as indicated above, Europe stood at the zenith of civilisation, whereas its nadir was variously occupied by the inhabitants of Tierra del Fuego, African slaves or, in their turn, Melanesians and Australian Aborigines. By contrast, from their first encounters with European explorers, Tahitians became idealised as the prototypical 'noble savages', who had been blissfully spared the trappings of a class system that hampered Europeans and enjoyed free love and the bounty of nature.

From Louis de Bougainville's enthusiastic accounts, Tahitians had assumed features that European critics, especially the so-called primitivists, used in order to censure what they saw as crude materialism in their own societies. This idealised image of Tahiti and its people survived through the ages, enduring even after it had been shown that their society was far from being carefree and not only did private property exist, but also wars and despotisms, perhaps comparable to those known to Europeans.

Interestingly, Spanish accounts of this voyage were largely devoid of this sort of idealisation. From the very beginning, the journals stress the same injunctions that were issued during the first voyage to Tahiti, concerning the humane and respectful treatment of the indigenous population, which were, again, duly observed. This is mentioned, for example, by Pantoja, who outlined the punishment to be inflicted on those breaching those rules. This was in contrast, according to Pantoja, with the

English who had displayed 'cruelty' towards the Tahitians by robbing them of their women and forcing them to have sex. In this vein, Pantoja also recorded the breach of Spanish rules by one sailor, Esteban González, who was arrested for having 'cooperated' with one woman, and given fifty lashes as punishment (1992: 129–32, 145).

Máximo's account pays little attention to the actual sea voyage, concentrating on the time that the 'mission' remained on the island and the contact with the locals. Upon arrival on Tahiti on 15 November 1774, the first event recorded by Máximo is taking part in a reconnaissance tour on a boat on which he was accompanied by, among others, 'Bonacorci' (Bonacorsi), Machao and 'the Indian of the said land, called Tomas and Pautu by the islanders' (1992: 44). In this and further references, the names given to the two Tahitians who had been to Lima become 'Christian' names, as given to them on their baptism, while their indigenous names are preserved like a surname or family name.

As the Spanish party sailed around the island, they were surrounded by various canoes, and people asking about the fate of the remaining Tahitians who had left on the previous voyage: 'Tomas Pautu, Manuel Tutanui... Francisco Ojeyao, y Tipitipia'. Máximo informed them that two of them had died on arriving on the South American mainland, one in Valparaíso and the other in Lima.[5] Pautu then recognised one of his relatives, who came on board and greeted him warmly, kissing him on the cheek and forehead (1992: 44). This effusiveness was also noticed by the padres, who observed how the father of one of these boys came on board and, when he saw his son, hugged him and did not want to let him go – demonstrations of love and tenderness that were equally extended to the Spaniards who had brought them back (1925: 98–9).

Heartfelt emotion was also displayed by Pautu's uncle when he went to the Spaniards crying and invited them to go to his house. The explorers obliged and they met there a big crowd 'some happy to see Pautu, and others crying and lamenting the death of the other two who had left with him. As they entered the house, the guests were received so effusively and with such noise that they could not even understand one another. Everyone embraced them so warmly that Máximo used the term 'burning' to describe the warmth of the embraces (1992: 45). Máximo was then taken to see relatives of the deceased Tipitipia and he tried to comfort them, indicating that the Spaniards had done all in their power to save him. He was relieved, however, when he saw Tetuanui's parents, who, while lamenting their missing son, were informed that he was alive on the ship, only prostrated by a recent wound in his shoulder.

The party was then led to the harbour of Tautira, referred to by Máximo as 'santisima Cruz (alias) Ojatutira', using the syncretism often applied by the Spaniards to local names. There, the two main *arii* of the island, Tu and Vehiatua, along with their respective families met with the Spaniards, who inferred that the chiefs were now at peace. As they took a stroll, they were met by a canoe, where Vehiatua's mother, O Purahi ('Opó')[6] and stepfather, Titorea, welcomed the Spanish warmly. Pautu displayed great respect for his chief, even taking his hat off and giving Vehiatua his own clothes. Although young, Vehiatua was disfigured, due to the frequency with which he got drunk on kava ('eaba'), to which Máximo attributed the flakiness of his skin ('escamas') (1992: 45–6).

Tu boarded the Spanish boat with his brothers, one of whom, Hinoi, became Máximo's close friend, his *taio*.[7] Hinoi, with whom Máximo exchanged names, was, according to the latter, a good-looking youth. The Pacific custom observed by Máximo of exchanging names as a token of friendship was, for Máximo, the highest 'finesse' ('mayor fineza') that may be bestowed (1992: 46).[8]

From these meetings, the Spanish learned that two English ships had been there when the Tahitians showed them an English flag belonging to Cook's second or third voyages (1773 and 1774). The Tahitians informed the Spaniards that the English had left Tautira, remaining, instead, on Matavai, which was Tu's domain. While this information was being imparted, so many Tahitians gathered around the Spaniards that the *arii* ordered that they be dispersed by beating them with sticks, a sign of authority on some Pacific islands that was later commented on by Francisco Mourelle in Vava'u.

The following day, the Spanish party set out to reconnoitre the 'Puerto de la Virgen (alias) *Anunji*',[9] which was on the land of the *arii* Pahiriro, who was called 'Eri Pajairiro' by Máximo, using Spanish phonology (1992: 47). This second day of exploration, according to the padres, was a colourful one in which barter became a source of amusement and entertainment for all. Besides recognising that the Tahitians had the upper hand in these exchanges, the padres also noted the islanders' remarkable skill in disposing of some older rugs, making them appear new in order to gain an advantage in the exchange. Other than blankets and rugs, the Tahitians carried fruit, poultry, pigs and additional items to trade.

> The same number of Indians as in previous days turned up at the side of the frigate loaded with fruit, blankets, rugs, pigs, wood pigeons, parakeets, chickens, snails and even the most despicable items that they had to exchange

with our people. We spent all day very amused, seeing the actions of the Indians and admired by the sagacity with which they disposed of their exchanges, tricking many with rugs and blankets that they were selling as new and were found afterwards to be full of patches. (1925: 98)

Mutual enjoyment and cordiality seem to have been prevalent in these exchanges, which included not only artefacts and names but also information about lore, beliefs and cultural knowledge. By this time, Máximo had already established a warm relationship with some islanders as shown, for example, on the occasion when Tu saw a rosary which Máximo wore around his neck. Máximo offered Tu an explanation that included terms to which Tu could relate, indicating that Christians wore those items so as to free themselves from the 'Demonio o *Tupapau*' (1992: 48), utilising both the Spanish and Tahitian words.[10] Frustratingly for contemporary readers, Máximo explained this type of exchange in greater detail in his *Extracto*, a narrative that remains lost to date.

In sharing and interpreting each other's cultures, the Tahitians who had been to Lima had some advantage, especially Pautu, who was of a reasonable age when he visited the South American city. Thus, on this particular occasion, Pautu was able to display his cross-cultural knowledge, explaining to Tu that he had become a Christian through the ceremony of baptism. Tu then asked Máximo to give him a cross, to which Máximo replied that he would do so 'in time', inferring that he would once Tu became more fully acquainted or integrated with the Christian faith (1992: 48).

Exchanges continued when the Spanish met Pahiriro and his wife, who offered blankets, receiving from the 'caballero oficial' an axe and two knives. Pahiriro returned with a pig but the Spaniards did not accept it as a gift, probably because they had run out of items with which to repay. In this, the Spanish followed the pattern already displayed by islanders in earlier voyages, implying that they were aware of the role of gifts in cultural and social exchanges, and the fact that gift-giving entails obligations that ought to be reciprocated.

While the Spanish party went to survey the land, they were often invited to local houses, with Máximo writing once that they were surrounded by so many Tahitians that they were hardly able to cook (1992: 49). This seems to have been always the case when moving around the island, with the padres also remarking on the number of Tahitians surrounding them, and their curiosity (1925: 112). To relieve themselves of this multitude, the Spaniards even resorted to asking the Tahitians to fetch some rats for them, which they promptly did, returning with many, some of which were still alive.

By and large, the Tahitians seemed to be pleased with the presence of the Spaniards and with the knowledge gained. Above all, they were eager to participate in barter although it is worth remarking that, when gifts were swapped, the Spanish acknowledged or even stimulated the hierarchy that they perceived to exist on the island. Thus, they gave more presents to the daughters of the *arii* O Reti ('Oreti'), whose rank Máximo assimilated to 'Governador' (1992: 48).

Throughout an early conversation held by the Spanish and the Tahitians, the former indicated their delight at the fact that Máximo would remain on the island with the padres. Máximo was, moreover, the willing recipient of many gifts, which continued when the Tahitians brought coconuts and blankets. Similarly, when the Spaniards went to the harbour of Tautira ('Ojatutira'), Vehiatua gave Máximo some blankets and a rug. Vehiatua, however, rejected an axe which was offered to him, which surprised Máximo because, he wrote, it was a precious item for Tahitians. Again here, the obligations entailed by the exchange might have caused Vehiatua to refuse a gift which he would be unable to repay in kind or even tenfold, as a chief would be expected to do. Máximo also received the willing support of the islanders in describing the landscape and artefacts on the island. For example, Máximo enquired about the canoes called *paepae*, which had a sort of platform on top, and he was answered that they were used for warfare with Moorea. By contrast with these canoes, there were others called *pajies* (*pahi*), which were used for travelling long distances (1992: 50).

Wherever the Spanish went, they were surrounded by many people, some of whom prevented them on one occasion from approaching the sepulchre of the late Taitoa, whom they had met on their previous voyage.[11] Máximo also observed that the Tahitians threw a piglet at the grave, which he interpreted this as part of a ceremony performed to ward off the devil ('temor del *Tupapau*'). The Spaniards tried to get closer to other corpses, one of which was rotting, but they were informed that *Tupapau* would take revenge on the living if they did so. Although, according to Máximo, the Spaniards tried to convince the Tahitians of their 'error', the visitors showed some degree of understanding and respect for the different customs, and avoided upsetting the Tahitian taboo (1992: 52). This deference is also noticeable in the absence of the type of moral censorship we might expect in earlier accounts.

The ritual display of sorrow, which was normally associated with mourning and in which women actively participated, was observed by Máximo when he saw Pautu's sisters crying and making their heads bleed, which both shocked and impressed him. As Pautu saw Máximo's discomfort, he asked his sisters to stop the ritual, which they promptly did and cleaned the blood that they had extracted using a shark's tooth. When interrogated about the meaning of the ceremony, Pautu obligingly responded that when a relative returned they first celebrated with joy, which was then followed by the lamentation in which the close female relatives, meaning mothers or sisters, were required to prick themselves in the manner observed. Máximo asked Pautu not to do that again, but Pautu answered that, for him, this was a good ritual. Subsequently, Máximo appreciated that Pautu was politely trying to change the conversation to avoid lying to, or disappointing, his friend (1992: 52).

It is remarkable to read how Máximo understood the process of learning, which, for him, required careful and constant study and observation, remarking how he had been disabused and was subsequently able to understand the reasons for the Tahitian women to prick their heads (1992: 56). This concurs with Barbara Stafford's observations regarding the approach to inspection from a scientific, supposedly objective, standpoint during the eighteenth century.[12] In this, Máximo followed the pattern of enlightened travellers – an approach, however, which was associated with higher-class subjects and with a type of unemotional rapport quite unlike Máximo's involvement with his subject.

Máximo's participation allowed him to notice religious rituals, such as praying in their stone temple, which he rendered as *emarae*, and which belies the supposed absence of religious cults to which Bonacorsi had referred on the previous voyage. From this *emarae*, the Spaniards went together to the ship, where they hosted and welcomed the *arii* Tu and Vehiatua, an occasion that allowed Máximo to acknowledge that misinterpretation was not a Spanish prerogative, as the Tahitians inferred that the visitors were taking their beloved *arii* to Lima against their will. Their fears were not allayed for four days, however, as the weather prevented the Spaniards from taking the *arii* ashore and the laments continued throughout that time. Nevertheless, the Tahitians' concern dissipated when their chiefs returned and told them that they had been treated well, which was corroborated by the gifts received (1992: 53–5).

Mutual misunderstandings, as well as curiosity, were also shown in relation to the items associated with European might: their weapons. To test them, Vehiatua asked to borrow a gun, which he was offered, and which was held at all times by someone in order to help him direct it against a canoe, lest he did something 'extraño' (Rodríguez 1992: 56). In spite of this restraint or 'guidance', Vehiatua seemed to be pleased with his new friends, whom he introduced the next day when Boenechea enquired whether he thought that the padres could have a house and garden among them. Not only was Vehiatua delighted at the prospect, but he also urged them to choose the setting themselves, which they did. The padres' account of these events emphasises the role played by Máximo as interpreter, noting how Boenechea talked to the *arii* and to various 'principales' to inform them that the house was needed for the mission, which was the main objective of this visit:

> He [Boenechea] asked them if they were pleased that such house might be built; whether they would give the necessary land for its foundations and whether they would commit themselves to treat well the two religious men and the interpreter. They all replied with untold joy that they would and that they would give people and all the necessary equipment to build the house and to use the land which they would find better suited to the purpose. (1925: 97)

The padres further observed how far Vehiatua would go to please the visitors in this matter when the land for the mission was found to be a plot belonging to his mother. Vehiatua told them that he would ask her, adding that he had no doubt that she would consent to cede it to them. His mother, O Purahi, certainly obliged, likewise showing a ready willingness to please the visitors with her generosity. The Spanish demands on Vehiatua's goodwill did not end there as, when they started building, they realised that two 'ranchos' were too close to theirs and demanded that Vehiatua evacuate them, which he did (Rodríguez 1992: 57).

However, not every exchange was wholly devoid of conflict and, as before, theft spurred on the most unsettling friction of these engagements. In one instance, a sailor who had a shirt stolen threatened the Tahitians in such a way that they all started to flee. Only after negotiations took place, using Máximo as interpreter, did Gayangos agree to find the guilty sailor and punish him. The *arii* interceded on the sailor's behalf and a lesser punishment consisted of his being tied to the cannon with shackles (Rodríguez 1992: 58–9).

Despite the degree of openness in our approach to different cultures, contemporary readers may feel some discomfort because of our expectations of mutual respect. Likewise, our ecological concerns are heightened when we become aware of the environmental damage inflicted by those expeditions. In many of the accounts, it is written as a matter of fact that, when the visitors went onshore, they had three objectives: water, food and wood. Thus, we learn of the tree felling that often accompanied the caulking of ships. In a particular instance from this 'mission', different sources inform us of the potential harm visited on the population by such actions. This happened when the Spaniards started building the mission house and felled twenty *euros*, the breadfruit trees that provided a staple food source for the islanders. The Spaniards were asked to stop chopping those trees to prevent the Tahitians from suffering famine. Nevertheless, Máximo tried to mediate on behalf of the visitors, insisting to the islanders that only the wood from the *euros* was of the required quality for the ships, adding that the same ruthless behaviour had been done by Otute (Cook). In this particular instance, however, it is easy to endorse Corney's remarks that Máximo ought to have shown a clearer understanding of the situation.[13]

To dispel the Tahitians' fears in this regard, Máximo bombastically reassured them that they would be protected by the king of Spain and indicated that the Spaniards would leave their island if they did not get help with the necessary wood (1992: 60).[14] Nothing more is heard of this event in Máximo's account, although other writers, such as Pantoja also recounted the incident, highlighting the important role that the trees played in Tahitian life. In fact, Pantoja gave a very detailed explanation, including the fact that the Spaniards had selected only those trees that did not give 'good fruit', following the advice of 'one of their captains', Taitoa (1992: 144).

As shown in this particular instance, Máximo's role as go-between gradually increased in importance, and he became an effective mediator. In fact, Máximo interceded on many occasions on behalf of one of the parties although mostly, especially early on in the visit, this intercession was for his countrymen. Eventually, he became quite an expert at conciliating the hosts and the visitors, ironing out even small misunderstandings regarding food or theft. For example, Máximo resolved a conflict when a Spanish sailor had offered a handkerchief to a woman as payment for sex and had then refused to give it to her. Acting as interpreter, Máximo informed the captain, who then put the sailor in the stocks and ensured that the handkerchief was given to the aggrieved woman (1992: 61).

The fact that Máximo's account was written with a Spanish audience in mind invites readers to consider carefully his words and deeds. It certainly implies that we ought to accept his sometimes subtle and sometimes overt criticism of Spanish ways, as well as his explicit acceptance of

Tahitian lifestyle, as commitments to knowing, living and enjoying another culture. Indeed, it is likely that the visitors were accepted peacefully and hospitably in Tahiti for so long because of Máximo's skills.

The only event during which a Spaniard lost his life on the island resulted from an accident and was detailed by Máximo, who interpreted the attitude of the Tahitians when the death occurred. While building the house for the padres, the Tahitians pulled down a palm which landed on a sailor and broke his spine, causing him to die instantly. Tu and all the locals who were present began to flee, fearing that they would be blamed and punished. However, the Spaniards soon asked them to return and reassured them that it had been an accident for which they were not to blame (1992: 62).

Many interesting local ceremonials and festivities are also highlighted in Máximo's account, and he was careful to include the Tahitians' replies to his enquiries as to the meaning of several rituals. Some of these explanations are, nonetheless, sadly missing, as they were recorded in his lost *Extracto*: for example, with regard to a festival that Máximo simply called *Jeiba* (heiva), which would have been detailed in the *Extracto* (1992: 63). Among the customs that Máximo detailed in the journal is the exiling of people and their families from the land under the control of a particular *arii*. On one occasion, not giving Vehiatua food meant that the culprit and their family were banished but, not taking their fate silently, these people rebelled against their chief the very next day (1992: 62–4).

At some stages in his narrative, Máximo's status among Tahitians recalls the experiences of Cabeza de Vaca two centuries earlier. After eight years surviving among Amerindian tribes in the inhospitable south of today's United States, Cabeza de Vaca became what for some contemporary critics is the epitome of many settlers: neither an indigenous person nor a coloniser but a mediator or 'participant observer' who was able to use that sense of non-belonging to his advantage, as Rolena Adorno has demonstrated.[15] Like Cabeza de Vaca, Máximo used healing as an instrument of power, and tried to enhance and maintain his reputation as a knowledgeable medicine man among Tahitians. The first time that he recorded this skill is when they took him to see a sick woman and, on looking at her, diagnosed that it was the retention of her menstruation that had caused her to become unwell. Máximo asked her whether she would consent to be bled, to which she agreed. They bled her from one arm and gave her some medicines provided by Máximo but, when they tried to continue with the second arm, she offered some resistance, relenting thereafter. The fact that her health improved the next day meant that Máximo started to get further requests for assistance and that his status was raised considerably among the Tahitians (1992: 65–6).

Máximo's healing abilities were tested again when they took him to see a sick man, whom he assessed as having a cold and, because the Tahitians kept fanning him, he did not improve. The islanders informed Máximo that fanning was also a way of calling on their god, and Máximo decided that if the sick man were to be cured, the Tahitians should bring him to his own house so that he might be kept warm. During this particular visit, Máximo remained there for the night, sharing a bed with Vehiatua, whose drunkenness prevented Máximo from sleeping (1992: 84).

Again reminiscent of Cabeza de Vaca's healing was the request that Máximo resurrect a dead woman. Máximo denied the claim that he could perform such an action, and also refused to pray with the Tahitians for her because they were not Christians. Furthermore, he expressed his wish that she not be buried near his abode, as the stench of the rotting corpse would reach them in the mission (1992: 117). During another incident, later on during their stay on the island, Máximo was asked to cure a woman suffering from what he described as a liver condition, 'tiricia'. This time, Máximo's diagnosis seems to have been a felicitous one, for he recommended that she enjoy herself so as to cure an illness that was due to 'melancolia' (1992: 156).

No healing remedy, however, halted the rapid spread of influenza among the Tahitians, many of whom began to die. For Máximo, they were dying of 'cold', because they had a habit of not covering themselves when it rained. Like Máximo, the padres attributed the 'epidemics of catarrh fevers' to the Tahitians' disregard for keeping dry and warm, while the Tahitians believed that their god, Teatua, was angry with them on account of the Spaniards having mowed grass from their temple. Although such belief was qualified by the padres as a superstition, Boenechea, 'moved by their superstitious preoccupation', showed respect for their customs and sacred grounds and 'ordered that no more grass be mowed from that setting and that no fruit from the *marae* be eaten' (1925: 107). Even if it were for different reasons, the Tahitians accurately assessed that their situation could be rightly attributed to the arrival of foreigners on their shores.

Unlike the Spaniards in regard to the Tahitian sacred house, the islanders showed a readiness to forgive the visitors and to recognise that their mistakes might be due to their ignorance of the local customs and environment. For example, when Máximo cut grass from the ground of their 'emarae', Vehiatua argued with him and expressed his disappointment but could appreciate that he had not acted out of ill-will and they made up the very next day (1992: 66). Later on, however, Máximo committed the same mistake and again desecrated another *emarae* by taking plants from it, making a woman cry because her son was buried there (1992: 123).

The Tahitians were also ready to learn about Spanish ways in relation to food and table manners. Vehiatua, in particular, not only thanked the Spaniards when eating with them, but also made a point of celebrating the food, indicating that it was to his taste and, after a few visits, he even made use of cutlery, asking those next to him to help him learn how to handle it. The padres, however, noted ironically that Vehiatua's pleasure at sharing their meals and customs might have been heightened by the fact that he was normally intoxicated with kava:

> On taking his leave from us, he said that he had liked very much our food the previous day. The Commander told him to go to eat on board whenever he liked, and he did so for some days. He learnt to make use of the spoon, fork and knife, observing with attention our actions, and when he found difficulty with the execution of some action, he begged whoever was next to him to teach him. None of our sauces was repugnant to him; he ordered in his own turn, and praised everything much. But it is not surprising that he liked it, because he was inebriated most days with that bitter concoction that his servants made of the root called *Eava*. (1925: 99)

In spite of some of these events where we can discern a level of arrogance, by and large, the explorers seem to have accepted and followed Tahitian customs. This is especially true of Máximo, who became increasingly at home among the Tahitians, as attested to by the fact that, when Pahiriro died, Tu's mother invited Máximo to attend the ceremonies on the grounds that Máximo had now became a relative of all the *arii*. Nevertheless, when participating in these rituals, Máximo reacted adversely to the loud wailing, describing it disparagingly as howling like dogs (1992: 67–8).

Other parts of the ceremony on which Máximo remarked seem to have had greater significance for him, as, for example, the offering of plantain leaves. It is interesting to note that, according to the padres, Máximo followed Boenechea's design in trying to infer the meaning of the Tahitian's ceremonies by integrating himself in these actions. On the occasion of a burial, Boenechea asked Máximo to mix with the islanders and observe them in order to relate his interpretation back to the Spaniards, much as Boenechea had seen done in the narratives of English voyages (1925: 107).

Once again during this ceremony, the Tahitians showed their good disposition towards learning about Spanish culture and ways of living. While Máximo was attending the ritual, his Tahitian friends approached him to enquire about his own customs and, more specifically, about his country's conduct in war and the use of the cannon. They went on to discuss religion, which gave Máximo the opportunity to assume an air of superiority. This occurred when they told him that the *Tahuas* ('priests') could make him a cripple and that he ought to be scared, at which Máximo laughed (1992: 69).

Máximo must have been, however, a warm friend and conversationalist, a quality much admired by the patient Tahitians, as some of his inconsiderate gestures did not offend his hosts. In fact, Máximo shared their house and slept with them on banana leaves, which, on the occasion when he went to Pahiriro's funeral ceremonies, made for a rather uncomfortable night, because of the wet weather. Following the night-time conversations, Máximo took part in the rituals of mourning the following day, when the corpse was taken first to the *emarae* and then to the house for burial (1992: 69). After this, Máximo returned with the padres to help them with the building of their mission house.

Further misunderstandings between both parties arose from the appropriation of the Spaniards' personal property, although they were reconciled through the goodwill of the Tahitians and Máximo's effective mediation (1992: 72–3). For example, soon after Pahiriro's death, there was an incident during which a surly sailor had a shirt stolen and, in the midst of the arguments that followed, he was hit with a stone.[16] Upset by this event, some Spaniards 'threatened' to pull down the mission house and leave the island.

Equally important at this point for the padres was the animosity that they felt towards the Tahitians who had accompanied them to Lima. On their return to the island, they went to live with their kin, and the padres complained bitterly at their decision, while Máximo accused them of ingratitude (1992: 70). Later on, however, Máximo would show his endorsement of the Tahitians against the padres.

As exemplified by the complex rituals of possession displayed by European colonists, elaborate ceremonies were by no means exclusive to indigenous societies. The Spanish mission to Tahiti was no exception, as illustrated in relation to the Treaty or Convention of Ojatutira for the possession of the island. Besides this performance, while on Tahiti, the Spaniards also carried out some traditional rituals which must have been observed with curiosity, if not disbelief, by the Tahitians. For example, on one occasion they took their cross on land, where it was received by all the crew dressed in uniform and then taken on a procession led by the padres. Reminiscent of the famous processions organised by Quirós in Vanuatu, those participating sang the litany in chorus. They then shot in the air until they arrived at the place where the cross was to be raised. There, a mass was said and they all intoned the hymn *Salve Regina*, ending with the firing of the cannon. Unfortunately, there is little in Máximo's diary about the attitudes of those Tahitians who were onlookers or participants in this ceremony (1992: 74–5). Nonetheless, the padres observed how an 'infinite' number of Tahitians 'admired' the display and questioned the Spaniards about the meaning of the rituals. According to them, the Tahitians watched intently from trees as the Spaniards raised the flag and 'proclaimed' their king three times, following which they were 'greatly surprised and asked us many sharp and funny questions about the event' (1925: 111).

The padres further inferred that the power held by the *arii* was limited and that he could do little to contain people, only reacting when he was not given food, in which case the islanders could be exiled, and to return 'would cost them dearly, because they had to give the Eri either a canoe or other items' (1925: 116–17). The vision offered by the padres is, nevertheless, qualified by their inability to integrate with the locals, as shown by the insults which Tahitians levelled at them so as to provoke them:

> Some called us *guariro*, which means thieves; *neneva*, which means crazy; *porejo*, which means snail but among them stands for the shameful parts, making obscene mockery of us; others called us *jarimiri*, which means old. Those terms we understood, others, which were no doubt opprobrious, we did not. The women did with great laughter; the boys following the rest. We did not answer and this lasted more than half an hour and they returned home. (1925: 117)

Unlike the padres, then, by the time the Spanish rituals of possession took place, Máximo had become close to the Tahitians and was often welcomed in their houses as a guest. He continued his effective work as mediator for the padres when, for example, he was sent on an errand to swap a pregnant goat for one who already had milk. Máximo also observed the exchanges between Tahitians and those from neighbouring islands such as 'Teturoa', who, he remarked, often came laden with food, presumably to trade and barter (1992: 76). Likewise, the Tahitians travelled to Raiatea, probably for the same 'commercial' reasons.

Among the Tahitian festivities recounted by Máximo is one that he referred to as 'Taurua' and 'Paraparau', which involved lengthy conversations about 'good governance' (1992: 77).[17] Máximo also described briefly the 'fiestas of arrows with dances', about which he wrote in the lost *Extracto* (1992: 79) and to which Andía y Varela also paid attention (1947: 68–9). Although contemporary readers would appreciate greater detail about these festivities, we must be satisfied with what is offered.

If Máximo showed some surprise at the Tahitians' customs, the latter, he indicated, were also puzzled to observe his own adherence to his 'superiors', as he must have appeared to them of higher standing than he really was. When they asked him whether they could count on his support whenever they fought against Mooreans, Máximo, to their surprise, informed them that he would not do such a thing without the consent of his 'superiores' (1992: 78). Máximo's supposed respect for his betters was, however, belied by the brevity and detachment with which he recalled Boenechea's death, coming, as it does, as a surprise to the readers.

This momentous event is briefly recounted when Máximo went to deal with a bull which had gone on a rampage and was told that Boenechea was dying. Boenechea passed away on 26 January and Máximo used two or three sentences of his account to inform readers that Boenechea gave up his soul and the Spaniards performed the corresponding 'signs of feeling' (1992: 81). Boenechea's death, however, gave Máximo an opportunity to discuss with Vehiatua different practices regarding the care of corpses and to suggest that burial was a healthier alternative because of the smell and the flies that accompanied the laying-in-state practised by the Tahitians. This time, according to Máximo, Vehiatua informed his people of Máximo's views and all discussed the matter at length (1992: 83).

Like Máximo, the padres also recounted Boenechea's death without showing much sorrow, although informing us that the many Tahitians who went to the burial the day after Boenechea died were pleased to see that he was put in a coffin before being consigned to the earth, opposite the house where they had placed the cross 'as sign of possession' (1925: 119). Earlier in their account, the padres had noted the Tahitians' dislike of the Spanish burial practices because, for them, to put earth on top of somebody and to step on the soil above the corpse were signs of disrespect (1925: 103).

If death rituals were of interest to both parties, Tahitian lore and knowledge of their local environment were especially appealing to the Spaniards, especially as they related to navigational techniques and to knowledge of the neighbouring islands. This can be appreciated when, two days after Boenechea's death, the ship left to reconnoitre the surrounding area and took with them Tomás Pautu, whose knowledge of the islands was to be commended, according to Pantoja, who granted him a degree of respect as a local pilot ('práctico de todas estas Yslas'). The Spaniards' reliance on information, such as the charts that Pautu drew, illustrates a cross-cultural engagement where the explorers overtly adopted local knowledge.[18] The following quotation from Pantoja demonstrates the use and incorporation of such knowledge:

> This island was given by its inhabitants the name *Milagro* [Miracle], and even though it has no name, it is referred to as Tupuae ... That one was called *San Juan*, and by its inhabitants *Erua* ... The island of *San Simon* is called *Atapataitota* ... The names of these islands and those that follow were given to us by an Indian whom we brought from Lima and who is a práctico [harbour pilot] of all of them. And he affirms that he has been in all of them with his canoes, but that he has not reached the Island of *San Narciso* [Takapoto]. This means that he has seen all those we have discovered East of *Otajiti*, and he also affirms there are many more, because he has recorded eighteen of them. To know this was mere chance for us because, when our pilot was charting them, this Indian saw them ... asked what it was, and was answered in his language. He did not need to know anything else but he sat down and said what I have mentioned above: that he had seen them all and registered them carefully and knew all their entries and reefs, which he explained after he had been told in his own language about the four cardinal winds. Also, he knew the days that one could go from an island to another, using favourable winds. (1992: 122)

In this inventory, the syncretism in the naming of the islands is also ratified by Pantoja's affirmation that the 'Indian' informing him was an eye-witness of what he recorded. This was precisely the same procedure followed in those the places mentioned by Pantoja, which were drafted by Juan Hervé either individually or in groups reproducing that hierarchical compound naming, as shown at the end of this book. Pantoja's list is remarkable in the way it charts the processes of naming and incorporating foreign lands into the European (in this case Spanish) paradigm and for his overt recognition of indigenous habitation and respect for their knowledge.

Whenever shown, respect or admiration could bridge the differences that often took place in many encounters. Likewise, the giving and receiving of gifts were, as in previous voyages, probably the most important demonstrations of the effort made to facilitate a friendly relationship where hostility could just as easily prevail. Throughout Máximo's narrative, we read of the many times that gifts sealed the friendship between Spaniards and Tahitians, providing the base for mutual understanding or constituting a way of resolving conflicts. However, the gift, as Marcel Mauss explained and I have argued in relation to the earlier voyages, always has obligations attached to it, in the form of correspondence or social duties. Thus, at times in these exchanges, the parties involved felt compelled to refuse the gifts offered either because they had nothing to exchange or because they wished to avoid consolidating a relationship entailed by the acceptance of the gift. For example, when Máximo borrowed a canoe to visit the areas of 'Guayuru y Mataobae' (Vaiuru and Matavai) he was showered with gifts upon arrival in Vaiuru: 'all the islanders that were there were coming out of their houses as I was passing them and were giving me blankets, bananas and coconuts, and if I refused them they would get upset, so that it was necessary for me to collect the gifts'. Máximo had nothing to offer in return and felt quite embarrassed about the whole situation, not quite knowing how to proceed. He ended up accepting a blanket from the *arii* so as not to suggest that he felt contempt for his gifts, which might be worse than not reciprocating (1992: 84–5).

Whether or not they felt compensated in terms of gifts given, the Tahitians often went to visit the Spaniards laden with gifts or goods to barter, and on one particular occasion there were so many of them that Máximo asked them to stand on the plain, so that he could roughly calculate their number. He wrote that there must have been around 2000, plus the *arii* Tutea. The islanders then performed a '*Jeiba* or dance' in Máximo's honour and, at the end of it, they took off their blankets and presented them to their guest. Acknowledging their poverty, Máximo was rather embarrassed at their generosity and refused their donation for what they were giving was all they had to cover themselves. Moreover, he had been given enough already, and he told them so. Máximo's response seems to have puzzled the Tahitians, who tried to assess the ethics ('moral') of his 'disinterest' (1992: 85).

The gifts that Máximo was given were not always retained by him for, when he returned to Vehiatua's land, he had to give some of them to the *arii*. Máximo realised that many of the offerings which he received were, in great part, given to the chiefs themselves, especially to Vehiatua. We learn more about this custom when we read that, wherever Vehiatua went, either he was given or else he took with him pigs in part payment for the visit. These offerings, therefore, or the functions which they performed, found their way to the *arii* and constituted the affirmation of a relationship of power or respect (Rodríguez 1992: 86–7).

Máximo also noted the ceremonies that took place whenever Vehiatua arrived somewhere, where he was greeted by a plantain branch and yellow feathers which the Tahitians put before him on the floor. The islanders then prayed, thanking their god through their priest or *tahua* for the *arii*'s safe arrival. The ritual was completed by the sharing of food, which, in one particular example, was shark while, on another, a pig had been offered and Máximo believed the pig's sacrifice to be beyond what he should accept as a Christian. He told the Tahitians that he would not participate in that part of their festivity and, according to him, this refusal made the Tahitians reconsider their custom in the light of what he had said (1992: 87–8).

In spite of what would appear to us to be great differences, Máximo seems to have accepted, and to have been accepted gradually by, the Tahitians, perhaps in part because of his intimate friendship with the *arii* of the island. Progressively, then, Máximo spent more time with the Tahitians than with the padres whom he was meant to serve, and who reminded him of his duty every so often. Máximo was surprised at their displeasure, for he believed that his ability to integrate with, and win the sympathies of, the islanders, whom the padres were meant to convert, should be applauded. Instead, the padres admonished him for his long absences and accused him of having drunk *kava* and, worse, of having been 'married for a night' (1992: 88). Indeed, Máximo had 'gone native' to such an extent in the eyes of the padres that Padre Narciso thought on another occasion that Máximo might be an accomplice of the Tahitians in the theft of a pig (1925: 124). This time again, Máximo tried to justify himself, but he indicated his deep disappointment when, at the end of the voyage, he relayed these events to Amat, who endorsed Máximo's dislike of the padres' aloofness and criticised them in his own reports.

However badly the padres thought of him, it was Máximo who solved many situations for them, as, for example, when the padres' pigs roamed free, causing the Tahitians to complain. Máximo used his friendship with Vehiatua and told him that if they could not live as they pleased they would have to move out, which made Vehiatua act on their behalf. Moreover, Máximo took seriously his task of promoting the Christian god, who got an unexpected boost when Máximo performed a 'cure' by simply suggesting to someone that he should rest in bed and keep warm with blankets. As this man's condition improved, the Tahitians told Máximo that his god was 'big'. Nonetheless, Máximo's healing abilities had little or no effect on his friend and protector, Vehiatua, whose relapse Máximo attributed to his addiction to kava (1992: 89–91).

During his time on the island, Máximo was also able to dispel some doubts about the differences between gift-giving and bartering for the Tahitians. When his friend, Hinoi, who came with two 'good-sized' lobsters for him and the padres, was asked what he wanted in exchange he took offence at this suggestion, indicating that he did not treat in exchanges and was offering things out of 'friendship'. Hinoi stressed the difference between gift-giving as a marker of power and status, and trading or exchanging goods. Nonetheless, Padre Gerónimo thought that even an indication of friendship also had to be acknowledged somehow, which he did by offering Hinoi two biscuits: 'because these are items which they like very much'. Hinoi, however, refused the offer, boasting that, unlike the padres, he had plenty of food (1992: 92).

In contrast, the Tahitians working for the padres in their house and garden gladly accepted payment for their work and were given beads and hooks, which satisfied them. Thus, the padres counted on the help of many islanders, as well as the services of Máximo and the sailor, who alternated in cooking for them. Nevertheless, Tahitian food did not agree with Padre Narciso, who throughout Máximo's narrative is repeatedly said to have suffered from flatulence. In still more serious condition, as mentioned above, was Vehiatua, who had 'syncope' and deteriorated so much that he let the Spaniards take care of him, telling Máximo that he had ordered that they be provided with provisions and people as needed (1992: 92–5).[19]

Following upon Vehiatua's injunctions, Máximo requested the locals to fell cane so that they might make a patio and fence it, which they agreed to do. Once again, however, the Spaniards showed disrespect for Tahitian customs by taking stones from the *emarae* to use for their fireplace, disregarding the warnings issued to them by Vehiatua's mother (1992: 100). In spite of these displays of irreverence on the part of the 'missionaries', the Tahitians' acceptance of Spanish customs continued, and they also showed curiosity about Spanish social structure, which was satisfied by Máximo, who gave them 'news about the lands that our sovereign possesses'. They, in turn, informed Máximo of Otute's (Cook's) visit to Matavai, while telling him that Cook was now an owner of the island and would return to it. Máximo tried to counter Cook's claim and denied that he would come back, which was, eventually, rejected by Cook when he returned and attacked Máximo, accusing him of 'lying' (1992: 97).[20]

The lengthy conversations held by Máximo with the Tahitians seem to have fulfilled their mutual desire for information and communication, as well as Máximo's need for company. Thus, when the padres complained of noise from having so many people close to their quarters and they moved away, Máximo felt rather lonely (1992: 100). The padres' hostile attitude did not seem to be to the taste of the returned Tahitian, Manuel Tetuanui, either. Having abandoned Spanish clothes and habits to live with his people, Manuel was asked by Máximo to come back to help with interpreting for the padres, which he refused, indicating that they had threatened him and that he was rather afraid of them (1992: 103).

Later on in Máximo's narrative, when he was visiting Vehiatua during his illness, he met again with Manuel and reiterated his request that he return, only to receive the same reply. Manuel indicated that he would only go to see Máximo, but would not approach the house for fear of the padres and this time Máximo believed Manuel to have some grounds ('algun fundamento') for thinking and acting in the way he did. Máximo also emphasised that he and Manuel enjoyed each other's company, talking about the differences between the treatment according to him by 'His Excellency', meaning Viceroy Amat, and the present circumstances (1992: 154).

The padres' version of events, which is considerably shorter, talks about Manuel's attitude at the same time as Vehiatua's illness, which they saw in completely different terms. According to them, when they were informed of Vehiatua's condition, they provided what Taitoa had asked for: 'one piglet, biscuit, salted bacon from Lima and honey, all of which we gave with pleasure'. On their behalf, Máximo had gone to Taiarapu to ask Manuel to return and Manuel had 'absolutely' refused to do so, which he did again some fifteen days later when Máximo was sent by the padres to ask Vehiatua to mediate and ask Manuel to return. Manuel maintained his refusal 'resolutely', even though he was crying while doing so (1925: 122).

Máximo also quarrelled once with Manuel and, when Vehiatua found out, the *arii* threatened to set fire to Manuel's house and send him and his family into exile. At this point, Máximo had to change sides and intercede on Manuel's behalf, so that Vehiatua would not carry out his threat (1992: 112–13). A similar attitude was shown by the other Tahitian who had been in Lima: Pautu. While in Matatoe, Máximo met Pautu, who cried, telling him that he wanted to return to Lima but, like Manuel Tetuanui, did not want to go to Tautira ('Ojatutira'), because he had heard about the sailor and the padres. Pautu, according to Máximo, knew well about the antagonistic attitude of the padres and the enmities in the Spanish quarters (1992: 115).

In the padres' journal, Pautu, always referred to as Tomás, is said to have returned to the mission and to have been received with open arms, like a 'prodigal son': 'As another prodigal son, he came naked.' When the padres asked Pautu why he had left them, he indicated that it had been because of fear, and was scolded and reminded of the special treatment bestowed on him by the viceroy. According to the padres' version of events, although Pautu showed signs of repentance, they appeared to be false: 'We asked him why he had run away, and he replied that [it was] because of fear; we reprimanded him ... likewise, we asked him to remember the favours received from the Señor Viceroy, and he gave signs of repentance, but they were pretence' (1925: 114).

Throughout all these events, the Tahitians continued to work on the padres' house and land, planting more maize, though sometimes at a slow pace and with the familiar thefts and arguments about them. As mentioned, these workers were paid for their work, often with hooks, while they brought the Spaniards fish in return (1992: 104–9, 120). Things seemed to be relatively relaxed until the sailor took things a bit too far, in Máximo's opinion, and stabbed a local twice, simply because he thought be was being threatened with a gun (1992: 109). The sailor's attitude and that of the padres was summed up by Máximo, following a row between Padre Narciso and the sailor, saying that the four of them thought they had been born to be served: 'all of us are heads, and we lack feet with which to walk' (1992: 123). Their distance from one another was confirmed when the sailor asked Máximo to write a letter to give to the padres, complaining that he was being asked to be everything for them. Máximo copied what the sailor said and the sailor handed the letter to Padre Narciso who, in reply, slapped the sailor in the face and had to be constrained by those around him to prevent him from going any further.[21] Máximo concluded that the four of them were all too ready to argue with the others, and that there was no sense of solidarity whatsoever among them: 'for which it can be seen that there is no union among the four of us, for each is by himself, so that when some quarrel the others look on' (1992: 127).

Absent from Máximo's account is any indication that the Tahitian practice of human sacrifice could be extended to their guests, while the padres expressed fear that they might become unwilling victims themselves.[22] When the Tahitians went out in search of someone to sacrifice, they wondered whether they, being foreigners, might not become their next target: 'according to prudent and well-grounded judgment, we might be in danger of losing our lives, when these inhuman people tried to kill their countrymen, for, being foreigners, we determined to take out our weapons, which were hidden until them, and to get them ready and loaded in sight of everyone' (1925: 128).

By way of contrast, Máximo had no fear and was always treated kindly and amicably by the Tahitians, which was clearly demonstrated when he visited the Te Pari people in 'Matatoe'. The Tahitians came one at a time and offered Máximo blankets, snails and all sorts of foodstuffs, having also 'Jeybas' or *fiestas* in honour of their guest. Curiously, Máximo wrote that among the presents given to him there was a dwarf but, frustratingly enough, he did not explain further, and the dwarf was never referred to again. The fondness of the Te Pari Tahitians towards Máximo was also displayed when he left their land and everyone cried at his departure (1992: 115–16).

As Vehiatua's condition deteriorated, so did the relationship between Máximo and the padres. Thus, when Máximo asked them for permission to go and see Vehiatua because he was dying, the padres refused it. Nonetheless, Máximo ignored the order and departed, since he wanted to find out about his friend, as well as seeking some pearls and 'a seat made of black stone', the famous *umete*. Máximo arrived to find Vehiatua very sick, lying with everything he had been given around him. To help with the healing process someone, probably a priest, who Máximo affirms to be possessed by their god, talked while moving around 'clumsily' (1992: 129–30).[23]

Máximo was again welcomed as one of them and every *arii* wanted to receive him as their guest with such insistence, and showing such generosity, that Máximo stated that he found it difficult to attend to their kindnesses towards him. Also, Vehiatua wanted to demonstrate his liberality at this point and asked Máximo what he would like from him, to which Máximo replied that he would be satisfied with some nets and a canoe (1992: 130). However, Máximo was not always aware of the complexities attached to the special status of the *arii* in relation to gift-giving or the obligations inherent in exchanges with other people on the island and showed his confusion when he gave a net to a fisherman to fish for Vehiatua and was asked to give pigs, blankets and fruit, learning that even the *arii* were not exempt from that sort of payment (1992: 134).

The Tahitians also told Máximo that he could not keep the net given to him in the house because he was a commoner and his house was *efare-noa*, meaning a commoner's abode, warning that the punishment for failing to fulfil the requirement would be exile (1992: 134–5). That, for the

Tahitians, Máximo was a 'commoner' was also stated by Pahiriro's mother, who, after receiving him warmly, told Máximo when he asked to borrow a canoe that those that she had were royal ones (*evara*) and could not be used by him. Instead, she offered to look for one used by normal people, so that he could travel in comfort (1992: 139).

Throughout all these events the mutual curiosity of Máximo and his Tahitian friends appears to have been reciprocal and they exchanged all sorts of questions. For example, Máximo asked a woman who had 'divorced' Vehiatua the reasons why she had done so, while the Tahitians, in their turn, enquired about Máximo's customs and were pleased with all the explanations he provided, and even with his opinions. Nevertheless, they objected to his thoughts on their custom of segregation of the sexes when eating. After they told him that they would not eat with women because, if they did so, they would lose their hands, Máximo retorted that nothing would happen to them, but they did not believe him (1992: 131–2). As on other occasions, Máximo proved to be a good conversationalist, willing to hear and to discuss matters for as many hours as necessary, which seems to have been mutually rewarding.

After a certain time on the island, Máximo became quite fond of the people in his district, comparing them favourably with those of the island of *Matayba* (Mataiva), in the Tuamotus, who he thought were cowardly (1992: 150). By contrast, for the padres, all Tahitians were hypocritical and their friendliness dissipated when they received no gifts, in which case 'they say that we are bad friends, as we have experienced'. The padres could not make any converts, they said, because the Tahitians were completely uncivilised, which was proved by the fact that they did not live in towns and were 'proud, haughty, unruly, bellicose', having neither 'subordination nor administration of justice, which they do not know'. The padres added that even their *arii* had no power because, if he tried to do anything, his subjects would easily rise up against him (1925: 137). The same opinion was expounded in a letter to the Spanish authorities, where the padres showed their lack of appreciation of Tahitians in the following words:

> In relation to the quality and inclinations of the indigenous people of this island, we have conceived that they are naturally inclined to steal and to all sorts of vices, taking on their own hand satisfaction for any injustice which they receive, being fair or not, because they have no subordination whatsoever to the Heri, and only recognise him as such in bringing him food, and, not doing so, he exiles them from his domains and to return they go to other domains to steal either canoes, pigs or blankets . . . And with this, they restore his goodwill. (1925: 153)[24]

Unlike the padres, however, during the days Máximo spent with Vehiatua he received gifts of kava and fish from the Tahitians.[25] Also, Máximo was given a book, 'Tablas de Matemáticas', which had been stolen from the English and was of no use to the Tahitians on account of the language (1992: 132). Sometimes, it is worth noting, gifts are only mentioned as having been warmly received but, in other instances, the return gift is also acknowledged, emphasising the reciprocity of the exchange, even in cases where there might be unevenness between those given and those received. Normally, however, both sides obtained something which they lacked and appreciated, which was habitually cloth or iron tools by the Tahitians and food by the Spaniards.

In relation to food, Máximo also mentioned the custom of giving provisions to chiefs, who, it seemed to him, owned everything and everyone on the island. The continuous and lavish gift-giving to the *arii* was also noted by the padres, who qualified the taking of gifts on such a scale as 'avarice' ('codicia'). The padres also noted that, on one occasion, Vehiatua's mother, O Purahi, came with a little boy to ask Manuel Tetuanui to give her all his clothes for the boy. When Tetuanui obliged, the Spaniards tried to dissuade her from taking everything that he had, to which she answered that all that Tetuanui had rightly belonged to her. They classed her attitude as 'excessive': 'On seeing this, we told Manuel's mother that he had nothing but those breeches and shoes to wear, or band to fasten them with ... to which she answered that those clothes belonged to her son, because he was Manuel's *arii* ... her avarice was excessive' (1925: 115–16).

Special items were given by the Spanish to the chiefs, as, for example, a mattress offered by the padres to Vehiatua (1925: 162). During the time Vehiatua stayed with them, Máximo was again showered with blankets and, on occasion, in such quantities that he had to refuse them because he had nothing to give in exchange. The Tahitians, however, insisted that he accept the gifts by placing them in his hands: 'They gave me several blankets and a fine mattress, and refusing to admit those gifts on account of not having anything in return they clasped my hands around them' (1992: 172). Among the local items Máximo wished to have or exchange, the most precious were those made of mother-of-pearl, especially some masks which were called *parae*.[26] These masks were so valuable that, in order to get them, Máximo had to give two sheets and two axes, which was what the Tahitians appreciated most from the Spaniards (1992: 118).[27]

If Máximo and the padres were sometimes surprised to see the local attitude towards gifts and bartering, their own was also a source of interest to the Tahitians, who were surprised to hear from Máximo that his king also gave gifts, and that this was a duty of a 'principal' in his country. Máximo also told them about the welfare system in Spain and Spanish America, whereby the destitute would be cared for in hospitals, information which met by the Tahitians with bewilderment: 'Vehiatua called me to give me gifts from his sick relative, because he was better, and I refused them, making it known that it was the duty of the highest chief, at which they were astonished when I said that our Sovereign also did this, giving alms to the incurable by having hospitals' (1992: 174).

It is at this point of the exchanges that the dealings in relation with the *umete* took place, after Máximo heard that Tu had 'a vessel of black stone' ('una batea de piedra negra') built in Maurua and asked him for it (1992: 168). Máximo acknowledged that, by offering him the *umete*, Tu had in effect gifted a 'unique jewel' and was delighted because, being a consecrated item 'to their God, *Eatua* . . . I doubted that I could obtain it' (1992: 180). To get the 'batea' from Tu, who had offered it to Máximo to give to his king, Máximo went to Tu's domains with his friend Hinoi. However, the *umete* was so large that it had to be carried by four men, and was stolen on the way to the mission. After making some enquiries, Máximo found it buried, and he slept with it thereafter to avoid losing it again (1992: 182).[28] The *umete*'s wanderings and hazards did not end there for it was located some years later in the possession of the Viceroy's butler after Amat had been replaced by Theodor de Croix.[29] Eventually, it somehow found its way to Spain, and even survived the plundering of the National History Salon by Napoleonic forces in the early nineteenth century, finding its way to the *Museo Arqueológico Nacional* in Madrid, where Corney identified it in 1912 (1914: xxvi).

By contrast with Máximo's successes in obtaining precious gifts from the locals, Padre Narciso was unhappy because Vehiatua did not want to give him a concave seat he desired 'after having assisted him with his illness' (1992: 173). This episode, for Corney, marked the 'mercenary trait in the *Padre*'s character', which was partly defined by 'ineptitude and petulance'. However, Corney also regrets that Padre Narciso was unable to get this 'concave stone seat', as this would have placed the artefact in a European museum 'as a companion' to the *umete* (1918: 162 n. 1). Corney also concedes that the level of assistance provided by the padres to Vehiatua could be subject to different interpretations, and that the padres' affirmation that they did all in their power to assist him should not be dismissed.

The controversy about the padres' attitude in relation with Vehiatua's illness arose because, in spite of gifts, *heivas*, and Tahitian or Spanish medicine, Vehiatua's health gradually deteriorated and his mother complained that the padres refused to share their own medicine with him (1992: 187, 190). The padres were spared the criticism of Vehiatua's mother which was not translated by Máximo, who remarked that O Purahi's assessment must have been right, because the padres guarded the medicine cabinet so zealously that he had failed in his attempt to steal from them (1992: 190, 192). However, according to Corney, the padres perhaps prudently refused to give Vehiatua their own medicine in order to avoid being seen as the cause of his death, which they saw fast approaching.

The islanders, in the meantime, contributed what they could to improve Vehiatua's health and spirits, and his relapses were accompanied by various ceremonies or festivities, designed to spur on or celebrate his cure, such as one called by Máximo *Taurua mahona* ('Taurua maona') (1992: 173). On this particular occasion, Máximo was disappointed because he believed that Vehiatua's last relapse was due to the fact that he had lost control ('haverse desmandado'), probably referring to his habit of drinking excessively. Eloquently, Máximo refused a gift of bananas brought by Vehiatua's mother to conciliate him so as to show his displeasure at Vehiatua's attitude, once again highlighting the multifarious role that giftgiving or, in this case (not) receiving a gift, could play (1992: 175).

Whether or not kava was the cause of Vehiatua's death, this came all too soon and, when it happened, Máximo praised him in the highest terms, describing him as a young man, much loved by his friends, family and vassals but sadly fond of kava. Máximo also acknowledged that Vehiatua and his family had shown great kindness towards him, adopting and lavishing love on him, and that these favours went on after Vehiatua's death. As proof of their esteem, they named him after a deceased grandfather, 'Oroytimoheajea', asking him to use that name instead of his own (1992: 191).

Following upon Vehiatua's death, the traditional mourning rituals were observed, with the women taking a leading role and crying loudly while bleeding themselves using shark's teeth to cut their skin. As they quickly stopped wailing and turned to conversation, Máximo inferred that their lamentation was an outward sign merely to observe the due ceremony, rather than a demonstration of true, inner sorrow. He also noted one taboo surrounding the death of an *arii* when the locals could neither fish nor light a fire for the duration of the ceremonies and that people from other districts came to pay their respects, with the women bringing gifts of blankets (1992: 193–5).

Once the mourning for Vehiatua's death was over, life returned to normal, and the Tahitians did not show the hostility feared by the padres after the *arii*'s protection had ceased to shield them. In fact, soon after Vehiatua died, and to prevent any wrongdoing to the padres, Vehiatua's mother, O Purahi, sent another son, whom the padres believed would be the next *arii*, to their compound for their protection. In the midst of her own sorrows, and of her own accord, Vehiatua's mother kindly sent her own servants to climb up the trees closest to the mission to observe whether anybody was coming to threaten them. The padres' fears, however, proved to be unfounded, as nobody came to bother them (1925: 133).

By this stage in their stay, Máximo had become quite familiar with the islanders, gaining information about the struggles taking place across the islands and investigated further into customs such as the ceremony of eating turtle, which was again frustratingly said to be explained in the lost *Extracto*. Máximo included in his journal some shorter explanations, such as how the plantain leaves were used not only to welcome people and to indicate peace, but also to make up and restore friendship. He also expanded on some aspects of the traditions he had itemised throughout the narrative, such as banishment, in relation to which we read the interesting fact that, when exiled, a man had to leave not just with his family but also with the bones of the deceased kin, which were normally kept in the house. This information appears in relation to one instance in which Máximo pleaded for a Tahitian to be pardoned from being exiled and, after being initially ignored, he was eventually granted his wish that the people concerned be allowed to remain in their district. Máximo was successful again when he begged for the life of the thief who had stolen some of his property and who, when apprehended, was given the lesser punishment of exile following Máximo's entreaties (1992: 201–7).

On the custom of gift-giving to the *arii*, we learn from Máximo that it was often preceded by a ceremonious walk around him, before the offer of feathers or blankets. Máximo named of the ritual *etatára jara* (*E tatara hara*) and that it was devised as some sort of atonement for one's fault and to ask for forgiveness: 'literally translated, it means the same as *satisfaction or payment for it*' (1992: 206). A breach of this custom would lead to warfare, as happened once when the Spaniards were asked to be careful because there was 'Erabé' ('war') between 'Oparé y Tallarabú'. To the padres' question as to what this conflict was about, the Tahitians replied that when an *arii* visited another in order to take foodstuffs to him, he would obtain whatever he pleased and leave the rest to the 'plebeians'

(1925: 102). A fight had started because this custom had not been observed by those paddling the canoe, who kept everything for themselves.

In relation to food, Máximo also referred to the custom that he called *epori*, which entailed the fattening of some selected boys during a few months, in which they were not allowed to move at all (1992: 151).[30] The last interesting ceremony about which we are taught a little more towards the end of Máximo's account concerns the theatrical plays enacted by the Tahitians.[31] Máximo went in the night with Tu to a theatre-like place and saw what appeared to him to be a comedy which he found 'ridiculous', acknowledging it to have been amusing to the locals: 'I was led by *Eri Otú* . . . to a ranch with props as in a theatre, where, as in our coliseums, some *entremeses* or *mogigangas* ('interludes or mummeries') were represented, quite ridiculous, but fun and entertaining for them' (1992: 205). Again here Máximo indicated that this would be explained in greater detail in the *Extracto*.[32]

At the time these celebrations took place, the padres' compound was completed, and the fence finished, for which they paid the workers with cotton (Rodríguez 1992: 194, 196). They proceeded to clean the patio and the house, paying those who did the work with 'bujerias' ('bagatelles'), which pleased them (Rodríguez 1992: 203). No sooner had they finished than Máximo informed the padres that he would move out of their house to his own place and had a house speedily made the following day when up to 'five hundred souls' joined in the building effort, after which Máximo started to make some improvements to it and to widen his patio (1992: 209).

One day later, however, on 30 October, the Spanish ships returned and Máximo spent the night talking to the captain, Cayetano de Lángara, about the events on the island during their absence. It is interesting to note here that de Lángara received Máximo's information first and then went to see the padres, who told de Lángara of their wish to depart from Tahiti because the Viceroy had not sent more people on the ship to help them out, knowing the 'danger' they faced among such 'barbarous people' (1925: 136). De Lángara agreed to take them back to Lima, which hastened their departure from the island, and the end of the 'mission'.

According to Máximo, his Tahitian friends were very sad to see him depart and some even asked to be taken along to Lima. The Spaniards refused to do so because two out of the four who had left on the previous occasion had lost their lives and they did not want the Tahitians to infer that they might have been killed (1992: 211–12). Like Máximo, the padres remarked on the many Tahitians wanting to travel to Lima, going to the extent of stowing away in the most remote parts of the ship. The Spaniards were forced to look carefully over every corner prior to their departure, expelling those they found hiding. They took with them two men, however: 'one for being a good pilot of all the eastern islands, called Paloro, and the other called Barbarua, one of the chiefs of *Orayatea*, and brother in law of *Eri Otu*, whose insistence made us admit him' (1925: 119).

As they left, the Spaniards tried to reward the services rendered to them by the *arii*, giving two shirts, which were rejected in spite of their insistence. According to the padres, the chiefs and 'distinguished' islanders remained close to the departing crew, showing 'feeling' and urging them to return and, when they left, 'the islanders departed in their canoes, many of them crying bitterly' (Padres 1925: 119). The fleet departed from the island never to return again, arriving back in Callao on 3 February 1776. In Lima, the voyagers were received by Viceroy Amat who, like de Lángara before him, met first with Máximo and believed his assessment that the padres' attitude was cowardly and was not due to any specific threat.[33] Consequently, Amat sent a letter to the king of Spain, stating that he would proceed with the intended conversion of the Tahitians only if other religious men with a 'more ardent spirit' were sent there 'so that they could profit that which these others wasted because of their fear'. Furthermore, Amat also suggested that the king should do so before too long, so that the Tahitians would not forget the friendship established with the Spaniards and the good treatment received. Also important was the fact that the English might obtain power in the area, 'as they had done previously'. Before ending his letter, Amat expanded on what he believed to be the flaws of the padres, to ensure that future missions were cared for (1925: 167).

Neither other missionaries nor another voyage followed, however, and the Tahitians were left to look after the mission for years to come. Nonetheless, their loyalty towards the Spanish visitors seems to have lasted long, as Cook and other voyagers appreciated.[34] More than one hundred years later, another Tahitian 'explorer', this time the scholar Bolton Corney, met with a descendant of one of those who had gone to Peru. Corney learnt that this man still kept alive memories of this voyage that had been passed on to him, which, though fading, were pleasant to recall. Perhaps, after all, that the voyage and the memories were remembered with a mixture of sympathy and satisfaction is a most remarkable achievement for what could be termed to have been Máximo's 'mission' in Tahiti.

NOTES

1 Amat's Questionnaire ('Interrogatorio') and Dictionary were translated and edited by Corney (1914: 2. 1–28).
2 For a list of these islands, see Mellén (Rodríguez 1992: 14).
3 A copy is kept at the *Real Academia de Historia* in Madrid, and is edited by Mellén (1992a: 19–20).
4 Of all the sources, the only one unavailable to Corney was the journal of Juan Pantoja y Arriaga (1775). For other sources extant from this journey, see the Appendix. The padres' account is entitled 'Relación de los principales acaecimientos durante el viaje y permanencia en Otahiti escrita de común acuerdo por el Piloto Dn. José Barela y los Misioneros Clota y González' and is here and in the Bibliography shortened as Padres.
5 Corney believes that 'Oheyao' should be 'O Heao'.
6 Mellén notes that Opo (Opoo) is the short version of O Purahi (Te Vahine Moe-atua) (Rodríguez 1992: 45 n. 51). According to Corney, the name Opo corresponds to 'Te Vahine Moeatua, better known as Purahi, or O Pu for short' (1914: 2. xxiv).
7 Máximo refers to him as Jinoy, while Corney observes that his name should be 'Hinoi-atua' and that he was 'a half-brother of Tu' (1918: 6 n. 2).
8 Máximo mentions this exchange of names with Hinoi elsewhere (1992: 177).
9 According to Mellén, the harbour is Auhi, into which one enters via Rautea, opposite Faraari (Rodríguez 1992: 47 n. 58).
10 Mellén adds that *tupapau* means deceased and that Máximo confused the devil with the dead (Rodríguez 1992: 48 n. 60).
11 See Corney's remarks regarding the contradictions of Máximo's references to Taitoa, concluding that the puzzle of whether Taitoa was the old Vehiatua is impossible to unravel (1918: 12–13 n. 1).
12 'Faced with a proliferation of new scenery, travelers in search of substantiality pondered the problem of what was the correct, least distorting point of view from which to scrutinize the world ... The traveler consciously observes himself in a situation and attempts to describe it accurately' (Stafford 1984: 399).
13 'One would have expected Máximo to realise what this ruthless felling of bread-fruit trees meant to the natives, especially as he had been on the island with the previous expedition. But his function was to interpret, and further the work of the frigate's carpenters in any way he could within his province; he had to tide over, rather than espouse, any objections the natives might put forward, and we know that he had an unwavering respect for the orders of his official superiors' (Corney 1918: 24 n. 1).
14 This threat was used on other occasions, as when the padres told Vehiatua via Máximo that, should the Tahitians continue committing sacrifices, the

Spaniards would return to Lima. Vehiatua said that they should remain, but listened in silence without promising anything (1925: 131).

15 Adorno (1991) has studied the paradigm of fear and healing negotiated successfully by Cabeza de Vaca in order to survive.

16 The padres also recounted the episode of the shirt's theft and the sailor's anger, noting how the Tahitians interceded so that the sailor would not be punished (1925: 100).

17 Mellén associates them with the contemporary *taupiti* and *parau*, indicating that *parau* simply means to talk or to converse (Rodríguez 1992: 77 n. 144 and n. 145).

18 This was the case with Tupaia's map. Tupaia, a local Tahitian, drew a map which is not extant, but which was printed in George Foster's account of the voyage and is preserved in a copy at the British Library.

19 For references to Vehiatua's ailment, see also Rodríguez (1992: 97, 107, 123 and 174).

20 To quote Cook's words: 'When these ships left the island, four Spaniards remained behind. Two were priests, one a servant, and the fourth made himself very popular among the natives, who distinguish him by the name of Mateema. He seems to have been a person who had studied their language, or at least to had spoken it so as to be understood; and to had taken uncommon pains to impress the minds of the islanders with the most exalted ideas of the greatness of the Spanish nation, and to made them think meanly of the English. He even went so far as to assure them that we no longer existed as an independent nation; that *Pretane* was only a small island, which they, the Spaniards, had entirely destroyed ... all this, and many improbable falsehoods, did this Spaniard made these people believe' (1784: 76). According to Mellén, when Máximo found out that Cook was censuring him, he took issue with these claims in a prologue ('prologuito'), which he added to his journal. However, the only extant copy of the journal does not include this section (Rodríguez 1992: 26). In the introduction to his translation of Máximo's journal, Corney also cites the praise accorded to Máximo by two surgeons travelling with Cook, William Anderson and David Samwell (1918: xv–xvi and xvii).

21 Later on, Máximo had to calm the sailor, who felt offended (1992: 163ff.).

22 There are references in Máximo's journal to human sacrifice (1992: 187, 189, 196).

23 Corney indicates that: 'Transient attacks of this character were of common occurrence in members of the Melanesian race; but less so, perhaps, in Polynesians of the Tahitian type. The visual hallucinations they suffer at such times were very vivid, and were accompanied as in the case Máximo relates with temporary delusions, ecstasy, tremors, muscular spasms, and sometimes cataleptic rigidity.' As regards the padres' fear that they might become the victims of a sacrifice to heal Vehiatua, Corney adds that Melanesians would have acted

differently, in which case, he infers, 'the white intruders would have been the first to come under the ban of the soothsayer' (1918: 138 n. 1; 181 n. 1).
24 They finish by adding that otherwise the Tahitians would just as easily join in with others and stage a coup to depose the *arii*.
25 Fish was gifted to the Spaniards on other occasions throughout their stay and they reciprocated with fried fish on one instance, giving it to Vehiatua, also asking for fresh fish, which they paid for with 'bagatelles' (Rodríguez 1992: 140–1, 143, 146–7).
26 Mellén suggests it to be *paa rae*, which refers to 'the pearl mask used by the chief when leading a duel' (Rodríguez 1992: 118 n. 221). Corney remarks that: 'Several specimens of this singular garb exist in museums' and that Cook brought back with him a complete one, as did Banks, who donated it to Trinity College, Dublin. Corney also notes that he had 'found parts of one in the ethnological section of the Museo Nacional at Madrid, which I believe to have been collected by Máximo and brought away in the *Águila*' (1918: 94 n. 1).
27 Later on, Máximo confirms that cotton sheets and axes were the best items of exchange, permitting the Tahitians to trade pearls for them (1992: 132).
28 Corney, who refers to the *umete* as a 'mystic bowl', notes that its provenance, which Máximo places in Taputapuatea, is confusing, for there existed more than one *marae* with that name (1918: 159 n. 1).
29 Corney explains this as follows: 'In a Despatch from the Viceroy of Peru ... to the Secretary of State for the Indies, the *umete* is also alluded to. De Croix indicates that Máximo has informed him that the *umete* "was in the possession of D^n Jayme Palmer" and that Máximo had told him "of the high esteem with which those Islanders regarded it, having dedicated it to their God in his sanctuary". De Croix indicates that he "should send it forward to Your Excellency, in order that it may be installed in the Gallery of Natural History as a specimen from that Island wrought by men who had no knowledge of iron and no tools adapted for carving such a thing"' (1918: 212).
30 Mellén describes the tradition of fattening boys as a function of *arioi*, noting that fat was a sign of elegance for Tahitians, as for other Polynesian cultures (Rodríguez 1992: 151 n. 284). For Corney, Máximo's 'is a very inadequate description of an Arioi function' (Corney 1918: 135 n. 3).
31 The padres' journal also mentions the representation of an 'interlude', lasting one and a half hours about one 'Indian' whose wife was jealous (1925: 125).
32 On the occasion of this show, Máximo was also able to realise the appreciation that Tu had for him when he invited him to sleep over, which not even his own father did (1992: 205).
33 In this letter, Amat noted that Cook took down the cross raised by the Spaniards and erased its inscription, adding on it Wallis's name and the year 1767 (1925: 166).

34 One of these was Lieutenant Mortimer, who called in at Matavai in 1789 and met one of those who had gone to Lima, who 'seemed very partial to the Spaniards, and spoke much of the favourable reception he had met with at Lima' (Corney 1913: xxxv). Cook's words, which have been often quoted, read as follows: 'Whatever the intentions of the Spaniards, in visiting the island, might be, they seemed to had taken great pains to ingratiate themselves with the inhabitants; who, upon every occasion, mentioned them with the strongest expressions of esteem and veneration' (Qtd. Corney 1913: xxvi). Elsewhere, during his third voyage, Cook mentioned the Spanish visit, indicating that the islanders 'told us these ships came from a Country called *Rema* which undoubtedly must be Lima the Capital of *Peru*; that the first time they came they built a house and left four men behind them viz. two Priests, a boy or a servant and one *Mateama*, who was much spoken of at this time; that after a stay of ten Months the same two Ships returned and took them away, but the house was left standing and near it a Cross (as they described it) at the foot of which the Commodore of the first two Ships, who died while they lay in the bay, was buried. They call him Oreddee' (2003: 495).

4

Mourelle and Vava'u (1781)

IV

As far as difficulties and hardship go, the gruelling journey of Francisco Mourelle de la Rúa across Pacific waters harks back to those of earlier centuries. Indeed, the discomforts, illnesses and sheer hunger, as well as the utter despair that took hold of Mourelle's crew, remind readers of Magellan's men or other sixteenth-century voyagers. The challenging journey led by Mourelle took more than two years, departing from the Mexican port of San Blas on 21 February of 1780. Under Mourelle's command, the frigate *Princesa* navigated across the stretch of the Pacific, stopping at, among other places, the Vava'u islands of the Tongan archipelago. It returned to San Blas nineteen months later, on 27 September 1781 (Figure 4.4).

New geographical knowledge notwithstanding, Mourelle had to find his way in the Pacific with charts that had not been updated since the 1750s and he used maps that were remarkably similar of those of the late sixteenth century.[1] The voyages of Samuel Wallis or Louis de Bougainville and, especially, those of James Cook, remained for Mourelle verbal descriptions that afforded him more frustrations than a sense of direction. In his journal, Mourelle lamented the lack of information from the voyages of 'Byron, Carteret, Wallis, Bougainville, and, particularly, those of Cook and Dampier' in the following words: 'the continuous sight of many islands, shoals, etc. which were not on Mr Bellin's chart, which was the only one I had for my governance, obliged me to live with the unrest that arises from repeated discoveries and the inability, for the said reason, to compare my islands with those which the mentioned navigators discovered in their navigations' (1970: 278–9). It was, according to Mourelle, only his drive to serve the king and to contribute to the 'perfection' of the geographical knowledge of the world that spurred him on to continue and complete his voyage and to 'forget at times the unhappy situation in which my journey originated' (1970: 279).

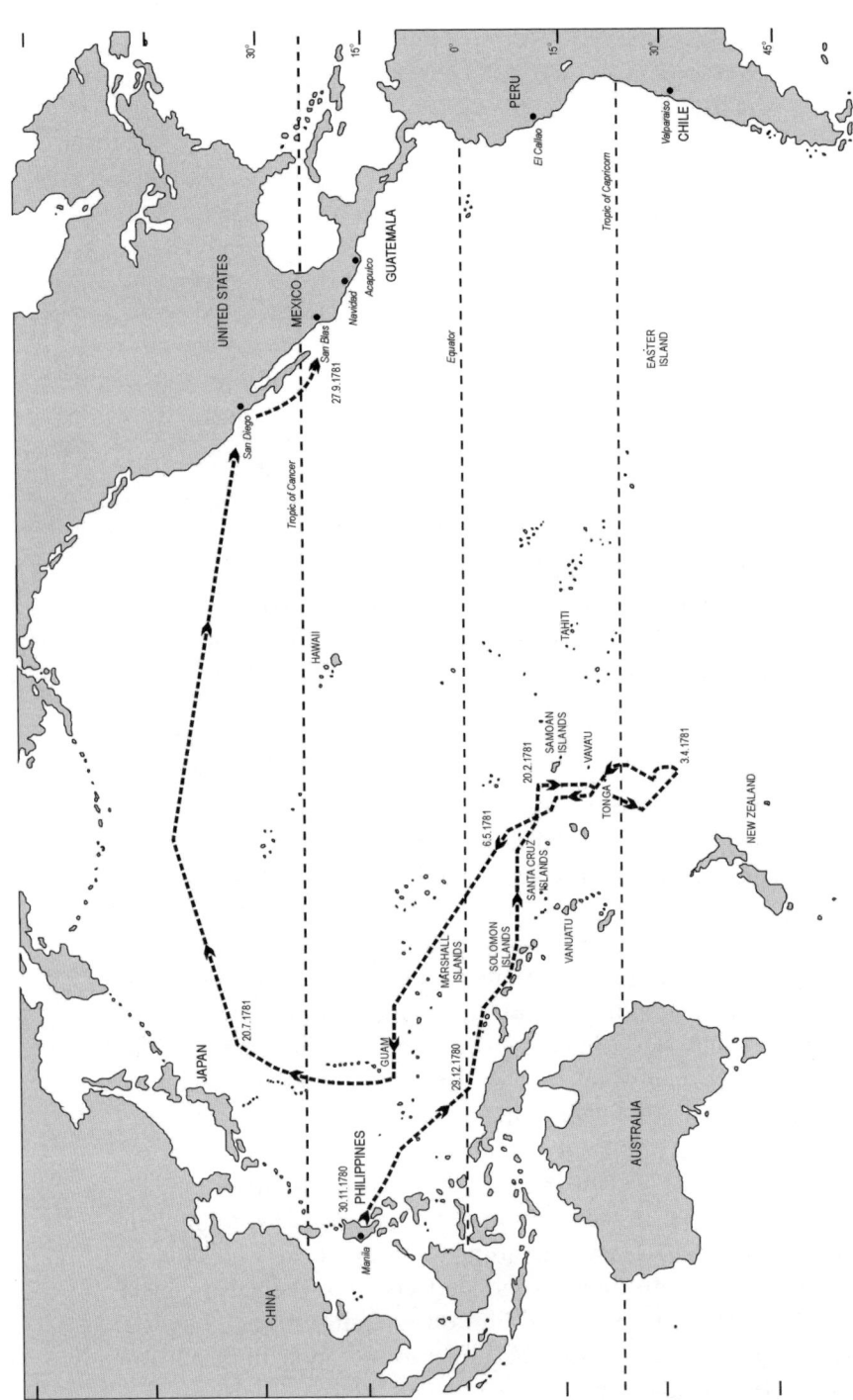

4.4 Itinerary of the voyage of Francisco Mourelle de la Rúa to Vava'u (1780–81). Mourelle is attributed with discovery of these islands of the Tongan archipelago.

Mourelle's *Princesa* first discovered an island north of Vava'u which the Spaniards named, significantly, *Amargura* ('Bitterness'). Ten years later, the island was named Gardner by the English and is known today as Funale, Faunale or Fonualei. Next, Mourelle's expedition found Late, an island explored by La Pérouse six years later, which was also sighted in 1791 by Edward Edwards, who called it Bickerston (Landín 1970: 79). However, the lack of geographical data meant that Mourelle wisely decided not to name any more places in order to avoid causing future confusion:

> From this time onwards, the names that I gave to all the lands which I discovered but were not found on my map will be avoided. Because they are clearly marked each of them in the attached chart with their locations and sizes, so that one day, their comparison with those discovered by the voyagers of these seas, will make it easy to recognise them with their original names. (1970: 280)

Contacts with the islanders were largely friendly throughout this voyage, especially during the days they spent in the Vava'u islands towards the later part of the journey. The inhabitants of these Tongan islands seemed to the Spanish welcoming and well provided for by their environment. By contrast with the abundant supplies of the Vava'u islanders, Mourelle's first contacts with Pacific peoples showed him islands on which foodstuffs were in rather short supply. In the first place they arrived, the crew of the *Princesa* was met by some islanders who came out in twelve canoes and refused to board Mourelle's ship but urged the Spaniards to land, while asking for food with 'greed'. The Spaniards threw some coconuts and biscuits from the frigate and the scrambling for the food that followed created such chaos that Mourelle was worried that some islanders might die as a result. In this way, the islanders 'gave away their miserable condition, unable therefore to provide the slightest refreshment for the sailors'. The resulting 'disenchantment' led Mourelle to sail onwards, after making some notes in his journal about the environment and people met (1970: 281).

Mourelle's description of the islanders follows the pattern already seen in previous voyages, first concentrating on the colour of their skin and hair, and in the manner of dressing or, in this particular case, lack of it: 'These people are no different from blacks from Guinea, because their hair, colour, lips and eyes are perfectly similar, and they were completely naked.' Nakedness, it is worth remembering, was considered to be a sign of lacking culture for Europeans, who often used standards of dress, or its absence thereof, as a way to classify the stages of civilisation of the cultures encountered on their voyages of exploration. Also, nakedness could be seen as a marker of innocence and closeness to that state of nature in which humans had supposedly lived before the fall from paradise. In this line, after assessing their appearance, Mourelle referred to the weapons these islanders carried, which equally afforded him with a way of placing them in an 'earlier' stage of civilisation because they were rudimentary arrows with no bows to shoot them. They had, however, fishing nets, from which Mourelle inferred that fish was their main means of subsistence (1970: 281).

Leaving this deprived environment, the Spaniards continued northwards, encountering six more small islands which Mourelle tried to locate on his chart – unsuccessfully, because of the distance from their ship (1970: 281). Mourelle wondered whether one of these islands belonged to the New Britain archipelago, but decided instead that it must be the one named Don Juan by Bellin. The same source of information, Bellin's world map, was used to identify a second island, which Mourelle thought to be Hohondaba. Sailing further, Mourelle saw three more islands south of Hohondaba, and, like the previous ones, he placed them on his chart (1970: 283). From the last of these islands, six canoes came out to meet the Spaniards, but Mourelle could not wait for them owing to the prevailing winds. Nevertheless, he observed that the men on board the canoes were very similar to those seen before, and also seemed to be 'unhappily' served by their environment: 'they returned to their small possessions, which, even though they had a few coconut trees, demonstrated with their size and other circumstances the unhappiness of those living beings' (1970: 284).

It was at this point that a most distressing plague of cockroaches took hold of the ship. Mourelle's description of their vast numbers and the devastating effect they had on the food supplies, and the people on board, is remarkable in its detail. It is especially memorable to note how the fury of the assault of these insects caused men to bleed in their fingers and eyebrows. To get rid of the plague, Mourelle had to resort to placing containers full of precious water and honey, which were thrown overboard full of cockroaches every four hours:

> It is impossible to imagine the sheer number of that devouring insect: to be persuaded of the reality, it was necessary to have seen with one's own eyes the lamentable situation to which they reduced us, and to observe how those individuals of the crew who, for the softness or sweetness of their flesh,

offered agreeable pasture to them, found no place in the ship where they could take refuge from their terrifying persecution. There were many, whose brows and eyebrows and fingertips dawned daily skinned to the point of bleeding, not being enough to diminish such plague the many measures that we took of spreading all over the place pots full of water and honey, which every four hours were filled and were then emptied into the sea. (1970: 286)

After this, Mourelle arrived on the island of Late, where bartering with the islanders commenced and he pleasantly observed their trust, comparing them favourably with the 'barbarians' of the southern Californian coast (1970: 288). Mourelle was pleased to see the faith shown in the Spaniards by the people on the island and believed that the demonstrations of affection ('afabilidad y cariño') shown by the islanders in the form of dances and other performances had to be returned somehow. For Mourelle, any sign of friendship between sailors and islanders ought to be strengthened to ensure the mutual advantage of both parties, and he attempted to set an example with one of the islanders, who appeared to him to be a chief: 'I tried to correspond with him in terms that his gratefulness would strengthen my friendship, and, in effect, he could not dispense with offering me that island, whose name was Late, of which being chief he wanted to supply me with several fruits and water.' However, Mourelle saw nowhere to anchor and could not, therefore, reciprocate those 'humanas expresiones' (1970: 288).

The barter taking place in Late and the neighbouring islands seems to have been quite profitable and to the common satisfaction of both parties, 'contracting' local produce and foodstuffs in exchange, initially, for iron tools with a certain degree of confidence, on a daily basis. The daily trades followed the same pattern, starting normally in the morning, when the locals received the Spaniards in their canoes and were already well prepared for the ensuing negotiation. Canoes numbering 'fifty to one hundred' approached the ship, carrying foodstuffs, such as piglets, hens, bananas, coconuts, roots and breadfruit or *ufis*, as well as cloth made of palm and flax and 'those bedspreads or blankets which they gave greater value, verifying the trade on the side of the frigate, without [there] being any suspicion of bad faith in the contracts on either side' (1970: 289).

The exchange of tools and utensils on board reached a dangerous point, however, and Mourelle eventually forbade his crew from exchanging any more, and persuaded them to trade other items ('otras especies'). According to Mourelle, the islanders viewed their eagerness to offer them clothing and cotton as 'obstinación' on the part of the Spaniards and continued demanding tools, in an interesting bargaining duel in which neither party held the advantage: 'even though at the beginning they remained constant with that pretension on their part, our obstinacy in offering them only handkerchiefs and other items of this sort, the proximity of night made them cede the first day, because they were forced to retire' (1970: 289).

Finally, the persistence of the Spaniards in wishing to exchange items of clothing succeeded, and everyone started selling what they had to wear, as well as household utensils, including pottery, which they had obtained in Manila. This 'public contract' saw the sailors disposing of items that they were taking to the Americas or Spain and their own shirts or jackets in exchange for food supplies:

> They then opened public contract, admitting the most despicable rags for all they had in their canoes; so that the sailors tore their shirts, breeches, coats, bands &c. to be able to provide themselves with those refreshments. And, since they had brought from Manila some pottery to use in their houses, they also tried to trade it to apportion themselves as many supplies as they could. (1970: 289)

At this point, Mourelle believed that the Spanish gained more from the exchanges, because even some old items of clothing seemed to please the 'rustic' islanders (1970: 289–90). Nonetheless, there is no way of ascertaining whether the islanders thought that they were obtaining goods that were of no value to them, and we cannot take the assumption about the Spaniards' advantage at face value. If the islanders felt at disadvantage in these exchanges, they did not demonstrate it, which means that both parties may have achieved the slippery concept of mutual satisfaction. Mourelle certainly gained himself, for the food obtained allowed him to cut his ration of meat altogether and halve that of bread because his men were supplied in abundance with local food.

The sense of camaraderie did not extend to a comparison of physiques, in which the islanders asserted their own superiority. Mourelle commended their physical form, indicating that the men there were all 'well-built' and 'proportioned', alluding to their size and bodily shape. Indeed, the hosts were fully aware of those qualities and went so far as to mock the size and countenance of the visitors, especially those working as servants: 'this difference provided a source of some mockery of those whom I had sent in search of water and firewood because they were less useful with weapons' (1970: 290). While the islanders made sure that their contempt was clear, Mourelle could not see any local with bodily handicaps, with even the smallest among them being taller than the 'best on my ship'.

Mourelle's description gives readers some information not only about the relative sizes of Spaniards and islanders but also about the hierarchy on the boat and the distribution of chores in relation to physical ability. Thus, the 'best' among Mourelle's men took arms, while those 'less useful' ('menos útiles'), meaning smaller in size, were deployed to carry water and fetch wood.

That this hierarchy was important for Mourelle is shown in relation to the exchange of gifts, as had happened also in the voyages to Tahiti. Thus, when he received an offering of fruit, he tried to 'court' its carrier because he believed him to be the main chief's own son 'so that his friendship might bring me that of his father, and he would not bother me when I had to fill my water vessels, instead being helpful'. Mourelle treated this boy with preference, thereby emphasising the reciprocity and the obligations entailed in gift-giving, as well as the hegemonic relations implied. Given these assumptions, it became of paramount important for Mourelle to identify the chiefs and the different social strata on the island, which he tried to do by locating the 'egui' (*arii*) and investigating whether he was the only one with power over the islanders (1970: 290).

As also happened in previous voyages, Mourelle was offered a woman, but he refused the gift with an 'air of contempt and indignation', while trying to indicate that nobody on his boat could receive such 'help': 'Tubou's son brought me on behalf of his father a woman of 22 to 25 years of age; and when he offered her to me, I tried with an air of contempt and indignation to refuse a present that nobody in my ship could receive, making sure she was taken back to land at once, and assuring him that we did not need such succour'. In case he might be misunderstood by his readers, Mourelle highlighted that his behaviour obeyed orders which were put in place so as to avoid the jealousy and hate that might otherwise arise, explaining that: 'This behaviour, even if it were not in accordance with the purity of my passions, was a policy that, when followed uniformly in successive events, would remove from the hearts any reason for jealousy, which in discoveries are regularly the origin of discord and interminable hates' (1970: 291).

Mourelle's rejection of the young woman did not prevent him from receiving and accepting daily a canoe full of breadfruit given by the chief, whose obesity is reiterated throughout the narrative. In exchange for the food, Mourelle placed a red cord with a medallion bearing the portrait of the king of Spain around the necks of the chief and his wife to offer proof that the Spanish ship had been on the island. The friendship was thus marked by gifts and by demonstrations of affection, and the chief and his wife left from this visit to the ship 'newly regaled', ratifying the 'alliance' with 'kisses and embraces that the old man did not cease to give me' (1970: 292).

In spite of the friendly relationship with the islanders, Mourelle's orders not to harm anybody were accompanied by his injunctions that should be careful not to blindly trust their hosts, in order to avoid unpleasant surprises. To this effect, he asked the Spaniards to shoot at rocks so that the islanders would appreciate the power of their weapons, which the 'around 1200 to 1500 souls' present did and were duly terrified, begging Mourelle to cease his display. Thus, Mourelle indicated, 'with little expense I could infuse terror' in order to prevent the use of weapons 'more rigorously' on other occasions (1970: 292).

Despite such display of might on the part of the Spaniards, the islanders had the upper hand in their access to local resources and willingly helped the visitors in their search for water. Their 'fine expressions' of friendship towards Mourelle continued, with 'kisses and embraces as proof of their love', feelings corroborated when they invited the Spaniards to take part in their kava ceremony. This ritual put Mourelle in a rather uncomfortable position, especially after seeing that the fermentation of the kava was produced by chewing and spitting it. Mourelle, repulsed by the sight and guessing the bitterness of the final product, could not bring himself to take it, but his refusal did not offend the islanders, who placed before him a basket of roasted breadfruit and bananas, from which Mourelle ate before passing it on to his soldiers (1970: 293).

Mourelle was very pleased to receive such treatment from both the 'king' and the 'queen' and praised them in the highest terms, especially the queen whose 'agreeable' disposition was complemented by sweet expressions. It was the 'king', nevertheless, who gave Mourelle food in sufficient quantities for his crew and also gifted him a carved stick, which Mourelle greatly appreciated.[2] Thus, Mourelle's visits were always welcomed with gifts of breadfruit and he was also helped in his search for water, which was carried back to the ship by the 'indios' provided by the *arii* (1970: 294–5).

As the departure of the Spaniards approached, more canoes visited to trade in a 'fair' ('feria o facatau') with so much 'satisfaction' that many islanders slept on board 'as though they were in their own rooms'. On the last day, the 'king' invited Mourelle to a 'fiesta', the preparation and performance of which are related in some detail in the journal. Before festivities started the islanders arrived in pairs, carrying long sticks on their shoulders, and with breadfruit, bananas, coconuts and fish, which they piled up, making up 'a cube of two yards in height'. Next, the 'king' led Mourelle by the hand to a circle, where 'more than two thousand Indians' were waiting for them. They sat on 'texidos de palma' ('palm mats') and Mourelle observed that the members of each clan ('ranchería') were segregated from those of other clans. After the king's initial offering of fruit to Mourelle, the islanders kept silent, with hardly a 'deaf murmur' between them, and only those who 'because of their standing sat close' to the king answering his words. The silence seemed to Mourelle ominous and, as he wondered whether some unpleasant surprise might be in store, he warned his people to be on the alert and to have their weapons ready (1970: 295). His fears proved unfounded, however, as what followed was a spectacle in which the islanders fought and then boxed.

After the men had boxed for about two hours, it was the women's turn to do likewise and this made Mourelle feel so uncomfortable that he asked them to stop. His plea was heard and Mourelle thought that the islanders celebrated what they appreciated as a compassionate gesture on his part. When the fights ended, the 'king' invited an old woman to sing, which she did for one hour, gesticulating while doing so 'in manner of representation'. At the end of the festivities, so many islanders gathered around the Spaniards that the *arii* ordered that they be dispersed and he came out beating them away with a stick, with two of them taken away as though they were dead (1970: 295–7).

While Mourelle was finalising the preparation for his departure, and resolving any associated problems, the *arii*, who called him 'son', kept sending him baskets with fruits, hens and fish. He also visited Mourelle regularly, eating on board and having his *siesta* there. When the time to depart came, the 'king' and 'queen' bid farewell to Mourelle, displaying sadness at the occasion, while some canoes with islanders accompanied the ship as it left until they were far from the island. At that point, Mourelle wrote that he had named the harbour between the three islands *Refugio*, and the group of islands in honour of Viceroy Mayorga, of 'Excelentísimo Señor Don Martín Mayorga' (1970: 298–9).[3]

Mourelle completed his narrative with a description of the physical and human features of the place and its inhabitants. Firstly, he mentioned the fruits and plants encountered, noting the extreme care with which the locals sowed and tended them, and indicating that the Spaniards left seeds for planting, much as happened on the previous voyage to Tahiti. The acceptance of these seeds illustrates the importance of receiving gifts graciously in order to seal an amicable relationship, and Mourelle commended that they were taken 'with particular appreciation, assuring us that they would place them in their best fields'. The beauty of the tilled fields and the care with which they were looked after and weeded were greatly admired by Mourelle, who commended their roads as being 'worthy of being imitated among people more polite and cultivated' (1970: 299).

To conclude, Mourelle extolled the islanders' wit ('genio') and docility ('docilidad'), signalled by the fact that they were pleased with the visitors (1970: 299). Harsher words were reserved, however, for the practice of theft, which was attributed to their ethnicity as 'indios'. When boarding the ship, according to Mourelle, the islanders always took with them everything that they could, going so far as to throw things overboard, even from the windows of the 'camarotes' ('cabins'). Mourelle's complaints were answered by the *arii*'s permission to kill those he might find stealing and assuring Mourelle that he had ordered that he could take the lives of thieves (1970: 300).

The journal also refers to the religion of the islanders, which was seen to lack ceremonies, and their language, which was easy for Spanish to pronounce, and vice versa. As for the islands themselves, to the confusion of those studying the journey, Mourelle was told that two frigates had visited them, and that those on board had given the islanders rosaries of beads, and axes. This information is puzzling, as Mourelle's voyage is widely acknowledged to be the first to reach these islands. While it is possible that the islanders exchanged those goods with neighbouring islands, whether there were others before Mourelle to Vava'u and, if so, who the visitors could have been, remains an open question.

The custom of cutting part or the whole of a person's little finger was also accounted for at the end of the narrative, with chiefs having not just one but both fingers missing. Another marker of distinction was the fact that the chiefs wore a mother-of-pearl necklace, probably to distinguish them from the other islanders. Such description of local customs and habitat sketched in these final pages of Mourelle's journal is given more attention in a separate section, which Mourelle wrote after the voyage, his 'Digresión'.[4] There, Mourelle included a lengthy description of the item most broadly celebrated by Europeans: the local canoes and the way they were navigated, which was a cause of 'great admiration'. The physical features, kindness, cleanliness and humanity of the women, whom Mourelle said he could never forget, were equally celebrated in the highest terms (1970: 300–4).[5]

Altogether, the inhabitants of these islands, according to Mourelle, showered affection on the sailors, with each family adopting one particular man, calling for him and bartering their fruit baskets with him, or even giving them to him for free. Once again, gift-giving and commerce acted on this journey as means of communication and markers of social cement, while also expressing the affection binding human beings.

In relation to food, Mourelle highlighted the fact that the islanders – men as well as women – cooked everything, and the fruit was ripe (1970: 305). This distinction between the raw and the cooked has traditionally been seen by Europeans as a sign of civilisation, distinguishing cultures that cook from those who do not. Like other Cartesian dualities, such as nakedness and dress, the categories of raw and cooked food have been used to classify different societies, in this case, to place the Tongans above other indigenous cultures.[6]

Not everything deserved praise, however, and Mourelle's journal censures the wearing of tattoos, which he disliked intensely. By contrast, he celebrated the ceremonies of mourning, recalling one occasion in which an 'indio' had been killed by accident, when he was stealing on the ship. The wailing and self-flagellation that followed revealed to Mourelle 'beautiful feelings' in the islanders which 'extend beyond death'. These, however, went to extremes, such as 'cutting their flesh that blood flew like a sea' or the fact that an old man, who could have been the father of the deceased, hit 'his cheeks with his fists, until they were reduced to black bruises' (1970: 305–6).

It is worth noting that, although Mourelle never so much as visited the chief's village, he observed that the locals 'venerated' him, remarking that they kissed his feet wherever he went (1970: 307–8). Because his rule was despotic, Mourelle was surprised to witness the level of social cohesion: 'With the crowd of people gathered there would be an excessive number of *Eguis*, all of which commanded their vassals despotically. This observation made me conceive of a great division among them; but the general harmony with which they managed themselves belied such concept' (1970: 290).

On the return voyage, Mourelle detailed the stopovers on other islands during which the Spaniards were met by canoes with fruits and local items which the islanders wanted to exchange. For example, on one of the islands which they visited, from dawn onwards, many canoes arrived in succession 'with the same fruit and effects as the previous ones, exchanging them likewise for any type of clothing offered to them'. Mourelle also met there with the local *arii* who, he believed, was trying to outdo that of the 'islas de Mayorga', which is the name that he gave to Vava'u, in feasting the Spaniards and giving them gifts. This chief sent Mourelle 'two piglets and some coconuts', insisting that Mourelle visit him until 'finally, he himself arrived on board' where he kindly assured Mourelle that he would also have fighting games and a pile of breadfruit to feast them, matching the festivities in the 'islas de Mayorga' (1970: 309).

Mourelle affirmed that, this *arii*, who was not shown the respect of the previous one, commanded a large number of islands, Ha'apai, which were named in honour of another personality of New Spain: 'Excelentísimo Señor don Josef de Galvez' (1970: 310).[7] Mourelle's ship then proceeded on to two more islands, which were given the name *Islas de Consolación*, where the Spaniards again bartered with the islanders all the goods they could, which served to 'alleviate their misery', as they exchanged breadfruit, coconuts, piglets and hens for around thirty hours. Bartering went to such lengths that the sailors traded all their clothes in order to provision themselves for 'more than eight days of navigation'.[8] Mourelle believed that the language and ethnicity of people on that island were closely related to those of the Vava'u islands, and they were equally friendly towards the Spaniards. As with Vava'u islanders, the trust of these men was shown by the fact that they slept on board the Spanish ship and had to be forced to leave the following day before the Spanish departed (1970: 314).

Finally, the *Princesa* approached another island, seeing that they were again short of food and, while some canoes approached them, they could not give them the coconuts they carried because the islanders could not get past the reefs. The Spaniards, therefore, did not land, having to release the ropes which they had been given by the islanders to help them approach the shore. For Mourelle, the people on this island were not as pleasant as those left behind and he likened them to 'infernal figures' on account of the 'varnish' with which they painted their bodies. Likewise, their language was different, 'and most of them had beard of such length that it reached their breast'. Mourelle also noticed many houses close to the forest 'in such number and so well disposed that the whole island seemed a big village' (1970: 315).

Soon after this visit, the Spaniards traversed the line of the Equator to the north, arriving in the Marianas, where the Governor, after checking Mourelle's commission, gave him supplies of rice, corn and pigs for fifteen days, providing for his crew while on the island (1970: 317–18). The desire of many sailors to remain in the Marianas was achieved by some 'deserters', like the sailor mentioned in relation to Quirós's second voyage in 1606, who became a 'beachcomber'. This sailor's decision demonstrates the cultural marginality felt by many explorers whose accounts failed to materialise and who attest to a type of cross-cultural exchange that has not made it to our historical records. Nevertheless these men, like the indigenous peoples who travelled to Europe or America, epitomise the engagements that underwrite much of our past and our present. For the majority, however, deserting was not an option. In spite of the expressed or repressed desire of many to remain on the islands, the remainder of Mourelle's fleet returned to their world. Mourelle's men left the Pacific islands on 20 June for the Americas, and reached Mexico three months later, on 27 September 1781, returning from a region that was to become, for many Europeans, the new Promised Land.

NOTES

1 Mourelle did not have with him anything other than the chart made by the French cartographer Jacques Nicholas Bellin, which was rather dated 'and some brief news of a journey made a few years prior to his from Manila towards Nueva Guinea' (1970: 73). Bellin's chart, according to Mourelle, indicated that they were only '107 leagues east' of the Solomons, with no other islands shown (1970: 286).
2 With the carved stick, Mourelle also received two fish, with which he retired to his bed 'with the hope of getting water the following day' (1970: 294).
3 Martín de Mayorga became Viceroy of New Spain after the death of Antonio María de Bucareli, in 1779.
4 The title reads: 'Digresión escrita después de concluido el viaje' (1970: 301–20).
5 Mourelle also emphasised his pleasure on seeing the women's bathing habits and the way the 'Reina' (Queen) brought him food (1970: 305).
6 This type of taxonomy became the foundation of structural thought. For Levi-Strauss, these 'empirical categories . . . can . . . be used as conceptual tools with which to elaborate abstract ideas and combine them in the form of propositions' (1969: 1). The categories he selects along the 'raw and the cooked' are: 'the fresh and the decayed, the moistened and the burned, etc.' This 'etcetera' would include dualisms such as young versus old, male versus female, and animal versus human.
7 Mourelle stated that this *arii* was chief of '48 islands, whose names they distinctly related, but I did not see them treat him with that submission and respect' that the *arii* of Refugio enjoyed. After boarding, Mourelle added that: 'he put on my neck his mother-of-pearl shell as sign of our friendship', follow-

ing which he retired to one island where he waited for Mourelle the next day (1970: 310). These are the Haapai islands, according to Landín, who mentions that Gálvez was 'visitador general' in Mexico and afterwards minister of the Indies and marquis of Sonora (1970: 90).

8 Mourelle also traded for food to provide sustenance for the remainder of the voyage (1970: 314).

4

Malaspina and Vava'u (1793)

The expedition led by Alejandro Malaspina received some deserving attention during the last years of the twentieth century.[1] Previously, his own journals were only published in 1885, after nearly one hundred years during which his name had been all but deleted from historical records on account of the political changes that cost him eight years in jail and the remaining seven years of his life in exile from Spain. Although the expedition was welcomed on arrival, in 1794, and Malaspina was promoted to brigadier (rear-admiral), the following year – by the end of 1795 – his celebrity came to an abrupt end. Malaspina paid a hefty price for presenting his own political programme and criticising the capricious minister, Manuel Godoy, who, at the time, was effectively running the country. Not only was Malaspina arrested and imprisoned, but the publication of works related to the voyage was halted and it was only the intervention of Napoleon Bonaparte in 1807 that brought his term in prison to an end, on condition that he never return to Spain. The recuperation and publicising of the sources relating to the remarkable voyage that Malaspina led intensified after the celebration of its 200th anniversary in 1989 and the publication of a scholarly three-volume translation of his journal by the Hakluyt Society (2001–4).

Originally from the Italian town of Mulazzo, Malaspina joined the Spanish navy in Sicily in 1774. In 1786 he was promoted and put in command of the frigate *Astrea* to circumnavigate the world via South America, the Philippines and the Cape of Good Hope. After this journey, Malaspina and his friend and colleague, José Bustamante, drew the plan of the five-year voyage that included the stopover in Vava'u on which this section concentrates. Both men took part in this momentous journey, which set out, primarily, with the intention of providing accurate hydrographical charts for use by the Spanish navy.[2] Secondly, Malaspina and Bustamante, together with the cartographers, geographers, scientists and draftsmen on the expedition, would write reports and make drawings of the places visited and of their flora and fauna.[3] More important for the present study is their concern to represent the people encountered, their customs and habitat, and to establish friendly relations with them.

With its mixture of political, commercial and scientific aims, Malaspina and Bustamante's plan remains an outstanding achievement on many fronts. However, in view of the limits of this study, this section focuses on the small portion of the journey, from 20 May to 1 June 1793, when Malaspina's fleet, like Mourelle a few years earlier, landed at the Vava'u islands of the Tongan archipelago.[4] The ships also made a short visit to the South Island of New Zealand, where contact with the locals was all but non-existent, although they left their footprint on the names of some geographical features (Robson 2002).

The visit to the Vava'u islands took place in the latter part of the journey, when the two ships from Malaspina's fleet, the *Descubierta* and the *Atrevida*, departed from Port Jackson in Australia to reach Vava'u. This was very much their last incursion into Pacific waters, for their projected visit to the Society Islands never took place. From Vava'u, the fleet left for South America, touching in El Callao before heading for Montevideo, from where they returned to Spain in 1794 (Figure 4.5).

As soon as the ships moored at a harbour of Vava'u, many canoes approached them, as on earlier voyages. On this occasion, an elderly man, Tupou, referred to by Malaspina as 'Eije Dubou', came on board with the usual presents of food, and gave away his club.[5] The Spaniards rubbed noses with the islanders as a sign of friendship, and gave the old man 'two yards of baize', inviting him to eat with them. Malaspina noted the confidence with which locals boarded the ship unarmed, remarking also on the need by the Spaniards to be alert to the thefts to which they were normally subjected. Both parties soon started to trade, establishing and sealing their friendship by means of the exchanges (2004: 101; 1984: 433–4).

Communication between Spaniards and islanders was facilitated by a vocabulary compiled by the pilot, Antonio Vázquez, who had travelled in Mourelle's frigate *Princesa* a few years earlier. With this basic tool at hand, people on board the *Atrevida* bartered items for food such as, for example, an axe for a pig and roots, which José Bustamante traded with 'Eije Tumoala'.[6] Problems, however, soon began to arise owing to the need to hide things from the islanders, including chiefs and 'plebe', whose 'inclination to every type of theft' appears to have been the sole cause of friction on this voyage. In fact, the islanders went so far as to steal a handkerchief from the pockets of José Robredo, and one man was found on board the

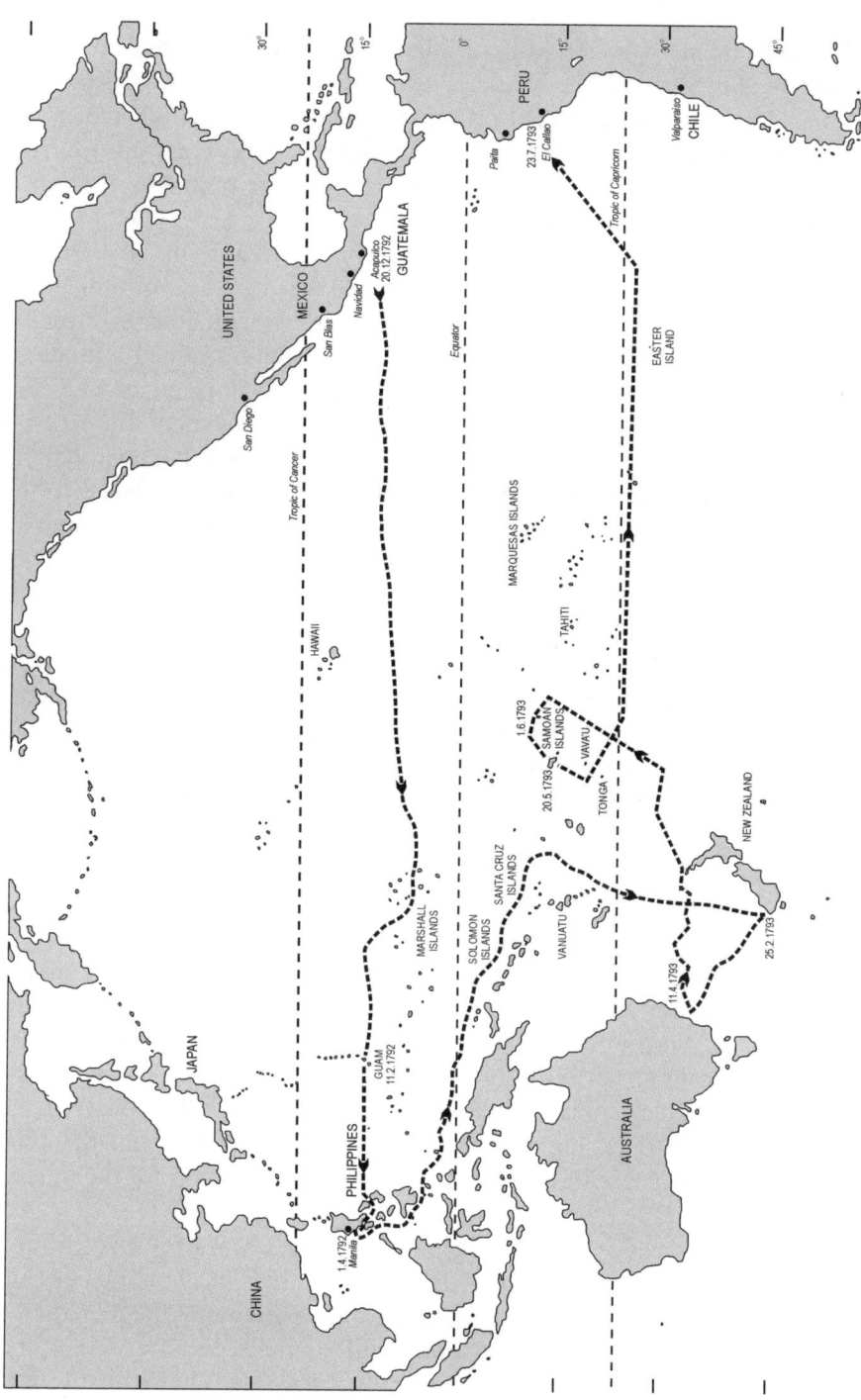

4.5 Itinerary of the voyage of Alejandro Malaspina to Vava'u (1793). Malaspina's 'scientific' journey (1789–94) visited, charted and drafted Vava'u and its inhabitants.

Descubierta making off with various pieces of clothing, which he had obtained by opening the windows of the chambers. To try to discourage more thefts, the man caught on the *Atrevida* with the handkerchief was given a few lashes on the cannon. This, however, did not seem to make too much of an impact on the others, as the same problems continued throughout the whole of the stay (2004: 101–3).

As with other voyages, women were also offered as items of exchange, with Malaspina commenting on the need to take care to avoid the problems that 'tolerance' in 'using' them could cause. As with other eighteenth-century Spanish officers, Malaspina compared the restrained attitude of the Spaniards with that of English and French sailors, suggesting that when officers of those nationalities went out with women it caused no interference with 'the maintenance of discipline on board' (2004: 104). By contrast, Malaspina observed that the English officers – more so than the crew – seemed to be more inclined to associate with island women, whereas, in his opinion, the opposite obtained in the Spanish case.[7]

Although they were inclined to steal, the islanders were friendly towards the Spaniards in all else, including helping them to fetch and carry water. It was difficult, however, for the visitors to determine the degrees of authority on the island, which they wished to so as to establish a hierarchy when trading. With Tupou, for example, Malaspina guessed that he had a lot of authority because he was the first to suggest 'some sort of monopoly' in relation to future exchanges (2004: 104).

As with other voyages, gift-giving was used as a means not just to bond with the people, but also to assess their degree and social standing. In this vein, Malaspina initially doubted the power held by Tupou because of the poor quality of his gifts: 'his offerings, even if intended for exchange, were very paltry'. His inference was confirmed when he met 'Eije Ko-Vuna', or Vuna, as he was later referred to, because he bestowed lavish gifts on the Spaniards.[8] Such opinion was confirmed when the explorers noticed the 'unequivocal signs of respect from the lesser chiefs', which revealed Vuna to be of a higher ranking. The Spaniards started to talk to Vuna, trying to cement their friendship with this most important man, and the chief exchanged names with Felipe Bauzá, issuing an invitation for the officers to visit him, which they accepted (2004: 104–7).

After the scientists Tadeo Haenke and Felipe Bauzá returned from a short trip with Tupou to explore the island on their small sailing boat, the pinnace, many of the locals gathered for a kava ceremony, the preparation of which, as had happened previously with Mourelle, disgusted Malaspina. In spite of their repugnance at the fact that a woman chewed the root to produce fermentation, the Spaniards took the drink 'with the required ceremony' to demonstrate their integration of local customs (2004: 107). After this, Malaspina went back to the ship and found that he needed to take some precautions to maintain order, including preventing women from boarding, or removing precious items from sight. In addition, he ordered that all exchanges be made with the items provided by the Spanish crown to that effect, to avoid the men bartering their own clothes. Again at this point, trading and gift-giving operated on different scales, ranging from the individual to the collective, and were used for material, social and emotional benefit.

The relationship between gift-giving and power was put to the test that afternoon when the Spaniards visited Vuna, who wished to receive them 'in fine style'. In order to display his power, Vuna had a local man guide the Spaniards to his 'hut', passing through a crowd of people surrounding him so that the visitors would become aware of his status on hearing the acclamations of his vassals. Not only did the Spanish hear those acclamations, but also men and women singing as part of the ceremony, which they did in reasonable unison, with 'well-arranged harmony' (2004: 108). The guests sat with Vuna accompanied by some local women and spent the afternoon 'in the greatest concord and cheerfulness', making good progress in learning the local language. Trading continued on the following day, this time with the Spaniards making some effort to stipulate a price that would suit them: 'We attempted to maintain a higher value for the objects of which we had a plentiful supply, hiding the axes and the feminine ornaments against a time when the former would have declined in value' (2004: 110).

The explorers also had practical reasons for appreciating the friendship of Vuna and of his nephew, Feileua, a boy around eight to ten years old, because, whenever these two were on board, items stolen were quickly restored. Indeed, Feileua became good friends with the Spanish and, as a sign of his friendship, exchanged names with José Espinosa and acquired Spanish dress. Alongside Latu, an older boy who accompanied and seemed to tutor him, Feileua informed the Spaniards about some 'some organised amusements' planned in honour of the visitors on the following afternoon. When writing about these events, Malaspina emphasised the islanders' taste and 'propensity to diversions of this kind' in which food and female company are said to have been important components (2004: 112).

While the Spaniards were attending to repairs on the ship, they received another visit from Vuna, who ate with them and received many gifts. Vuna was so pleased on behalf of himself and his family that he found 'it difficult to hide his pleasure in the many gifts which we either gave to him or directly to his wives or to young Feileua, which would eventually be added to his treasury' (2004: 115). The Spaniards showered gifts on Vuna directly although sometimes, as when Vuna offered them food, the gifts were given to his wives or to his nephew; albeit these normally found their way to Vuna, much as happened in Tahiti.

The 'tranquil idleness' in which the crew were submerged was, however, disturbed when Vuna believed that his people had not obeyed his orders diligently enough and commanded that they be dispersed by force. Perhaps, as Malaspina's journal suggests, Vuna did this in order to impress the Spaniards, 'to show us his boundless authority', which was duly demonstrated by turning to 'cruelty and violence'. The Spaniards were certainly surprised at the aggression and the fact that Vuna seemed 'well satisfied' with this demonstration (2004: 116).

When the time for the dances approached, Malaspina confided in his readers the need to be careful to avoid misunderstandings between the different parties, which might have tragic consequences. He attributed the many errors committed in the past to the ignorance of each other's language and of the due care required in observing social customs. Thus, he stated, it happened 'at such meetings that the slightest mistake may have the most serious consequences since, without much regard to the circumstances, the only concern is to reduce the risk by anticipating the [actions of the] adversary' (2004: 116–17). Similarly, in relation to women, although Malaspina warned against believing the stereotypes spread by 'travellers' tales' as true, while he also highlighted their kindness: 'the attractiveness with which fortune has endowed the fair sex in these happy climes, whose charms we still had only a very imperfect notion' (2004: 113).

Like gift-giving, ceremonies were often a way to display authority and to cement closer ties between visitors and hosts. In relation to the event attended by the Spaniards, Malaspina, like Mourelle before him, remarked on how people sat in circles, according to their rank, and of the large number present, which he estimated to be between 1,800 and 2,000. Following the offering of kava, the women invited the officers to sit next to them, and male dancers started to perform 'to the beat of the canes' (2004: 117). During these festivities, Vuna showed his despotic authority again by showing offence when the women refused to obey his orders to dance and 'began to attack men and women indiscriminately, dealing savage blows to any who did not escape as fast as they could' to show his displeasure.

Two chiefs tried to restrain him, and the women reluctantly obeyed his orders (2004: 118).

The Spaniards returned to their ship and the party of José Robredo and Luis Née found that they had to pay their way because their paddler threatened to take them elsewhere unless he was given a handkerchief, 'which, as can be imagined, they did not hesitate to hand over' (2004: 119). Once more, this accentuated the problems the Spanish encountered in differentiating between gift-giving and commercial exchanges, and the need to do so successfully in order to strike an amicable relation. Thus, after this event, Malaspina suggested that they exchange knowledge about the various ranks on the island and discuss how to proceed, for some of the islanders appeared to have become quite demanding in soliciting presents. At the same time, Antonio Tova warned against an old woman who appeared to come to distract people while others stole from the pockets of the Spaniards.

The intricate pattern of hierarchy that the islanders conveyed by means of gift-giving was corroborated the next day while the explorers installed an observatory. This time, the Spaniards were surprised and delighted to see Vuna and his nephew, Feileua, bringing them food, a gift which 'was generously reciprocated, and our mutual friendship could once more be considered as solidly established' (2004: 119). When commenting on Vuna's attitude on watching the setting up of the observatory, Malaspina used his contemporary assessment of gradation between civility and barbarism. In this 'enlightened' fashion, Malaspina noted that Vuna admired the Spanish works and implements, showing his own lack of 'civilisation' by so doing 'with that astonished admiration which peoples not yet civilized show at our achievements' (2004: 120).[9]

Malaspina's attribution of degrees of civilisation certainly concurs with prevalent notions established during the Enlightenment. Nevertheless, Malaspina appreciated the friendly treatment that he received, adding that their mutual friendship could never be taken for granted and had to be constantly cultivated, for 'a number of incidents which might have caused it to break down soon occurred'. This happened when Vuna, going to the second ship to request gifts after having been regaled on a previous occasion, found that the guard would not let him pass, and he considered this a great insult. Fortunately, an officer at hand solved the conflict, ensuring that Vuna received 'the gift of some highly valued metal goods' (2004: 119).

Gradually, during this short stay, the Spaniards' relationship with Vuna fell into some sort of routine, whereby Vuna received gifts in exchange for food, and checking that some of the items stolen were returned, and that the thief was duly punished. The constant struggle against theft continued, however, and Malaspina placed guards on board, although this was to no avail for, he admitted, the islanders always had the advantage and 'it was impossible to guard against all their ruses'. Malaspina went on to add that the Spaniards could not possibly exact retribution because Vuna suggested that they execute the culprit, which they objected to. In fact, on one particular occasion, the visitors even had to stop people who were about to carry out Vuna's order, while the 'delincuente' ('offender'), who had stolen a hammer, was kneeling ready to accept his fate with 'humillación' ('humility'). At this point, Vuna also offered Malaspina a woman 'for [his] use', a gesture rejected by Malaspina with some irritation ('un cierto enfado'), causing Vuna to send her away and entertain himself with kava (2004: 120–1).

As suggested, the islanders were graded on a scale of civility versus barbarism established by means of observation and description of local customs and ceremonies, the complexities of which were routinely described by Malaspina and other writers. These rituals included ways of cooking, which were of paramount importance in determining the evolution of non-European cultures, as shown in the section dedicated to Mourelle's voyage. Women's activities, and their role in cementing relations were also noted, as was the servility with which they complied with duties such as performing the *tuque, tuque,* which entailed using a 'soft rapid drumming with the fists on the back and thighs' of a man, usually a chief, who wished to relax and fall sleep. Vuna used *tuque, tuque* once to take a nap on board, and woke to the sound of glass and china when coffee was being served to the officers. Malaspina remarked on Vuna's whims and often-tyrannical attitude on this occasion, noting that no sooner had he woken up that Vuna wished to be given some of those utensils and offered women 'for our use' in exchange. Although Malaspina never accepted such gifts, he believed that this was Vuna's 'strongest weapon' (2004: 122).

To counter the offer of local women, the Spaniards asked Juan Ravenet to produce a likeness of an ideal European woman, which he did, drawing 'a woman graced with all the personal charms usually admired in our Europe . . . dressed in imitation of the ladies of Panamá and reclining languidly in a hammock'. This woman's posture certainly conveys the notion of women as objects of display prevalent in western art to which Malaspina referred.[10] They showed this portrait to Vuna, telling him that the wives of the officers were just as beautiful but would not go with them 'because we considered the hardships of life at sea to be far too great for their delicate constitutions' (2004: 123).

The idealisation of women in the portrait did, however, escape Vuna who, on seeing the portrait, according to Malaspina, assumed the woman to be real and proclaimed his wish to meet her, followed by a desire to possess her, very much like the gifts that he had already acquired. In exchange, Vuna offered Malaspina 'as many women as I might want from the islands of Vava'u'. When Vuna was finally disabused about the reality of the painting's referent, he contemplated the idea that his nephew, Feileua, should go to Spain with Malaspina's men, marry there, and return to the island with more women, some of whom would be destined for him. Malaspina concluded this account with a classical digression about the relationship between painting and original, saying that Vuna would prefer the 'imaginary subject of our tableau' to real women, such as Paulajo's daughters. To Vuna's insistence that Feileua should go to Spain with them, the Spaniards countered with the effective deterrent that only one wife was allowed (2004: 123–4).

On the same day that these events were taking place, one Spaniard deserted, wishing to remain on the island like the beachcombers referred to in previous sections. These 'traitorous' events, some of which became famous at this time throughout the Pacific, as the mutiny of the *Bounty*, also reveal a desire on the part of the crew to be part of a different culture, abandoning the trappings and structures associated with their own. Nonetheless, this man, who voluntarily left the Spaniards and wanted to hide and live on Vava'u, was eventually found with the help of the islanders and, on his return, and on account of his previous loyalty, was only punished by being chained for two days.

Thefts and exchanges continued during the remaining time that the Spanish spent on the island and Malaspina described theft and the insistent demand for gifts, which, on one occasion nearly acquired the dimension of ransom. This happened after a 'lantia de la bitácora' ('compass') was stolen and, when the thief was caught, Vuna and the other chiefs urged the Spaniards 'to have no scruples in executing any thief', reminding the visitors of the harsh punishments carried out by Captain Cook on Annamuka, Ha'apai and Tongatapu.[11] Malaspina rejected the offer, commenting with a degree of irony how Vuna devised methods to obtain a constant supply of gifts, which were not always impeccably ethical. Moreover, to satisfy his own wishes, Vuna offered the Spaniards women's sexual services as merchandise, which was obviously distasteful to Malaspina's sensibility.

The attitude of the women themselves was, nonetheless, also likely to be influenced by material gains, according to Malaspina, with gifts becoming a determining component of the affection shown. For example, on one occasion, Vuna took with him a dozen young women to sing for his guests and the women exchanged names, as well as 'pleasant and decorous banter' with the officers. Malaspina remarked that this had influenced the generosity of the gifts they received. Besides 'decorous' conversations with women, Malaspina and his crew exchanged knowledge with the islanders, very much in accord with the objectives of the expedition, enquiring not just about customs or religion, but also about the events surrounding the visit of Captain Cook to the archipelago or the *Bounty*'s famous mutiny. This was often done by Ciriaco Cevallos, who had managed to acquire 'extremely important notions of the language' (2004: 125–6). The importance of understanding the local language was also noted on other occasions, when we read that Latu was used as translator. By these means, Vuna acquired information about the domains and rule of the king of Spain, while the Spaniards learned about some aspects of local behaviour which puzzled them (2004: 458–9).

Communication and exchanges were furthered with some displays as, for example, when the crews of both ships were ordered to go ashore to practise some 'evoluciones militares' ('military drills') while the Spaniards undertook some astronomical observations. Vuna and his men were pleased to see the show, responding by gifting two pigs and with an invitation to honour the Spaniards 'with some entertainments which were to be better organized'. Before these ceremonies started, the Spaniards put on a display with their weapons, first marching and then firing some volleys in different directions. The islanders reciprocated by playing instruments, which Malaspina described as a hollow stick and 'split canes and the bass drums', while a choir of thirty-two men sung. At the same time, other men staged a battle, followed by some more dancers who performed with such skill that their movements inspired Malaspina to compare them to 'a vivid representation of the Golden Age', an analogy which became staple in many contemporary descriptions of Pacific life.

A similar association with a paradisiacal form of life is apparent in Malaspina's description of women's dances. Following some jigs by local men, the women performed in a circle, led by Vuna's sister, Tupou, and were praised by Malaspina for their 'determination, modesty and beauty of countenance'. Malaspina compared the atmosphere created with a classical Golden Age, with the scene suggestive to him of the temples of 'Cnidus and Amathus'. The endorsement of myths attached to the Pacific islands during the Enlightenment embedded in Malaspina's words was furthered when he rhapsodised about nature partaking of the 'delightful' spectacle thus: 'Everything spoke of pleasure; not only the spectators but nature itself seemed to take part in this delightful scene' (2004: 128–9).

The participation in, and interpretation of, local customs was complemented by the task of collecting information in the form of the charts made by Felipe Bauzá, and the specimens gathered by Tadeo Haenke for the 'Real Gabinete'. These chores were accompanied by the recurrent thefts, such as that of a chisel, for which one man received 'a hundred lashes, which were given by some of the chiefs sent by Vuna', and had his head shaved, a punishment inflicted, in Malaspina's words, after those used by the English, 'in imitation of Captain Clerke' (2004: 132).

To further the gathering of data about the islands, Malaspina sent an expedition to Leyaf'u, led by José Bustamante, and he included Bustamante's report of this journey within his own account.[12] Vuna, his father, four of his wives and Feileua accompanied the Spanish men on the expedition, which succeeded in its aims, recording, among other things, the environment and the construction of a sacred house, *Fale Otua*, the function of which was partly explained by Vuna, while Brambila sketched the building.[13]

On this excursion, the Spanish went to the house of 'la respetable Tubou',[14] who was held in high esteem by all the islanders, including Vuna, and who seemed to hold a rank similar to his on account of being not only Paulajo's widow of but also the mother of Fatafegi and Taufa, who was Feileua's father (Bustamante 1793: 103v). Tupou's high standing was confirmed when Vuna paid homage to her. Bustamante's praise for this woman, and for her dignified manner in accepting presents and addressing the visitors, permeates the passages about their meeting, which concludes with the assessment of Tupou's behaviour as thought she was an 'enlightened' European, affirming that it 'would be remarkable even if presumed to be the result of an enlightened education in the very heart of Europe' (Malaspina 2004: 141). Such recurrent association of features, as well as personages, in terms of an Enlightened Europe cast the islanders in a civilised light in the evolutionary scale of the time.

During this excursion, Bustamante's party also visited the tomb of Paulajo, the description of which affords a glimpse into burial practices and the islanders' respect for the dead. There, they noticed trees of 'two species, planted neatly and symmetrically ... used by the natives as a symbol of grief' (Malaspina 2004: 138). The trees were compared to the European cypress, following Michel Foucault's paradigm of resemblance prominent in earlier voyages, which shows that, in spite of the higher degree of complexity in enlightened descriptions, it is often difficult to trace a clear dividing line between the epistemological parameters of different times.

After this visit, the explorers went to Vuna's house, where they were offered kava in order of rank, with Bustamante rejecting the offer. The islanders went to the house with a bunch of coconuts each, which Vuna gave to Bustamante besides bestowing other gifts on the visitors. The Spaniards then visited other parts of the island, walking inland, led by Vuna along a path surrounded by lavish vegetation which, to Bustamante, appeared to be beautiful plantations and fruit trees, again evocative of a Golden Age and reminiscent of the paradisiacal landscape which associated the island with a Garden of Eden.

The Spanish could not, however, gain any further information about the islanders' religious beliefs, as grief seemed to plunge the chiefs, Vuna and Tagacala, into a state of lethargy. This show of feeling moved the visitors so deeply that it led Bustamante to wax lyrical about how the mood of these men fitted in well with their environment: 'The solitude of the place, the devout silence of the natives and the soft rustling of the sombre trees rocking in the wind, inspired deep thoughts and melancholy contemplation' (Malaspina 2004: 138). After visiting the cemetery of the *Eiguis*, the Spaniards departed, calling on their way at another settlement, Loutunaque, to the south of Vava'u, where they were met by the chief, Tuenuculaba with a gift of coconuts (Bustamante 1793: 106).[15]

Following Bustamante's return, Malaspina informed Vuna of their decision to leave the island and, after his first reaction of sorrow, Vuna seemed to be especially concerned with increasing the number of gifts and exchanges: 'the more urgent preoccupation of trading as much as possible, as well as the chance of receiving more presents'. Consequently, people were sent to the various villages, requesting foodstuffs to trade and the Spaniards agreed to set fixed prices in order to facilitate and speed up the barter, determining, for example, that 'the price of an axe was to be one large hog and one piglet'. With these arrangements in place, many successful exchanges soon started to take place (Malaspina 2004: 143).

Vuna let the explorers know that if their decision to depart was based on the thefts suffered he would ensure nothing more untoward happened. Many young women watched the preparations for departure, although, according to Malaspina, their cares swayed between the gifts that they craved for and their feelings: 'between the desire for presents, regrets at our departure, the disappointed hopes of lovers, and good-natured taunts which were directed at me'. They directed their criticism to Malaspina as 'the author of their present sufferings' (2004: 143).

To attest to their presence on the island, the Spaniards buried a bottle with a paper which claimed possession of the archipelago in the name of the king of Spain with, Malaspina wrote, 'the consent of Vuna'. Following such approval, the act of burial was ceremoniously carried out, with flags raised and the customary salutations to the king, which were echoed by 'the natives on board the *Descubierta*, following Vuna's example' (2004: 143).[16]

Leading towards the conclusion of his stay on these islands, Malaspina summed up the friendly relationships established with the islanders, emphasising how both parties were well disposed towards one another. Growing philosophical, Malaspina inferred that such attitude arose from the social 'instinct' that unites human beings across racial or cultural divides: 'that social instinct which draws us, without any specific reason, to our fellow men, and invites us to lighten the burdens of each other's lives'. Malaspina added that the most normal of those 'inclinaciones' is the mutual attraction between the sexes, accounting for some of the concerns and displays of affection between the local women and the men from his crew.

While this was happening, the exchanges continued and the Spaniards obtained an 'astonishing quantity of fruit and roots'. Even on the last day on the island, bartering took place from early on, and Vuna added a second pig to the one from the previous day. The chiefs repeated the word *ofa* to indicate their grief, showing sincere sadness, and frequently unable to contain their tears, embracing the Spaniards closely. On this occasion, Vuna also brought his wife with him and Ravenet made a portrait of her, while the rest of the officers talked to Vuna, hoping to be able to 'manifest' with greater certainty the 'character of the island' in their descriptions. The Spaniards promised Vuna that they would return with their wives, which pleased him, and Vuna's wife insisted that the Spanish women would be welcomed with due hospitality, and that no jealousy would arise (2004: 145; 1984: 463–4).

Lastly, the Spaniards left seeds of produce, including pumpkins, potatoes and melons, and gave Paulajo's daughter two kittens, to which she showed 'great care'. They all dined together, joined by a woman, described by Malaspina as 'decrepit', and whose status he found hard to ascertain. Short of items to offer, the Spaniards gave her an empty bottle, which she appreciated. Finally, to repay the services provided, the Spaniards presented the last items to Feileua and Latu, consisting of 'an axe, a length of baize cloth, some knives and some women's ornaments'. When they parted company, they saw that 'the women had hoisted a piece of canvas' in Vuna's house, as sign of 'farewell when their voices could no longer reach us' (2004: 146).

When the Spaniards made the final preparations to depart for El Callao at dawn, they said goodbye to their acquaintances on board where bartering took the centre stage. Also, as throughout the stay, both Spanish and islanders showed reciprocal signs of true affection and warmth, which were enhanced, created and ratified by the commerce taking place. The last of these eighteenth-century voyages and of all the journeys studied in this book could not provide a more fitting coda with which to conclude their stay on the islands of the South Pacific. Displaying the impossibility of separating emotional from material exchanges, Malaspina's journey epitomises and sums up the model of cultural encounters taking place on the islands of the Pacific, emphasising the essential role played by gifts and bartering in cementing human relations.

NOTES

1 Bernard Smith explains the contradictions within which the journey operated: 'One of the most important voyages modelled on those of Cook was the Spanish one under the command of Alejandro Malaspina, which set out from Cadiz in 1789. Despite their excellent work of collecting and describing, completed on the voyage itself, those on the expedition came home to Spain to confront a social and political situation highly unfavourable to the encouragement of the arts and sciences. The momentum of the French Revolution, with all its attendant excesses, threatened the values upon which the dynamics of Enlightenment science were based' (1992: 47).
2 According to Andrew David, 'the aim of the expedition was to produce hydrographical charts for the most remote parts of the Americas and to investigate the political state of Spanish possessions with regard to Spain and foreign countries and to record their trade, natural resources and defence, rather than discovering new lands' (1999: 3). David offers a thorough summary of the journey in this article, which was written while the Hakluyt edition of this voyage was being produced.
3 María Dolores Higueras grouped the materials related to this journey, cataloguing them in three volumes and also edited Malaspina's own journal (1985). Quotations from Malaspina's journal in this section are mostly taken from the translation and edition from the Hakluyt Society (2004). The Spanish version of Malaspina's journey used in this section is that of Mercedes Palau, Aránzazu Zabala and Blanca Sáez (1984).

4 This section takes up chapter 2 of volume 3 of the Hakluyt edition, and is entitled 'At Vava'u' (2004: 101–46).
5 The Hakluyt edition renders 'eixe' or 'eije' as '*eiki*, which translates roughly from Tongan as 'chief' or 'member of the aristocracy'. They are unable, however, to identify 'Tupou', as it seems to have been a common name, further noting that Tongans usually change their names several times during their lives (2004: 101 n. 1). All the notes for this section of the Hakluyt edition were provided by Phyllis Herda.
6 According to Herda's annotations for the Hakluyt edition, Tumoala must have been a lesser chief (Malaspina 2004: 103 n. 3).
7 Although Malaspina believed that to be the case, he was obviously simplifying a pattern of complex attitudes, as Cook's own restraint demonstrates.
8 On this chief's confusing identification, see Herda (1983: 217–24).
9 The Hakluyt translator amends 'stupid' for 'astonished', which is probably more in line with contemporary sensibilities.
10 This position is very much reminiscent of Albert Durer's 'Draughtsman doing Perspective of a Reclining Woman'. The division of subject and object and its implications are looked at by Rose (1992: 93–101) and Camino (1999: 111–12).
11 According to the Hakluyt edition, these included 'lashings, public whippings, musket fire and head shaving so as to mark the offender'. However, they went on to add that none of these methods 'proved effective' (Malaspina 2004: 125 n. 2).
12 Two different versions of Bustamante's account are kept at the Museo Naval. I use here the shorter one, while the longer has been edited by Higueras (Bustamante 1999). References to this report are to the Hakluyt's and my own translations of the brief manuscript.
13 Literally, *Fale 'Otua* means 'house of God'.
14 The Hakluyt edition uses Tupou, which reflects more accurately the phonology of a language with no voiced phonemes and which I have adopted here.
15 The settlement has not been located (Malaspina 2004: 141 n. 3).
16 According to the Hakluyt edition, the 'seven cheers' given by the Spaniards to their king were answered by 'the natives, led by their chief, Vuna, [who] repeated as many times "Vava'u foxa España", meaning "Vava'u is a child of Spain"' (2004: 143).

5 Viewing the Pacific

> Voyaging will always involve intrusion and injustice as well as gift giving and new knowledge. It will always foster stereotypes and misrepresentations as well as deeper appreciations of other people's stories and situations.
> (Thomas 1997: 230)

As seen in the narratives studied in this book, cross-cultural exchanges between Spanish explorers and Pacific peoples were never fully reciprocal, even though the outcome was influenced by both parties. Weapons and tools, as well as the interpretations of events, contributed to the creation of hegemonic relationships that, by and large, presupposed European supremacy. Although the voyagers may not have relied at all times on a favourable balance of power, all the visitors, including Máximo Rodríguez, took for granted the cultural superiority of Europeans. This, perhaps, was so even when the Spanish depended heavily on the Pacific islanders not only for food and material well-being but also for geographical and local knowledge.

European explorers routinely classified the indigenous peoples encountered, placing them variously along a scale, from barbarism to civilisation, as determined by occidental epistemology or religion. As a direct consequence, the accounts of the voyages often reveal more information about the producers, and other European travellers, than about the indigenous peoples of Oceania. While those early accounts of Pacific exploration provide insights into the lives and environment of the people inhabiting the area, these reports pre-eminently offer the scholar the opportunity to explore the worldview and thought processes of the explorers themselves, as shown throughout this book.

The relationship between Oceanic peoples and Europeans, which has been traced in this book, is eloquently summed up by the interesting coastal profiles that were produced during some of the voyages. While these views may be thought of as scientific and artistic products, they also provide social data that complement the accounts. Indeed, these views afford a suitable conclusion to this book, bringing together the various aspects investigated and some of the paradoxes outlined at the outset. For, on the one hand, the views could be seen to represent something in an artistic, disinterested or objective manner while, on the other hand, they fit within the paradigm of domination and appropriation obtaining in the colonial enterprise.

The coastal, panoramic or perspective profiles produced during these voyages follow a pattern that was inaugurated in the fifteenth century, which went on to influence charts and maps thereafter. With regard to the earlier voyages studied here, only four views of the Pacific, which were drafted by Diego de Prado y Tovar during Quirós's voyage to Vanuatu (1606), remain extant. By contrast with this scarcity, during the eighteenth-century Spanish voyages, many views were produced of Easter Island, Tahiti and other islands of the Pacific which, in style and content, are very much in line with those produced on the journeys of James Cook and others at this time.

Like journals and dispatches, bird's-eye views allow us to investigate the worldview of the explorers in that they engage in a dialogue not so much with the people whose land was being represented as with the local audiences in Spain or other European countries. These views characterise and symbolise an alien landscape for the people back home who acted as beholders of the representational hierarchy between observer and observed that these views embed. Nonetheless, in spite of this obvious exercise of power, the views also provide some relevant information about the contradictions inherent in the processes of mapping, as well as understanding or assimilating other lands and peoples.[1]

In this context, it is interesting to stress the obvious fact that the views foreground the foreshore and the beach, the paradigmatic sites of arrival and, as seen throughout this book, of material and cultural exchanges, including barter and gift-giving.[2] Indeed, the important role of the beach as the liminal environment in which two alien cultures meet has been highlighted by the 'beachcombers' mentioned throughout this book: the sailors who wished to 'jump ship' in order to join those cultures encountered.[3] From the sixteenth century onwards, references to these men underscore the readiness of some people to abandon their civilisation, wanting to explore, live and share in the lives and customs of others. In this sense, beachcombers exemplify the cross-cultural dimension that I have sought to illuminate, offering a clear example of the willingness to cross the divide separating Europeans from others. It goes without saying that a similar feeling towards embracing or creating a new culture was shared by other fellow travellers, as, for example, the settler men and women who accompanied Mendaña to the Santa Cruz Islands in 1595. It is, in this context, tragically suitable for the men and women who were lost in the *Almiranta* to have met their final destiny in the beaches of Pamua, leaving some pottery shards to remind later travellers of their passing (Greene and Allen 1972).

As sites of encounter, beaches and, by inference, their representation in coastal profiles, have been of vital significance to the colonial project.[4] Beaches are central in coastal views, which follow both artistic and strategic precepts already in use from the fifteenth century. Although to us these views may appear to be merely illustrative, they also had clear political uses. The military and tactical deployment of charts and coastal views did not escape the attention of European powers either in the sixteenth or in the eighteenth centuries. For example, on the occasion of one stopover in Brazil, Cook was suspected of taking sights of the harbour's dimensions and defences. The suspicions of the Portuguese colonial authorities were not without foundation, for it had been a long-standing practice for potential attackers to view and chart the coast and its fortifications with a view to future raids.[5]

Tracing the history of coastal views and their use, Rüdiger Joppien and Bernard Smith remark that these were an inherent part of Europe's mapping enterprise from the 1400s and 1500s. Initially, although Gabriel de Vallsecha included some views of important Mediterranean towns in 1447 their widespread use, especially as navigational tools, was a later development, and one which started to take shape from the 1520s onwards, becoming 'a regular feature on printed charts following the publication in 1584 of Lucas Janszoon Waghenaer's *Spieghel der Zeevaerdt*' (Joppien and Smith 1985–88: xxxviii). Views were used during Elizabethan times, and they were certainly important on Francis Drake's voyages.[6]

Other than their strategic value, coastal views often present ideal scenery, which is obviously achieved by disregarding the real lives of the local people and their means of production. Indeed, it is also hard to find one view which shows indigenous habitation, farming or gardening, although references to those activities may appear in the legend. The views offer a vision of a peaceful, hospitable and friendly environment, which is one of nature dominated, as it presupposes the control of the landscape by its inhabitants. In this, it may be said that coastal views do not simply represent or misrepresent the place portrayed but that they create it for the benefit of the viewer. Moreover, the process of constructing these views is very much one of distance and of detached observation, which privileges the eye of the observer, whose imagination, as Ken Hillis has eloquently illustrated, is 'disembodied' (1984). The drawing in itself creates a sort of panopticon where one can look at others without, however, being observed – a feeling which is transferred to the person holding the view.

Like maps, coastal bird's-eye views have descriptive and political functions, the history of which is linked to European military and imperial design.[7] As geographic or ethnographic sketches, these views can be considered part and parcel of colonial discourses in that the land and its inhabitants are assimilated into the empire by means of representation.[8] Coastal views form part of the inscription of alien lands and peoples into a system of representation that conforms to Michel de Certeau's appraisal of history as 'writing that conquers' (1988: xxv). Like the narratives of voyages quoted throughout this book, bird's-eye views endorse Certeau's idea that inscription can effectively reify the effects of arrival as conquest. Most of the views are either plans or bird's-eye views, which use a rising background of 30° to 90° to suggest visual apprehension and, by implication, possession.[9] This is the case of the four sixteenth-century views of Diego de Prado y Tovar, where the beach and coastal profile are vital features, as may be seen in the view of Santo's 'La Gran Baya de S^n Philippe y S^n Santiago' ('Big Bay of Saint Philip and Santiago') (Figure 5.1). In its simplicity, this view, like the remaining three from Quirós's voyage, stresses the emptiness of the land, as well as its lushness. In fact, these views reify an invitation to the viewer to partake in the containment and possession of land and sea, remarking on the absence of human habitation and thus inferring a sense of availability, which the actual explorers could not corroborate.

From the eighteenth-century voyages, one of the plan views of Tahiti, Juan Hervé's 'Plano de Ysla de Amat llamada por sus naturales Otajeti' (Figure 5.2), illustrates these points. Like Prado's, this view offers a 90° perspective of the island of Tahiti, which, unlike Prado's view of Santo, deploys writing to construe its content. The view displays in broad characters on the top a composite title that reflects the hierarchical syncretism underlying this voyage and contains information graded 'downwards' both in terms of the writing and of the importance of what it stands for.

First and foremost, this view of Tahiti presents in large font the given, imperial name of Amat in honour of the Viceroy under whose auspices the enterprise was launched, and after whom the island was christened.

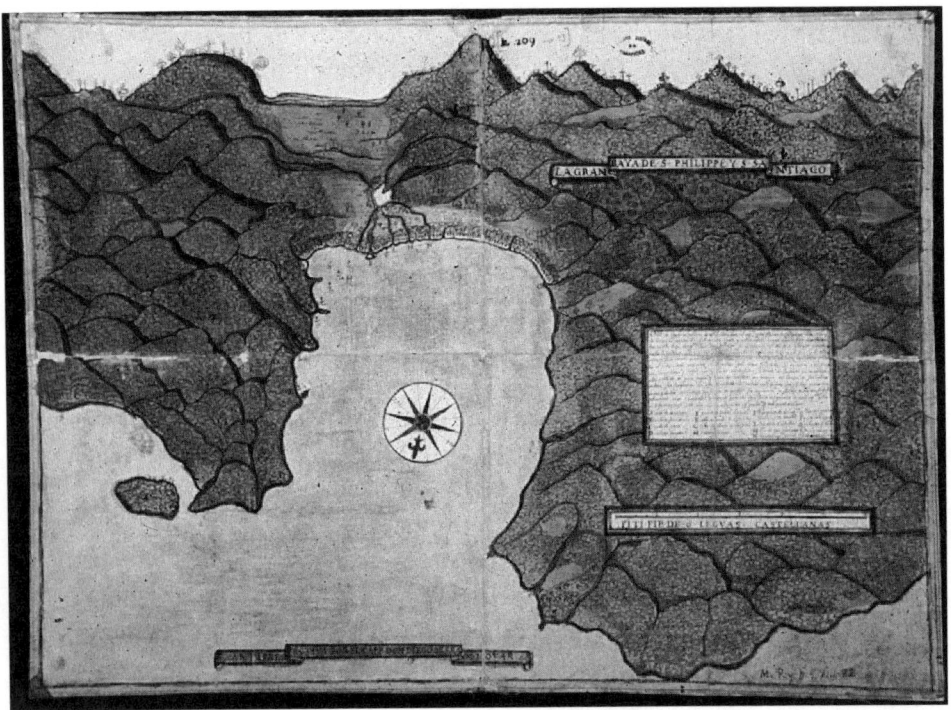

5.1 Diego de Prado y Tovar, 'Baya de Sn Phelippe y Santiago' (1606). This view from Quirós's voyage represents Big Bay in Vanuatu's Santo.

Thus, the Viceroy is the most important figure in this context, coming even before the king, who is recognised in smaller writing as having given orders for the voyage: 'Reconocida de Orden de S. M.'. Next, in line of priority, comes the captain of the fleet and the name of his ship, with the date of the journey, 'Don Domingo de Boenechea, Capitan de Fragata de la Armada y Comandante de la nombrada Aguila, 1772' ('Don Domingo de Boenechea, Captain of Army's Frigate and Commander of the said Aguila, 1772'). This script, like the legend illustrating the main geographical and strategic points of the island, is placed at the right-hand corner, fitted within the gulf that splits Tahitian land into Tahiti-iti and Tahiti-nui. The location of this text in a partially opened scroll, which is in the process of being unfolded, dynamically invites the viewer to partake in a process of discovering the land and unveiling its secrets.

Although produced nearly two hundred years apart, these coastal views use the post-Renaissance paradigm of the individual viewer located in the position of the eye of God. In both cases, the raised point of view is

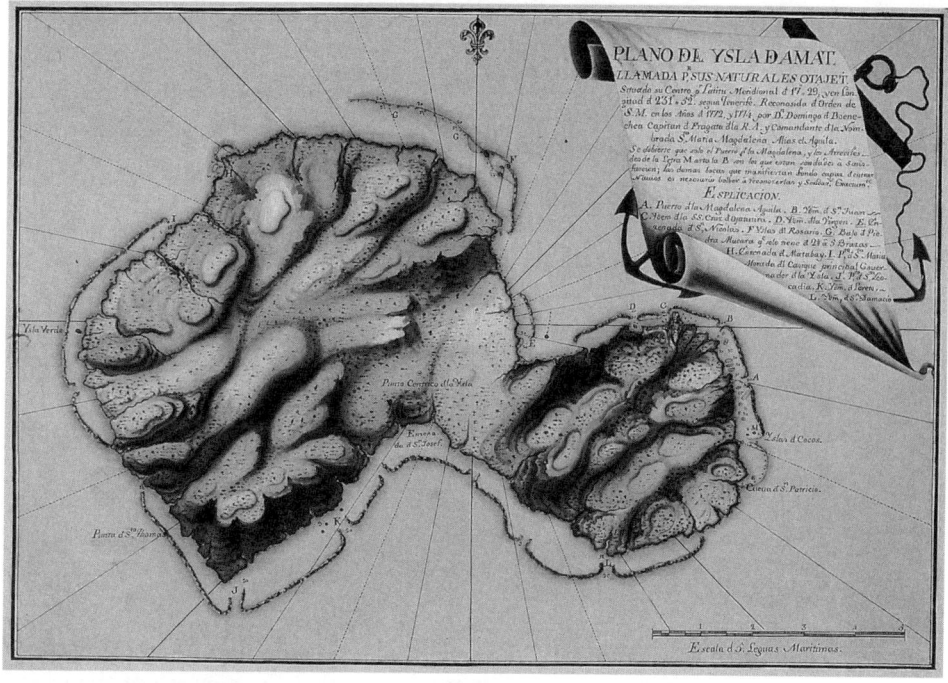

5.2 Juan Hervé, 'Plano de Ysla de Amat llamada por sus naturales Otajeti' (1772). Hervé's view acknowledges the indigenous name of the island.

the most convenient position for empowering vision, implying that all inhabitants may be perceived as anonymous beings, with their trajectories clearly visible to the viewer.[10] Elevated views give the impression that observers may be able to stand in the position traditionally occupied by God and thus participate in the apprehension of humans as individuals located at the centre of the universe, and in the bolstering of individualism associated with perspective viewing. This arises from the fact that the point from which such a perspective is drawn is associated with that of an individual artist or viewer. Consequently, the most immediate suggestion conveyed by these particular views is that everybody on the island would be part of the view's design and within the field of vision, and that their movements and settlements could be measured, controlled and even predetermined.

Elevated bird's-eye views, therefore, render the viewer as an observer who is implicated in a fantasy of appropriation. In spite of the references that record indigenous names and habitation, eighteenth-century views, like their forerunners, present the islands as targets for appropriation and as spaces that seem to be largely uninhabited or uncivilised. The views certainly fail to transmit visually the level of settlement and cultivation of the islands, which curiously contrasts with the emphasis on their overpopulation exposed in many journals. The significant deletion of obvious signs of human habitation or civilisation in these views helps to render them effectively ready for occupation or settlement. A relation of dominance is, therefore, embedded in their production, which is very much in line with that conveyed by maps of colonial or proto-colonial territories, as explained by Brian Harley (1988).[11] The apparent emptiness of the landscape, as Harley observes, is an idiosyncrasy of colonial maps that encourage viewers to make their mark on the blank spaces before them.

Prado's and Hervé's views thus offer the observer an implicit acknowledgment of the fact that designation can be equated with appropriation. In this sense, the naming of the islands on the maps is also an act of possession.[12] However, whereas Prado's only represents the Spanish name given to the bay, in Hervé's view this is followed by the native Otajeti for O Tahiti, which serves to acknowledge indigenous presence, even if it is given a subordinate place.[13] Paradoxically, the fact that the local name is given as a prominent alternative recognises that the naming of the island as Isla de Amat can be perceived as a rather meaningless ritual. This is especially apparent because, like the explorers, we know that the island had already been named St George or King George by Samuel Wallis in 1766 and would be named Nouvelle Cythère by Louis de Bougainville a few months later.[14] In fact, in this case, naming is used in conformity with the well-worn Christian and proto-imperial tradition that previous travels had accustomed us to, but that, in this instance, is already perceived as transitory and of fleeting significance.

The title given by the Spaniards to Vanuatu's Big Bay, and the names appearing on the Tahitian view, largely follow the religious criteria that became the hallmark of Spanish nomenclature. However, Hervé's view also acknowledges the presence of Tahitians and the mark that they made on the land in a reference to the harbour where their main chief lives, 'Puerto de Sta María donde vive el Cacique principal' (H), as well as the name Matavai in the 'Ensenada de Matabay' (G). This harbour is one of the only places where the indigenous name has remained, which is also detailed in a separate view, the 'Plano de Enzenada de Matabay' (Figure 5.3). Again, as with the naming of the island, native inhabitation is noted, even though it is given a less important role than the arrival of European powers. Nevertheless, such recognition very much contrasts with the

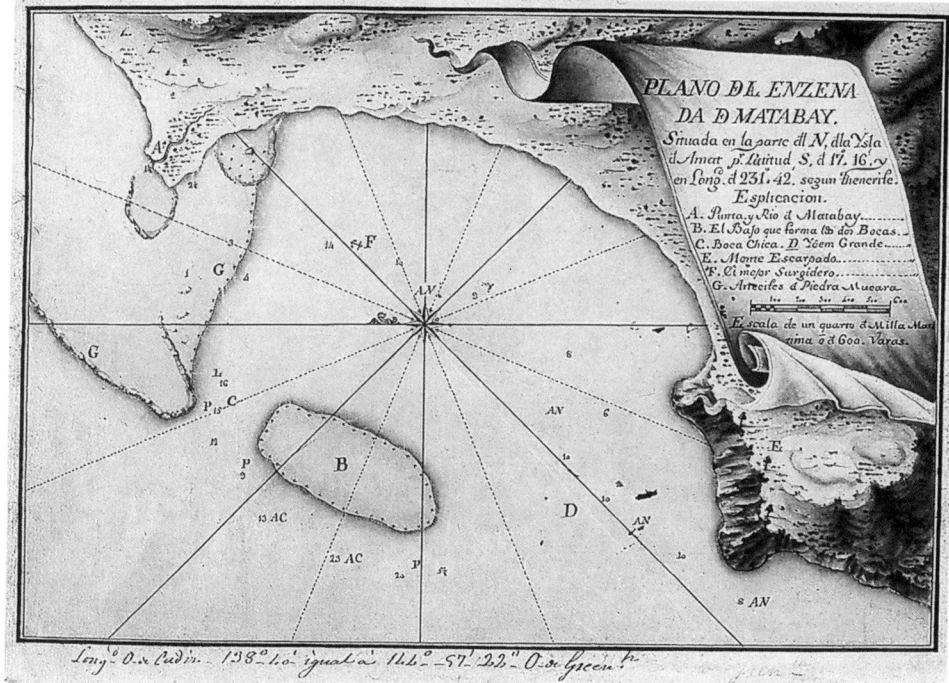

5.3 Juan Hervé, 'Plano de Enzenada de Matabay' (1772). Matabay is one of the few indigenous names used by the explorers.

bareness of colonial North American maps or of the *terra nullius* that was Australia.

While Prado's views do not indicate human presence on the island, they were complemented and matched in number by four drawings of indigenous peoples in various guises. Immaculately preserved, these are the earliest representations of South Pacific people from Vanuatu and coastal New Guinea. In a rudimentary fashion, these drawings offer a sketch of life on the islands, which foregrounds the islanders' dress, implements and weapons (Figure 5.4).[15] As with the journals and the views, the representation of the Pacific islanders given by Prado in the drawings is one filtered and graded by the explorers' way of seeing and classifying the world. Thus, weaponry, dressing, physical characteristics and, above all, colour are emphasised, very much as happened in the journals studied in this book.

The zeal for representing, baptising and naming displayed in the views and the drawings corroborate the dimensions of cross-cultural

5.4 The people of Big Bay are described as 'black... with ordinary bodies', wearing loincloths made from leaves to cover their 'shameful parts'.

engagements studied throughout this book. Like the itineraries traced in some narratives, the scenes presented are encompassed by the individual point of view from which they are drawn, and which is shared by the observer. This is precisely the notion of superior European civilisation that was largely extended to the appreciation of local knowledge from the early to the later voyages. Even if the eighteenth century witnessed an increasing curiosity to observe other cultures and to represent them in a detached, objective manner, as happened in the earlier voyages, many Europeans did not consider they could be taught much from their hosts, especially in terms of religious beliefs or scientific lore. Europeans were often more concerned about what they could learn about themselves by looking at others than about the indigenous populations encountered.

In the case of Tahiti, as on islands visited before, the islanders displayed a remarkable interest in observing and interpreting others, while those islanders who travelled overseas quickly adapted to the local cultures, making every effort not to offend their guests. They showed in these voyages to Europe and to South America that they could be worldly wise, adopting the customs of their hosts, while showing respect for them. In fact, Pacific islanders such as Puhoro, Pautu, Tetuanui, Omai or Ahutoru exhibited a considerable level of curiosity for the societies that they were visiting and proved to be quite capable of incorporating foreign knowledge into their way of thinking. This often contrasted with those Europeans who were wholly reliant on the assumed pre-eminence of their interpretation of phenomena.

Some comments on the acumen of the indigenous people from the journal of Juan Pantoja from the second Spanish voyage to Tahiti in 1774–75 corroborate the notions remarked on, and serve to bring this book to a close. After noting that the Tahitians had agreed to give land to the Spaniards in order to allow for the construction of the 'mission', Pantoja commented on their motivation. In doing so, Pantoja admitted that the Tahitians had sound reasoning comparable to that of Europeans and their system of beliefs, contesting the assumption that those who did not share that system were 'barbarians' or inferior in the scale of civilisation: 'I do not think that they ought to be called barbarians in everything just because they do not love our religion, because their mode of thinking and pondering is very different from the concept that we had made of them' (1992: 143).[16]

The Tahitians, Pantoja admitted, had embraced difference, thereby contesting some assumptions made about them. For Pantoja, therefore, the Tahitian mode of thinking and reasoning, even if alien, could be as valid as that of Europeans, a fact corroborated by his own recognition of local knowledge when writing about the role of Pautu as pilot, as mentioned above. Like the bird's-eye views looked at in this chapter, Pantoja's words substantiate some of the paradoxes inherent in the cross-cultural engagements. And, like some other explorers from the voyages studied in this book, Pantoja was willing and able to perceive some degree of cultural relativism. It is precisely instances such as this that make many occasions in these journeys unique and illuminating episodes of human communication, which recognise that there are always, to borrow James Boon's construction, 'other tribes' and 'other scribes'.

The Spanish-Oceanic cross-cultural exchanges arising from these voyages often created hegemonic relationships that assumed European superiority, even while the explorers depended on the locals for food and information. However, as Anne Salmond remarks: 'these expeditions were collaborative accomplishments, to which men like Tupaia and Puhoro and their knowledge systems made significant contributions' (2005: 183). As seen in the bird's-eye views and drawings of Vanuatu and Tahiti reproduced here, the acknowledgment and, at the same time, the relegation of indigenous lore reveal contradictions inherent in the European approach to other lands and peoples. These cultural products stand as exemplary witnesses of the paradoxes of belonging and not belonging that some voyagers adopted and which became the hallmark of Creolisation and colonial settlement.

The letters, dispatches, journals, drawings and views that substantiate this study allow us to explore the worldviews of those who travelled the Pacific Ocean, affording a glimpse into the environment and the peoples encountered. More importantly, the cross-cultural engagements in which these voyagers participated point toward mutual recognition and acceptance as modes of being in a world made up of multiple differences. These voyagers, following the steps of a Christopher Columbus or a Bartolomé de Las Casas, encompass all the paradoxes already signposted by the famous discoverer and missionary: zeal for conversion, zest for freedom and, above all, the wish to find, recreate or invent a paradise on earth.[17]

NOTES

1 'Although the art of drawing was itself a kind of assertion of European power, a pre-emptive acquisition of knowledge for the future, including future action, it could not be asserted, as other modes of power were, simply by the use of physical force' (Smith 1992: 93–4).
2 John Pocock suggests that: 'the beach ... is the *locus classicus* of encounter with the Other: the human culture for which one has no interpretative paradigm; and here clearly is a point at which the stereotype of the savage can reassert itself' (2000: 40).
3 Some important studies, including Greg Dening's *Islands and Beaches*, highlight the role of 'beachcombers', who Dening defines as 'those who crossed beaches alone. They crossed the beach without the supports that made their own world real into other worlds that were well-established and self-sufficient ... They left behind them the roles that made their world orderly and its gestures meaningful ... Whatever they did on the beach, they had to carve out a new world for themselves' (1980: 129).
4 'The coast', Paul Carter posits, 'not only harboured harbours, the longed-for object of every colonizing expedition, it paraded a variety of geographical objects ... A coast was a generalization, an abstraction ... it was a condition of knowledge, an analogue of the associative reasoning essential to the orderly progress of reason (and the legitimation of colonialism as the project of bringing formerly isolated peoples into contact with the West – or putting them on the map)' (1999: 125).

5 'From 13 November to 7 December 1769 the *Endeavour* was anchored in Rio harbour taking on provisions. Despite Cook's protestations that he was engaged upon a voyage of a purely scientific nature, the Portuguese viceroy in Rio did not trust him. Had he been able to see Buchan and Parkinson making their drawings of the harbour... and Cook's comments upon the weaknesses of the harbour's fortifications, he would have felt justified in his distrust' (Smith 1992: 54).

6 'Elizabethan seamen certainly appreciated the value of coastal views. An unknown artist on board the *Defiance* during Drake's last voyage (1595–96) drew some very elegant coastal views, which compare favourably with similar views drawn on Cook's first voyage'. The importance of bird's-eye views, these writers go on to show, was demonstrated in the following centuries: 'An early advocate of coastal views was the Royal Society... The importance of coastal views was further emphasised by the inclusion of a drawing master on the staff of the Royal Naval Academy on its opening in 1733 to provide education and training for future naval officers' (Joppien and Smith 1985–8: xxxviii).

7 As Neil Smith and Cindi Katz observe, colonisation 'is predicated on the deliberate, physical, cultural and symbolic appropriation of space' (1993: 70).

8 'Everything in the European dream of possession rests on witnessing, a witnessing understood as a form of significant and representative seeing. To see is to secure the truth of what might otherwise be deemed incredible' (Greenblatt 1991: 122).

9 Although the line between them is often difficult to trace, views can be classed following John Short's division as either 'prospect', 'plan', 'aerial', and 'bird's-eye view': 'In Renaissance times, cities were mapped using three types of view: 'prospect' view (from the side); 'plan' or 'aerial' view (from directly above); and 'bird's-eye views' (obliquely from above)' (2003: 120).

10 This point of view is, as Lucia Nuti has shown in relation to the views in the *Civitates orbis terrarum*, the more suitable position for empowering vision: 'the land was surveyed from an angle-shot of about 30 to 60 degrees... when the mapper reaches a 90 degree angle (the zenith), the eye will lose its power again' (1988: 547).

11 'Maps as an impersonal type of knowledge tend to "desocialise" the territory they represent. They foster the notion of a socially empty space. The abstract quality of the map... lessens the burden of conscience about people in the landscape. Decisions about the exercise of power are removed from the realm of immediate face-to-face contacts' (Harley 1988: 303).

12 As usual within the colonial enterprise, this naming is part and parcel of the process of appropriation. Tom Conley has observed that: 'Because the unknown was located by being *named*, it became a form of a relation rather than an unfathomable menace or delusion' (1996: 8).

13 In the views of the islands drafted by various artists voyaging with Cook, Tahiti is named King George's Island, while the indigenous names are the only ones recorded in the remaining islands (Joppien and Smith 1985–88).
14 Wallis was in command of the expedition to the South Pacific which left in August 1766 in which he was captain of the *Dolphin* and Lieutenant Philip Carteret of the *Swallow*. A few months later Louis Antoine de Bougainville sailed from France towards the Falklands and then the Pacific, in command of the ships *Boudeuse* and *Etoile*.
15 The transcription of the legend in the view of Santo's Big Bay runs as follows: 'This people are from the Bay of St Philip and St James, where the *Capitana* went. They are black and with ordinary bodies, and their weapons are arrows, darts and billy-clubs. The land is fertile and they cover their shameful parts with leaves from trees'.
16 Pantoja also wondered about the suitability of the term barbarian when he heard a 'mozo' ('lad') reason about warring tactics. He concluded that the lad in question was clever, although not the most intelligent among Tahitians: 'Would it be reasonable to call this lad a barbarian? And he is not even among the most skilful or learned' (1992: 162).
17 As John Elliott puts it, 'there existed another, and dissident Europe which had not yet exhausted the possibilities of the New World so unexpectedly revealed ... This was a Europe which rated freedom above authority, equality above hierarchy, and inquiry above acceptance. This other Europe would continue to turn, as it had turned in the days of the humanists, to America as a source of inspiration and hope. For if America nurtured Europe's ambitions, it also kept its dreams alive. And perhaps dreams were always more important than realities in the relationship of the Old World and the New' (1970: 104).

Appendix: notes on sources and English translations

ABBREVIATIONS

AGI	Archivo General de las Indias (Sevilla)
AGS	Archivo General de Simancas (Valladolid)
ATL	Alexander Turnbull Library (Wellington, New Zealand)
BC	Biblioteca Colombina (Sevilla)
BL	British Library (previously British Museum)
BN	Biblioteca Nacional (Madrid)
BP	Biblioteca de Palacio (Madrid)
BUS	Biblioteca Universitaria de Sevilla
ML	Mitchell Library (Sydney)
MNM	Museo Naval (Madrid)
RAH	Biblioteca de la Real Academia de la Historia (Madrid)
RGS	Royal Geographical Society (London)

TRANSLATIONS

Spanish names are normally written in Spanish, using contemporary diacritical marks. In those names, which have a widely-known English appellation, such as Ferdinand Magellan, the English version has been used. Some recognisable Spanish words have been kept in their original form and are italicised or in inverted commas when they are part of a quotation. Whenever necessary, their translation is given in brackets.

I have made use of some English translations, notably those of Celsus Kelly for Fray Martín de Munilla in the section on Quirós's journey and the Hakluyt Society's for Malaspina's journal. Bolton Corney's translations and insights have very much been taken into consideration too, although I have translated the original sources myself in the sections on to the voyages to Easter Island and Tahiti. Elsewhere, translations are also mine, while I have provided references to existing English translations whenever appropriate in the main text, in footnotes or in this Appendix.

Sources

The summaries that follow are rather concise, giving merely a rough outline of the sources used and of available contemporary editions or English translations. Celsus Kelly produced a *Calendar of Documents* (1965) which, with a handful of additions, contains the most detailed outline of the sources on these voyages to date. More recently, Amancio Landín (1992) has compiled a remarkable digest of Spanish journeys to the South Seas, also rehearsing possible itineraries. Other scholars to whom I am indebted are: Francisco Mellén Blanco for the eighteenth-century voyages to Easter Island and Tahiti and Bolton Corney for the journeys to Tahiti. The investigations of these four scholars have also been used for the itineraries of the journeys illustrating the relevant sections.

2.1 *Álvaro de Mendaña (1567)*

The main sources for this voyage are the accounts by Mendaña, the pilot Hernán Gallego, Sarmiento de Gamboa and the treasurer, Hernández de Catoira. There are two accounts by Mendaña, one longer, which is incomplete, and one shorter, the originals of which are held at the RAH and AGI, respectively. There are also two extant reports by Gallego, equally referred to as shorter ('breve') and longer ('extensa'), original copies of which are held at Casa Loyola and the AGI (with copies at BL, MNM and ATL). Also important is the journal of Sarmiento de Gamboa, held at the AGI, and the lengthiest and more detailed account by the treasurer, Hernández de Catoira, 'Relación del viaje y descubrimiento...', the original of which is held at the BL. Landín attributes an anonymous 'Relación' held by the AGS to Gallego.

Mendaña's shorter account, also known as 'Breve relación de Mendaña', was edited by Kelly in the second volume of *Austrialia Franciscana*, where Kelly also edited Catoira's (1965: 1–26 and 27–220, respectively). It was also printed by Justo Zaragoza in his *Historia del descubrimiento de las regions australes* (2000: 542–77). Mendaña's long and incomplete report is also reproduced by Kelly in volume three of the same multi-volume collection, *Austrialia Franciscana* (1967: 179–245). Gallego's two accounts also appear in volume three of *Austrialia Franciscana* (1967: 67–91 and 93–177, respectively). Sarmiento de Gamboa's was edited by Landín (1945: 215–33). Landín lists letters and other documents related to the journey (1992: 2. 552–5).

Catoira's difficult narrative was transcribed and then edited and translated by Lord Amherst of Hackney and Basil Thomson for the Hakluyt Society at the beginning of the twentieth century. Kelly, however, found this translation to be based on an imperfectly copied document, leading to a large number of errors and inconsistencies. These have been perpetuated by the widespread use of this edition as an accurate source of the voyage by important Pacific scholars, including John C. Beaglehole (Kelly 1967: xiv–xvi).

2.II *Álvaro de Mendaña (1595)*

The documents related to this journey, including Mendaña's last will and testament, are edited in the sixth volume of Kelly's monumental *Austrialia Franciscana* (1973). Much of the evidence related to this journey is set out in the questionnaires ('interrogaciones') made to the few survivors of the fleet. The only account of the voyage itself is that of the pilot, Pedro Fernandez de Quirós, who produced reports of the three early modern voyages to the South Pacific (1567, 1595 and 1605). Two manuscript copies of these narratives are kept in the PR with an additional copy in the MNM. Both were printed by Justo Zaragoza in 1876–82, an edition which was reprinted in a single volume with continuous pagination in 2000, and which is used above. The account of this particular journey appears in Zaragoza (2000: 115–308) and a contemporary paperback edition by Roberto Ferrando for *Historia 16* was published in 2000. It was translated and edited by Sir Clements Markham for the Hakluyt Society (1967 [1904]: 1. 3–148).

Quirós is attributed the brief 'Relación del viaje del adelantado Álvaro de Mendaña...' (1596), which was given to Antonio de Morga and was included in his famous *Sucesos de las Islas Filipinas* (Mexico, 1609). This volume has been edited several times, appearing also in Zaragoza (2000: 51–61). It was translated by Markham (1967 [1904]: 1. 149–57).

A comprehensive summary of the sources of this voyage is given by Landín (1992: 2. 599).

2.III *Pedro Fernández de Quirós (1606)*

Quirós's complete narrative of this journey, supposedly put to paper by his secretary Belmonte Bermúdez, appears in Zaragoza (2000: 309–469). Copies of his manuscript are held by the PR and MNM. Another important source for this voyage is the journal of Gaspar González de Leza, who was the second pilot of the *Capitana*, the original of which is at the BN. This account is also printed in Zaragoza (2000: 605–718). Also from this voyage is the remarkable report of the 'comisario', Fray Martin de Munilla, which is held at the AGI and was edited by Kelly in *Australia Franciscana* (1963: 19–106) and also translated by him in *Austrialia del Espíritu Santo* (1966: 1. 134–270).

Quirós's and Gaspar González de Leza's narratives, along with some shorter accounts, were translated and edited in two volumes by Sir Clements Markham for the Hakluyt Society (1967 [1904]: 2. 149–260 and 321–406, respectively).

Also related to this voyage is the 'Relacion sumaria' written by Diego de Prado y Tovar, the original of which is kept at the ML, and which was translated by G. F. Barwick and edited by H. N. Stevens (1930: 87–215). This volume also includes Torres' narrative of the voyage from Vanuatu to Manila across southern New Guinea (1930: 215–37). The original of this letter is kept at the AGS and was firstly translated into English by Alexander Dalrymple and printed by James Burney in the eighteenth century.

Juan de Iturbe wrote a brief account, the *Sumario breve*, which is held at the AGS and was translated by Kelly (1966: 2. 273–93).

Lastly, a summary of the journey appears in Fray Juan de Torquemada's *Monarquía indiana*, which was published in 1615 and was edited by Kelly (1963: 107–46).

5.I *González de Haedo (1770)*

Francisco Mellén Blanco has edited all the documents related to this journey, the most important of which are: Felipe González de Haedo, 'Extracto del Diario...' (1986: 222–6) and his 'Descripcion de la Isla de San Carlos...' (1986: 270–5), kept at the AGI and BP, respectively. Gonzalez's 'Extracto' was translated by Corney (1908: 35–52). Also used in this section are Juan Hervé's 'Derrota del Navío...', the original of which is held by the MNM and was translated by Corney (1908: 112–28), and the 'Relación diaria de lo más particular...' by Francisco Aguera e Infanzón, copies of which are held at the RAH, AGI, BL and which was also edited and translated by Corney (1908: 83–111).

5.II *Domingo de Boenechea (1771–72)*

The main sources of the first voyage to Tahiti led by Boenechea are the following: from Boenechea's hand, 'Relación de la navegación... (1773)', the original of which is kept at the AGI, with a copy at the RAH. It was printed in Spain in 1945–46 and translated by Corney (1914: 284–345). Attributed to Raimundo Bonacorsi is a manuscript entitled 'Viaje á la Ysla de Otayty...', held at the MNM and translated by Corney (1914: 29–63). Copies of Amich's journal are kept by the AGI and the RAH. It was first published in *El Viagero Universal* (1798) and reprinted by Izaguirre (1925), which is widely available in libraries and is the version used above. It is translated by Corney (1914: 65–89).

5.III *Domingo de Boenechea (1774–75)*

One of the most important sources for this voyage is the journal of the captain, Domingo de Boenechea, which was completed by Tomás Gayangos after his death. The original of this account, 'Diario de la navegación que... (1775)', is held at the AGI, with a manuscript copy at the RAH. It was printed by Barras y de Aragón (1945–46) and translated by Corney (1914: 103–99). Widely used above is the journal of the interpreter, Máximo Rodríguez, 'Relación diaria, que hizo el intérprete... (1774–76)', the original of which is in London's RGS and which has been edited in Spain by Mellén (1992). Of all the extant sources, the only one unavailable to Corney was that of Juan Pantoja y Arriaga, 'Extracto del viaje... (1775)', which is kept at the BUS, with a copy at the MNM. It has recently been edited again in Spain by Mellén (1992). The original of José Andía y Varela's journal, 'Relación del viaje ... (1774–75)', is kept at the AGI with three manuscript copies at the MNM, BNE and RAH. It was printed in Spain in 1947 and translated by Corney (1914: 221–317). The account kept by the padres, Gerónimo Clota and Narciso González, is kept at the RAH, and was published by Izaguirre (1925: 92–145). It is divided into two parts, the first of which is written by the padres with Andía y Varela, and the second by themselves (93–120 and 121–45). Corney edited and translated it (1914: 208–18 and 319–49). I refer to both as a single document. Copies of Amat's Questionnaire ('Interrogatorio') and the Dictionary are kept at the AGI and BC. Both were translated by Corney (1914: 1–28).

5.IV *Francisco Mourelle de la Rúa (1780–81)*

All the sources for this voyage are kept at the MNM and include Mourelle's 'Relación del viaje ...' and his 'Noticia de la navegación de la fragata "Princesa"...' Copies of both are held at the AGI. Also important for this journey is the journal kept by José Antonio Vázquez, 'Diario de la navegación ...' and his 'Extracto del diario de la navegación ...' which contains drawings and itineraries. Mourelle's journal and description were edited by Landín (1945), which is used above. For further information on sources on this voyage see Landín (1992: 3. 809–9).

5.V *Alejandro Malaspina (1789–94)*

The materials about Malaspina's journey are indeed extensive, making the selection process an impossible task had not María Dolores Higueras undertaken the challenging chore of making them accessible to scholars. Higueras has painstakingly catalogued and annotated these materials, which include voluminous correspondence, many hydrographical and astronomical works, over 1,500 drawings, charts and more three hundred journals and summaries of the voyage. The most important sources are the accounts of Alejandro Malaspina and José Bustamante, which have been used in the relevant section on this voyage. The originals of these journals, as of most documents relevant to this voyage, are held at the MNM. Also relevant are the journals of Felipe Bauzá, Ciriaco Cevallos, Antonio Pineda, Tadeo Haenke and Luis Née. For a summary of these sources, see Higueras (1985: 1. 22–7). The Spanish version of Malaspina's journey used is that edited by Mercedes Palau, Aránzazu Zabala and Blanca Sáez (1984); Bustamante's references are to the original manuscript, which has also been edited by Higueras (1999: 353–62). The Hakluyt Society has published a remarkable edition and translation of Malaspina's journal in three volumes (2000–3), which is liberally quoted above.

Bibliography

Adorno, Rolena (1991), 'The Negotiation of Fear in Cabeza de Vaca *Naufragios*', *Representations*, 33, 163–99.

Aguera Infanzón, Francisco (1908), 'Journal of the principal occurrences . . .' in Bolton Glanvill Corney (ed.), *The Voyage of Captain Don Felipe Gonzalez in the Ship of the Line San Lorenzo with the Frigate Santa Rosalia in Company, to Easter Island in 1770–71* (Cambridge: Hakluyt Society), 83–111.

Amat, Manuel de (1925), 'Instrucción dada por el Virrey Amat a los RR. PP. Predicadores Apostólicos Fray José Amich y fray Juan Bonamó destinados a la expedición que se va a hacer a la Isla de O'taeti . . . 1772', in Bernadino Izaguirre (ed.), *Historia de las misiones franciscanas y narración de los progresos de la geografía en el oriente del Perú* (3; Cajamarca: Tipografía San Antonio), 23–45.

Amherst of Hackney, Lord and Thomson, Basil (eds) (1901), *The Discovery of the Solomon Islands by Alvaro de Mendaña in 1568*, 2 vols (London: The Hakluyt Society (Second Series, Nos VII and VIII)).

Amherst of Hackney, Lord and Thomson, Basil (1901), 'Introduction', *The Discovery of the Solomon Islands by Alvaro de Mendaña in 1568* (London: The Hakluyt Society (Second Series, Nos VII and VIII)), i–lxxxiii.

Amich, Fray José (1925), 'Relación del viaje a la isla de Otaheti en la embarcación de guerra La Aguila, al comando del Capitán de Fragata Dn. Domingo Boenechea por el padre Fray José Amich, Diario de Gayangos y Amich and Descripción de la Isla de Otahiti por el Padre Amich', in Bernadino Izaguirre (ed.), *Historia de las misiones franciscanas y narración de los progresos de la geografía en el oriente del Perú* (3; Cajamarca: Tipografía San Antonio), 46–61, 63–77 and 77–91.

Andía y Varela, José (1947), *Relación del viaje. . . .* (Madrid: Joaquín Sarriera).

Badger, Geoffrey (1996), *The Explorers of the Pacific* (Kenthurst, NSW: Kangaroo Press).

Baert, Annie (*c.*1999), *Le Paradis terrestre, un mythe espagnol en Océanie: les voyages de Medaña et de Quirós, 1567–1606* (Préface de Christian Huetz de Lemps. Paris and Montreal: L'Harmattan).

Bakewell, Peter (1991), 'Spanish America: Empire and Its Outcome', in John H. Elliott (ed.), *The Hispanic World: Civilization and Empire: Europe and the Americas: Past and* Present, 65–84.
Beaglehole, J. C. (1966), *The Exploration of The Pacific* (3rd edn; London: Black).
Bellwood, Peter (1993), 'The Origins of Pacific Peoples', in Max Quanchi and Ron Adams (eds), *Culture Contact in the Pacific: Essays on Contact, Encounter and Response* (Cambridge, New York and Melbourne: Cambridge University Press), 2–14.
Berger, John (1972), *Ways of Seeing* (London: BBC and Penguin).
Bonacorsi, Raimundo (1772), 'Viaje a la isla de Otayty', 101–36.
Boon, James A. (1982), *Other Tribes, Other Scribes: Symbolic Anthropology in the Comparative Study of Cultures, Histories, Religions, and Texts* (Cambridge, UK; New York: Cambridge University Press).
Bourdieu, Pierre (1984), *Distinction: A Social Critique of the Judgement of Taste*, trans. Richard Nice (London, Melbourne and Henley: Routledge).
Bouzas, Pemón (2005), *El informe Manila* (Madrid: mr).
Bustamante, José (1793), 'Viaje a Leyafu', 103–6.
—— (1999), 'Viaje del comandante de la Atrevida a *El Sitio de Leyafu...*' in María Dolores Higueras Rodríguez (ed.), *Diario general del viaje* (La expedición Malaspina 1789–1794, 9; Barcelona: Lunwerg), 353–62.
Calder, Alex, Jonathan Lamb and Bridget Orr (eds) (1999), *Voyages and Beaches: Pacific Encounters, 1769–1840* (Honolulu: University of Hawai'i Press).
Callender, John (1766–68), *Terra Australis Cognita* (Edinburgh).
Cameron, Ian (pseud. Donald Gordon Payne) (1966), *Lodestone and Evening Star: The Epic Voyages of Discovery 1493 BC–1896 AD* (New York: Dutton).
Camino, Mercedes Maroto (1999), 'A Waxen World: Early Modern Women and Geographical (Un)Awareness', *Parergon*, 16 (2), 101–32.
—— (2005), *Producing the Pacific: Maps and Narratives of Spanish Exploration (1567–1606)* (Portada Hispanica, 18; Amsterdam and New York: Rodopi).
Carter, Paul (1999), 'Dark with Excess of Bright: Mapping the Coastlines of Knowledge', in Denis Cosgrove (ed.), *Mappings* (London: Reaktion), 125–47.
Catoira, Hernández de (1965), 'Relación del viaje y descubrimiento...1569', in Celsus O. F. M. Kelly (ed.), *Austrialia Franciscana* (2; Madrid: Franciscan Historial Studies and Archivo Iberoamericano), 27–220.
Certeau, Michel de (1977), *Culture in the Plural*, trans. Tom Conley (Minneapolis and London: University of Minnesota Press).
—— (1988), *The Writing of History*, trans. Tom Conley (New York: Columbia University Press).
Clifford, James (1986), 'On Ethnographic Allegory', in James and George E. Marcus Clifford (eds), *Writing Culture: The Poetics and Politics of Ethnography* (Berkeley, Los Angeles and London: University of California Press), 98–121.

—— (1988), *The Predicament of Culture: Twentieth-century Ethnography, Literature, and Art* (Cambridge, Mass. and London: Harvard University Press).
Clifford, James and George E. Marcus (eds) (1986), *Writing Culture: The Poetics and Politics of Ethnography* (Berkeley, Los Angeles and London: University of California Press).
Conley, Tom (1996), *The Self-Made Map: Cartographic Writing in Early Modern France* (Minneapolis: University of Minnesota Press).
Cook, James (2003), *The Journals* (London: Penguin).
Corney, Bolton Glanvill (1908), *The Voyage of Captain Don Felipe Gonzalez in the Ship of the Line San Lorenzo with the Frigate Santa Rosalia in Company, to Easter Island in 1770–71* (Cambridge: Hakluyt Society).
—— (1913), *The Quest and Occupation of Tahiti by Emissaries of Spain in the Years 1772–1776* (1; London: Hakluyt Society).
—— (1914), *The Quest and Occupation of Tahiti by Emissaries of Spain in the Years 1772–1776* (2; London: Hakluyt Society).
—— (1918), *The Quest and Occupation of Tahiti by Emissaries of Spain in the Years 1772–1776* (3; London: Hakluyt Society).
Cosgrove, Denis (1998), *Social Formation and Symbolic Landscape* (University of Wisconsin Press).
Dalrymple, Alexander (1770), *An Historical Collection of the Several Voyages and Discoveries in the South Pacific Ocean* (London).
—— (1967), *An Historical Collection of the Several Voyages and Discoveries in the South Pacific Ocean* (Amsterdam and New York: N. Israel and Da Capo Press).
—— (1996), *An Account of the Discoveries Made in the South Pacifick Ocean* ([1767] Potts Point, NSW: Hordern House Rare Books).
Dampier, William (1697), *A New Voyage Round the World* (London).
David, Andrew (1999), 'The Voyage of Alejandro Malaspina 1789–1794', *Annual General Meeting of The Hakluyt Society 7 July 1999* (London: The Hakluyt Society), 3–24.
De Brosses, Charles (1756), *Histoire des Navigations aux Terres Australes* (Paris).
De Morga, Antonio (1997), *Sucesos de las Islas Filipinas* (Madrid: Polifemo).
Defoe, Daniel (1719), *Robinson Crusoe* (London).
Diamond, Marion (1993), 'Trade Interactions', in Max Quanchi and Ron Adams (eds), *Culture Contact in the Pacific: Essays on Contact, Encounter and Response* (Cambridge, New York and Melbourne: Cambridge University Press), 58–72.
Douglas, Bronwen (1993), 'Pre-European Societies in the Pacific Islands', in Max Quanchi and Ron Adams (eds), *Culture Contact in the Pacific: Essays on Contact, Encounter and Response* (Cambridge, New York and Melbourne: Cambridge University Press), 15–30.
Duncan, Carol (1999), 'From the Princely Gallery to the Public Art Museum: The Louvre Museum and the National Gallery, London', in David Boswell and

Jessica Evans (eds), *Representing the Nation: A Reader* (London and New York: Routledge), 304–31.

Edgerton, Samuel Y. Jr (1987), 'From Mental Matrix to *Mappamundi* to Christian Empire: The Heritage of Ptolemaic Cartography in the Renaissance', in David Woodward (ed.), *Art and Cartography* (Chicago: University of Chicago Press), 10–50.

Edmond, Rod (2000), 'Missionaries on Tahiti, 1797–1840', in Jonathan Lamb, Vanessa Smith, and Nicolas Thomas (eds), *Exploration and Exchange: A South Seas Anthology 1680–1900* (Chicago and London: University of Chicago Press), 226–40.

Elias, Norbert (1978), *The History of Manners*, trans. Edmund Jephcott (New York: Pantheon).

Elliott, John H. (1970), *The Old World and the New 1492–1650* (Cambridge: Cambridge University Press).

—— (2006), *Empires of the Atlantic World: Britain and Spain in America 1492–1830* (New Haven and London: Yale University Press).

Estensen, Miriam (2000), *The Quest for the Great South Land* (New York: St Martin's Press).

Fabian, Johannes (1983), *Time and the Other: How Anthropology Makes its Object* (New York: Columbia University Press).

Foucault, Michel (1973), *The Order of Things: An Archaeology of the Human Sciences* (New York: Vintage Books).

Gallego, Hernán (1967a), 'Relación extensa', in Celsus O. F. M. Kelly (ed.), *Austrialia Franciscana* (3; Madrid: Franciscan Historical Studies and Archivo Iberoamericano), 93–177.

—— (1967b), 'Relación breve', in Celsus O. F. M. Kelly (ed.), *Austrialia Franciscana* (3; Madrid: Franciscan Historical Studies and Archivo Iberoamericano), 67–91.

Gates, Henry Louis (1991), 'Critical Fanonism', *Critical Enquiry* 17 (3), 457–70.

Gil, Juan (c.1989), *Mitos y utopías del descubrimiento* (2; *El Pacífico*; Madrid: Alianza).

González de Haedo, Felipe (1908), 'The Voyage of Captain Don Felipe Gonzalez in the Ship of the Line San Lorenzo with the Frigate Santa Rosalia in Company, to Easter Island in 1770–71', in Bolton Glanvill Corney (ed.), *The Voyage of Captain Don Felipe Gonzalez in the Ship of the Line San Lorenzo with the Frigate Santa Rosalia in Company, to Easter Island in 1770–71* (Cambridge: Hakluyt Society).

González de Leza, Gaspar (2000), 'Relación verdadera del viaje y suceso que hizo el capitán ... (1605)', in Justo Zaragoza (ed.), *Historia del descubrimiento de las regiones austriales hecho por el general Pedro Fernández de Quirós* (Madrid: Manuel G. Hernández, 1876, 3 vols. Facsimile in one volume. Madrid: Dove), 605–714.

Granada, Fray Luis de (1583), *Introducción al Símbolo de la Fe* (Salamanca: Herederos de Mathías Gast).
Graves, Robert (1950), *The Isles of Unwisdom* (London: Cassell).
Greenblatt, Stephen (1991), *Marvelous Possessions: The Wonder of the New World* (Chicago: Chicago University Press).
Greene, Roger C. (1973), 'The Conquest of the Conquistadors', *World Archaeology*, 5 (1), 14–31.
Greene, Roger C. and Allen, Jim (1972), 'Mendana [sic] 1595 and the Fate of the Lost 'Almiranta': An Archaeological Investigation', *The Journal of Pacific History*, 7, 73–91.
Harley, J. B. (1988), 'Maps, Knowledge, Power', in Denis Cosgrove and Stephen Daniels (eds), *The Iconography of Landscape: Essays on the Symbolic Representation, Design and Use of Past Environments* (Cambridge: Cambridge University Press), 277–312.
Hau'ofa, Epeli (1993), 'Our Sea of Islands', in Eric Waddell, Vijay Naidu and Epeli Hau'ofa (eds), *A New Oceania: Rediscovering Our Sea of Islands* (Suva: The University of the South Pacific).
Herda, Phyllis (1983), 'A Translation and Annotation of the Journals of the Malaspina Expedition during Their Stay in Vava'u Tonga, 1793' (University of Auckland).
Hervé, Juan Antonio (1908), 'Derrota del Navío de S. M. San Lorenzo a la Isla de David. Octubre 10 de 1770', in Bolton Glanvill Corney (ed.), *The Voyage of Captain Don Felipe Gonzalez in the Ship of the Line San Lorenzo with the Frigate Santa Rosalia in Company, to Easter Island in 1770–71* (Cambridge: Hakluyt Society), 112–28.
Higueras Rodríguez, María Dolores (1985–1994), *Catálogo crítico de los documentos de la expedición Malaspina (1789–1794)*, 3 vols (Madrid: Museo Naval).
Hilder, Brett (1980), *The Voyages of Torres: The Discovery of the Southern Coastline of New Guinea and Torres Strait by Captain Luis Báez de Torres in 1606* (St. Lucia: University of Queensland Press).
Hillis, Ken (1984), 'The Power of the Disembodied Imagination: Perspective's Role in Cartography', *Cartographica*, 31 (3), 1–17.
Hobsbawm, Eric (1983), 'Introduction: Inventing Traditions', in Eric Hobsbawm and Terence Ranger (eds), *The Invention of Tradition* (Cambridge and New York: Cambridge University Press), 1–14.
Hulme, Peter (1986), *Colonial Encounters: Europe and the Native Caribbean 1492–1797* (London and New York: Routledge).
Iturbe, Juan de (1966), 'Sumario Breve', in Celsus O. F. M. Kelly (ed.), *La Austrialia del Espíritu Santo: The Journal of Fray Martín de Munilla O. F. M. and Other Documents Relating to The Voyage of Pedro Fernández de Quirós to the South Sea (1605–1606) and the Franciscan Missionary Plan (1617–1627)* (The Hakluyt Society, 2; Cambridge: Cambridge University Press), 273–93.

Jack-Hinton, Colin (1969), *The Search for the Islands of Solomon 1567–1838* (Oxford: Clarendon Press).
Joppien, Rüdiger and Smith, Bernard (1985–88), *The Art of Captain Cook's Voyages* (New Haven: Yale University Press).
Kelly, Celsus, O. F. M. (1965), *Calendar of Documents: Spanish Voyages in the South Pacific from Álvaro de Mendana to Alejandro Malaspina, 1567–1794, and the Franciscan Missionary Plans for the Peoples of the Austral Lands, 1617–1634* (Madrid: Franciscan Historical Studies and Archivo Iberoamericano).
—— (1966), *La Austrialia del Espíritu Santo*, 2 vols (The Hakluyt Society; Cambridge: Cambridge University Press).
—— (1971), 'Introduction', in Celsus Kelly O. F. M. (ed.), *Austrialia Franciscana* (5; Madrid: Franciscan Historial Studies and Archivo Iberoamericano), 3–46.
—— (ed.) (1963–73), *Austrialia Franciscana*, 6 vols (Madrid: Franciscan Historial Studies and Archivo Iberoamericano).
Kelly, Celsus, O. F. M. and Gerard Bushell, O. F. M. (eds) (1973), *Austrialia Franciscana*, 6 vols (6; Madrid: Franciscan Historial Studies and Archivo Iberoamericano).
Kirch, Patrick Vinton (2000), *On The Road of the Winds: An Archaeological History of the Pacific Islands Before European Contact* (Berkeley, Los Angeles and London: University of California Press).
Landín, Amancio (1945), *Vida y viajes de Pedro Sarmiento de Gamboa* (Madrid: Instituto Histórico de la Marina).
—— (1992), *Descubrimientos españoles en el mar del Sur*, 3 vols (Madrid: Editorial Naval).
Langdon, Robert (1975), *The Lost Caravel* (Sydney: Pacific Publications).
Las Casas, Bartolomé de (1552), *Brevísima relación de la destrucción de las Indias*.
Lévi-Strauss, Claude (1969), *The Raw and the Cooked: Introduction to a Science of Mythology I*, trans. John and Doreen Weightman (London: Jonathan Cape).
Macpherson, C. B. (1962), *The Political Theory of Possessive Individualism: Hobbes to Locke* (Oxford and New York: Oxford University Press).
Malaspina, Alejandro (1984), *Diario de viaje de Alejandro Malaspina* (Mercedes Palau, Aránzazu Zabala, Blanca Sánchez; Madrid: Museo Universal).
—— (2001–2004), *The Malaspina Expedition, 1789–1794: Journal of the Voyage by Alejandro Malaspina*, ed. Andrew David, Felipez Fernández-Armesto, Carlos Novi and Glyndwr Williams (London/Madrid: Hakluyt Society and Museo Naval).
—— (2004), 'At Vava'u', in Andrew David, Felipe Fernández-Armesto, Carlos Novi, Glyndwr Williams (eds), *The Malaspina Expedition, 1789–1794: Journal of the Voyage by Alejandro Malaspina* (3; London: Hakluyt Society and Museo Naval), 101–46.
Malinowski, Bronislaw (1922), *Argonauts of the Western Pacific: An Account of Native Enterprise and Adventure in the Archipelagoes of Melanesian New Guinea* (London: Routledge).

Marcus, Jane (1989), 'The Asylums of Antaeus: Women, War, and Madness – Is There a Feminist Fetishism?' in H. Aram Veeser (ed.), *The New Historicism* (New York and London: Routledge), 132–51.

Marshall, P. J. and Williams, Glyndwr (1982), *The Great Map of Mankind: Perceptions of New Worlds in the Age of Enlightenment* (Cambridge, Mass.: Harvard University Press).

Mauss, Marcel (1950), *Sociologie et anthropologie* (Paris: Presses Universitaires de France).

—— (1967), *The Gift: Forms and Functions of Exchange in Archaic Societies*, trans. Ian Cunnison (New York and London: Norton).

McKendrick, Melveena (1974), *Woman and Society in the Spanish Drama of the Golden Age: A Study of the Mujer Varonil* (London and New York: Cambridge University Press).

Mellén Blanco, Francisco (1986), *Manuscritos y documentos españoles para la historia de la isla de Pascua* (Madrid: Centro de Estudios Históricos de Obras Públicas y Urbanismo (CEHOPU)).

—— (1992), 'Introducción', in Francisco Mellén Blanco (ed.), *Espanoles en Tahití* (Madrid: Historia 16), 7–34.

Mendaña, Álvaro de (1967), 'Relación de Álvaro de Mendaña al Licenciado Lope García de Castro ...' in Celsus O. F. M. Kelly (ed.), *Austrialia Franciscana* (3; Madrid: Franciscan Historical Studies and Archivo Iberoamericano), 179–245.

Mendaña, Álvaro de (1965), 'Breve Relación de Álvaro de Mendaña al Rey Felipe II', in Celsus O. F. M. Kelly (ed.), *Austrialia Franciscana* (2; Madrid: Franciscan Historial Studies and Archivo Iberoamericano), 1–26.

Mitchell, Scott (2000), 'Guns or Barter? Indigenous Exchange Networks and the Mediation of Conflict in Post-contact Western Arnhem Land', in Robin and Anne Clarke Torrence (eds), *The Archaeology of Difference: Negotiating Cross-Cultural Engagements in Oceania* (London and New York: Routledge), 182–214.

Mitchell, W. J. T. (1994), *Picture Theory: Essays on Verbal and Visual Representation* (London and Chicago: University of Chicago Press).

Montaigne, Michel de (1965), *The Complete Essays of Montaigne*, trans. Donald Frame (Stanford: Stanford University Press).

Montrose, Louis A. (1989), 'The Poetics and Politics of Culture', in H. Aram Veeser (ed.), *The New Historicism* (New York and London: Routledge), 15–36.

Mourelle de la Rúa, Francisco (1970), 'Noticia de la navegación de la fragata Princesa, al mando del Alférez de Fragata, Don Francisco Mourelle, desde Manila a San Blas, por el Océano Pacífico, en 1780 y 1781 ', in Amancio Landín Carrasco (ed.), *Mourelle de la Rua, Explorador del Pacífico* (Madrid: Cultura Hispánica), 273–320.

Mullaney, Steven (1983), 'Strange Things, Gross Terms, Curious Customs: The Rehearsal of Cultures in the Late Renaissance', *Representations*, 3, 40–67.

Munilla, Fray Martín de (1963), 'Relaciones de Fray Martín de Munilla, O. F. M. y Fray Mateo de Vascones', in Celsus O. F. M. Kelly (ed.), *Austrialia Franciscana* (1; Madrid: Franciscan Historical Studies and Archivo Iberoamericano), 19–106.

Munro, Doug (1993), 'Patterns of Colonial Rule', in Max Quanchi and Ron Adams (eds), *Culture Contact in the Pacific: Essays on Contact, Encounter and Response* (Cambridge, New York and Melbourne: Cambridge University Press), 114–25.

Nuti, Lucia (1988), 'The Mapped Views by Georg Hoefnagel: The Merchant's Eye, The Humanist's Eye', *Word and Image*, 4, 545–70.

Padres, Gerónimo Clota and Narciso Gónzalez (1925), 'Relación de los principales acaecimientos durante el viaje y permanencia en Otahiti escrita de común acuerdo por el Piloto Dn. José Barela y los Misioneros Clota y González', in Bernadino Izaguirre (ed.), *Historia de las misiones franciscanas y narración de los progresos de la geografía en el oriente del Perú* (3; Cajamarca: Tipografía San Antonio), 92–145.

Pagden, Anthony (1995), *Lords of All the World: Ideologies of Empire in Spain, Britain and France c.1500–c.1800* (New Haven and London: Yale University Press).

Pantoja y Arriaga, Juan (ed.) (1992), *Un diario inédito sobre la presencia española en Tahití (1774–1775)*, ed. Francisco Mellén Blanco (Revista española de estudios del Pacífico, 2; Madrid) 109–81.

Pedley, Mary Sponberg (1992), *Bel et Utile: The Work of the Robert de Baugondy Family of Mapmakers* (Tring, Herts: Map Collector).

Pigafetta, Antonio (1969), *Magellan's Voyage: A Narrative Account of the First Navigation*, ed. R. A. Skelton, trans. R. A. Skelton (New York: Dover).

Pocock, J. G. A. (2000), 'Nature and History, Self and Other: European Perceptions of World History in the Age of Encounter', in Jonathan Lamb, Vanessa Smith, and Nicolas Thomas (eds), *Exploration and Exchange: A South Seas Anthology 1680–1900* (Chicago and London: University of Chicago Press), 25–44.

Pratt, Mary Louise (1992), *Imperial Eyes: Travel Writing and Transculturation* (London and New York: Routledge).

Quanchi, Max (1993), 'Being Discovered: Perceptions and Control of Strangers', in Max Quanchi and Ron Adams (eds), *Culture Contact in the Pacific: Essays on Contact, Encounter and Response* (Cambridge, New York and Melbourne: Cambridge University Press), 45–56.

Quanchi, Max and Adams, Ron (eds) (1993), *Culture Contact in the Pacific: Essays on Contact, Encounter and Response* (Cambridge, New York and Melbourne: Cambridge University Press).

Quirós, Pedro Fernández (1986), *Descubrimiento de las regiones austriales*, ed. Roberto Ferrando (Crónicas de América 25; Madrid: Historia 16).

—— (2000), 'Viajes de Quirós', in Justo Zaragoza (ed.), *Historia del descubrimiento de las regiones austriales hecho por el general Pedro Fernández de*

Quirós (Madrid: Manuel G. Hernández, 1876, 3 vols. Facsimile in one volume. Madrid: Dove), 115–308.

Rabinow, Paul (1986), 'Representations Are Social Facts: Modernity and Post-Modernity in Anthropology', in James and George E. Marcus Clifford (eds), *Writing Culture: The Poetics and Politics of Ethnography* (Berkeley, Los Angeles and London: University of California Press), 234–61.

Rainbird, Paul (2000), '"Round, Black and Lustrous": A View of Encounters with Difference in Chuuk Lagoon, Federated States of Micronesia', in Robin Torrence and Anne Clarke (eds), *The Archaeology of Difference: Negotiating Cross-Cultural Engagements in Oceania* (London and New York: Routledge), 32–50.

Robson, John (2002), 'Somebody knows what!: The Cartographic Results of the Visits by Vancouver and Malaspina to New Zealand in the 1790s', *New Zealand Map Society Journal* (15), 35–47.

Rodríguez, Máximo (1992), *Españoles en Tahití*, ed. Francisco Mellén Blanco (Crónicas de America, 69; Madrid: Historia 16).

Roggeveen, Jacob (1970), *The Journal of Jacob Roggeveen*, ed. Andrew Sharp (Andrew Sharp edn; Oxford: Clarendon Press).

Rose, Gillian (1993), *Feminism and Geography: The Limits of Geographical Knowledge* (Minneapolis: University of Minnesota Press).

Rosenthal, Earl (1971), 'Plus Ultra, Non plus Ultra, and the Columnar Device of Emperor Charles V', *Journal of the Warburg and Courtauld Institutes*, 34, 204–28.

Sahlins, Marshall (1963), 'Poor Man, Rich Man, Big-Man, Chief: Political Types in Melanesia and Polynesia', *Comparative Studies in Society and History*, 5 (3), 285–303.

Salmond, Anne (2003), *The Trial of the Cannibal Dog: Captain Cook in the South Seas* (London: Allen Lane).

—— (2005), 'Their Body is Different, Our Body is Different: European and Tahitian Navigators in the 18th Century', *History and Anthropology*, 16 (2), 167–86.

Short, John Rennie (2003), *The World Through Maps: A History of Cartography* (Toronto, On; Buffalo, NY; Abingdon Oxon, UK: Firefly).

Skelton, R. A. (1958), *Explorers' Maps: Chapters in the Cartographic Record of Geographical Discovery* (London, New York, Sydney, Toronto: Spring Books).

Smith, Bernard (1960), *European Vision and the South Pacific 1768–1850: A Study in the History of Art and Ideas* (Oxford: Clarendon Press).

—— (1992), *Imagining the Pacific: In the Wake of the Cook Voyages* (Haven and London: Yale University Press).

Smith, Neil and Cindi Katz (1993), 'Grounding Metaphor: Towards a Spatialized Politics', in Michael Keith and Steve Pile (eds), *Place and the Politics of Identity* (London and New York: Routledge), 67–83.

Sobel, Dava (1995), *Longitude: The True Story of a Lone Genius Who Solved the Greatest Scientific Problem of His Time* (New York, London: Penguin).
Spate, Oskar H. K. (1979), *The Pacific Since Magellan* (1. *The Spanish Lake*; Canberra: ANU).
Spriggs, Matthew (1997), *The Island Melanesians* (Oxford, UK and Cambridge, Mass: Blackwell).
Stafford, Barbara Maria (1984a), *Voyage into Substance: Art, Science, Nature, and the Illustrated Travel Account, 1760–1840* (Cambridge, Mass.: The MIT Press).
Tcherkézoff, Serge (2004), *Tahiti-1768: Jeunes filles en pleurs* (Pirae, Tahiti: Au Vent Des Isles).
Thomas, Nicholas (1997), *In Oceania: Visions, Artifacts, Histories* (Durham and London: Duke University Press).
—— (2000), 'Liberty and License: The Forsters' Accounts of New Zealand Sociality', in Jonathan Lamb, Vanessa Smith, and Nicolas Thomas (eds), *Exploration and Exchange: A South Seas Anthology 1680–1900* (Chicago and London: University of Chicago Press), 132–55.
Torrence, Robin (2000), 'Just Another Trader? An Archaeological Perspective on European Barter with Admiralty Islanders, Papua New Guinea', in Anne Clarke and Robin Torrence (eds), *The Archaeology of Difference: Negotiating Cross-Cultural Engagements in Oceania* (London: Routledge), 104–41.
Torrence, Robin and Clarke, Anne (2000a), 'Negotiating Difference: Practice Makes Theory for Contemporary Archaeology in Oceania', in Robin Torrence and Anne Clarke (eds), *The Archaeology of Difference: Negotiating Cross-Cultural Engagements in Oceania* (London: Routledge), 1–31.
—— (eds) (2000b), *The Archaeology of Difference: Negotiating Cross-Cultural Engagements in Oceania* (London and New York: Routledge).
Trussell, Denys (1977–78), *The Two Worlds of Omai* (Art New Zealand; Auckland).
Van Linschoten, Jan Huyghen (2001), *The Voyage of John Huyghen van Linschoten to the East Indies* (New York: Elibron Classics).
Wallerstein, Immanuel (1974), *Capitalist Agriculture and the Origins of the European World-Economy in the Sixteenth Century*, 3 vols (The Modern World-System, 1; New York and London Academic Press).
—— (1980), *Mercantilism and the Consolidation of the European World-Economy, 1600–1750* (The Modern World-System, 2; New York and London: Academic Press).
—— (1989), *The Second Great Expansion of the Capitalist World-Economy, 1730–1840's* (The Modern World-System, 3; San Diego: Academic Press).
White, Hayden (1987), *The Content of the Form: Narrative Discourse and Historical Representation* (Baltimore and London: Johns Hopkins University Press).
Williams, Glyndwr (1966), *The Expansion of Europe in the Eighteenth Century: Overseas Rivalry, Discovery and Exploitation* (London: Blandford).

Williams, Patrick, 'Philip II, the Philippines and the Hispanic World', in Damaso de Lario (ed.), *Re-Shaping the World. Philip II of Spain and his time*, Manila, Ateneo de Manila University Press, 2008, 13–33.

Wroth, Lawrence (1944), 'The Early Cartography of the Pacific', *The Papers of the Bibliographical Society of America*, 38 (2), 87–265.

Zaragoza, Justo (2000), *Historia del descubrimiento de las regiones austriales hecho por el general Pedro Fernández de Quirós* (Madrid: Manuel G. Hernández, 1876, 3 vols. Facsimile in one volume. Madrid: Dove).

Index

Note: Given their number and the similarity in their names, the ships of the various fleets are listed under each explorer's name, e.g. Magellan's fleet. The number of a note on a page is indicated by 'n' after a page reference. Page numbers for illustrations are in italics.

Acapulco 29, 32, 98, 99
Admiralty Islands 22, 29
Adorno, Rolena 157, 178n.15
Africans 2, 3, 39, 58–9, 149
  see also slaves
Aguera Infanzón, Francisco Antonio de 124, 126–31 *passim*, 132n.9
Amat, Manuel de, Viceroy of Peru 9, 16, 123–4, 133, 137
Amherst of Hackney, Lord 36, 52n.3, 224
Amich, José 133, 140–3, 144n.2
Andía y Varela, José 146–7, 162, 227
Anson, George 8, 106–7, 123
arii 91, 115, 138, 140, 147, 151–76 *passim*, 179n.24, 187–9, 191–2, 193n.7
  see also individual entries
Australia 35n.26, 38, 83, 84, 101n.7, 103, 104, 108, 196, 217
Austrialia del Espíritu Santo 6, 83–4, 100n.1
  see also Vanuatu

Bakewell, Peter 113, 119n.14, 121n.30
Banks, Joseph 108, 114, 119n.11, 179n.26
'barbarians' 51–2, 74n.29, 92, 185, 219, 222n.16
Barreto, Diego 66
Barreto, Isabel 6, 32, 61, 66–7, 71, 76–80, 8n.9
Barreto, Lorenzo 66–7, 74–8 *passim*
Bauzá, Felipe 198, 205, 227
Beaglehole, John C. 83, 100n.3

Bermúdez, Belmonte de 66–7, 89, 90, 97, 101, 225
Bile 42–6, 48–50, 52–4, 63n.16
Boenechea, Domingo 133–40 *passim*, 146–7 *148*, 155, 158–9, 162–3, 214, 226
  Boenechea's ship, 1770:
    El Águila (Santa María de Magdalena) 133
  Boenechea's fleet, 1774–75:
    Águila 146, *147*
    Jupiter (San Miguel) 146
Bonacorsi, Raimundo 133–43 *passim*, 150, 154, 226
Bougainville, Louis Antoine de 8, 107–8, 114, 119n.8, 123, 149, 181, 216, 222n.14
  Bougainville's fleet, 1766–69:
    Boudeuse 107, 222n.14
    Etoile 107, 222n.14
Bustamante, José 195–6, 205–6, 209n.12, 227
  see also Malaspina
Byron, John 107, 123, 181
  Byron's ship, 1764: *Dolphin* 107

Cabeza de Vaca 157, 158
Callao, El 9, 32, 36, 39, 61, 62n.4, 84, 87, 131, 133, 143–4, 176, 208
cannibalism 8, 48–50 *passim*, 63n.24, n.25, 64n.26, 109, 112, 119n.11
capitalism 10, 11, 111
Carolines, The 22, 23, 29, 30
Carteret, Philip 107, 181, 222n.14

INDEX

Castro, López García de 36, 39
Castro, Mariana de 66, 73, 81n.3
Catoira, Gómez Hernández 39, 40, 42–4, 46–54, 56–65 passim
Charles III (King of Spain) 106, 113, 119n.6, 121n.30, 123
Charles V (King of Spain, Holy Roman Emperor) 21, 24, 26, 28
christianising 138, 143, 146, 152, 165
Christianity 8, 41, 48, 51, 88, 112–13, 128, 132n.9, 137
Christians 21, 61, 65n.45, 91, 98, 99, 152, 158, 165
Clifford, James 6, 13n.5
Clota, Jéronimo see padres
colonialism 11, 12, 13n.6, 14n.7, 15n.18, 16, 48, 64n.25, 118, 211–13, 216, 220, 220n.4, 221n.12
colonies 11, 26, 106, 111, 113, 143
Columbus, Christopher 8, 20–1, 23, 56, 64n.39, 82, 95
Cook, James 8, 10, 16, 19, 101–3, 112, 114, 120, 144, 156, 166
   Enlightenment and 109, 111, 136–7, 179n.26
   island peoples and 137, 203, 222n.3
   voyages 105, 108
   Spanish and 166, 176, 179n.33, 180–1, 204, 208n.1, 211–12
Corney, Bolton Glanvill 123–4, 132n.1, n.2, 137, 147, 172–3, 176–80 passim, 224, 226
Cortés, Hernan 38–9
Corzo, Felipe 66, 100n.2
Creoles 2, 3, 39, 58, 107, 110, 115
Croix, Theodor de (Viceroy of Peru) 116, 172, 179n.29
cross-cultural engagement 12, 15, 138, 163

Dalrymple, Alexander 62n.3, 84, 93, 225
Davis, Edward 105, 123
Douglas, Bronwen 17, 32n.4
D'Urville, Jules-Sébastien-César Dumond 17
Dutch East India Company 103–4

Easter Island 9, 34n.17, 104–5, 109, 114, 123–32 passim, 226
Edgerton, Samuel 21
Elcano, Juan Sebastián 20, 22, 24, 26–8, 34n.19

Elias, Norbert 54
Elliott, John 14n.12, n.14, 110, 120n.15, 222n.17
emarae 154, 158–9, 160, 166, 179n.28
Enlightenment, The 8, 17, 107, 110–11, 113, 120, 120n.20, 136–7, 201, 205, 208n.1
Enríquez, Hernando 47, 56–7
ethnocentrism 3, 10
ethnographic writing 1–14 passim, 108, 115, 122n.36, 131, 144, 213
   see also cross-cultural engagement

Feileua 199–201, 203, 205, 207
Forster, Johan Reinhold and George 108, 114
Foucault, Michel 53, 205
France 104n.36, 106–11 passim, 113, 120n.16, 123
Franciscans 9, 38, 42, 58, 91, 133, 145n.10
   see also Amich, José; Gálvez, Francisco de; Kelly, Celsus; missionaries; padres

Gallego, Hernán 38–9, 40, 42, 62n.7, n.8, 67, 224
Gálvez, Francisco de 42, 45, 56
Gates, Henri Louis 11
Gayangos, Tomás de 9, 133, 140–1, 144n.2, 147, 148, 155, 226
Gómez de Espinosa, Gonzalo 22, 26, 34n.16
González de Haedo, Felipe 9, 124, 125, 132n.5, 226
   González de Haedo's fleet, 1770:
     San Lorenzo 124
     Santa Rosalía 124
González, Narciso see padres
Greene, Roger 17, 67, 81n.6
Grijalva, Hernando de 22, 29–30, 34n.16
   Grijalva's fleet, 1536:
     Santiago 29
     Trinidad 29

Haenke, Tadeo 114, 198, 205, 227
Harrison, John 19, 33n.11, 105, 108, 118n.3
Hervé, Juan de 9, 124, 126–7, 129–33 passim, 136, 163, 213, 215, 216, 217, 226
Hervé, Roger 26
Hinoi 151, 166, 172, 177n.7
Hulme, Peter 48, 64n.26
human sacrifice 8, 109, 112, 119n.11, 168, 178n.22

INDEX

imperalism 10–11, 115, 121n.29
influenza 108, 139, 144, 158
 see also malaria
Isle of David
 see Easter Island
Iturbe, Juan de 81n.5, 95, 100n.2, 226

kava 151, 159, 165, 166, 171, 173, 188, 198, 200, 202, 206
Kelly, Celsus 38–9, 62n.4, 100n.2, 101n.6, n.11, 224–5
Kirch, Patrick Vinton 17, 32n.1, 33n.6, 132n.3

Landín, Amancio 29, 30, 34n.16, n.22, 35n.27, 36, 101n.11, 194, 222
Lángara, Cayetano de 116, 129, 175–6
 Lángara's ship, 1776:
  El Águila 116
Langdon, Robert 27, 28
Las Casas, Bartolomé de 14n.11, 220
Le Maire, Isaac 27, 104
 see also Schouten, Willem Corneliszoon
Leza, González de 88, 92, 101n.6-n.14, 102n.20, 225
Loaísa, García Jofre de 22, 26–8, 34n.16, 35n.25
 Loaísa's fleet, 1525:
  Anunciada 27
  Sancti Spiritus 27
  San Lesmes 27, 35n.26
  Capitana (Santa María de la Victoria) 27–8
  Santa María del Parral 27
  Santiago 27, 29
longitude 19, 33n.11, 36, 80, 105–6, 119
López de Legazpi, Miguel 18, 31, 34n.16
 López de Legazpi's fleet, 1564:
  Capitana (San Pedro) 31
  San Juan 31
  San Lucás 31
  San Pablo 31

Magellan, Ferdinand 5, 16–35 *passim*, 119n.5
 Magellan's fleet, 1519:
  Concepción 23, 24, 26
  San Antonio 23, 24, 27, 29
  Santiago 23, 24, 27, 29
  Trinidad 23, 26, 29, 34n.19
Magellan, Strait of 100n.1, 104

malaria 6, 32, 56–61 *passim*, 67, 76, 78
 see also influenza
Malaspina, Alessandro 2, 114, 195–211 *passim*
 Malaspina's ship 1786: *Astrea* 195
 Malaspina & Bustamante's fleet, 1793:
  Atrevida 196, 198, 207
  Descubierta 196, 198
  see also Bustamante, José
Malope 74–8 *passim*, 91
Manila galleon 18, 32, 102
Manrique 67, 70–7 *passim*
Maori 105
mapping 21, 92, 108, 211–12
Marianas Islands 21, 25, 28, 30–1, 79, 98, 192
Marshall Islands 22–3, 28, 30, 31
Matavai 151, 164, 166, 180, 216
Mauss, Marcel 11, 13, 14n.15, 41, 62n.12, 164
Melanesia 16–17, 33n.4, n.5, n.7, 81n.4, 110, 1459, 178n.23
Mellén Blanco, Francisco 124, 146, 224, 226
Mendaña, Álvaro de 5–6, 20, 32, 33n.16, 36–65 *passim*, 66–83 *passim*, 119n.5, 126, 224
 Mendaña's fleet, 1567:
  Los Reyes (Capitana) 38, 40
  Todos los Santos (Almiranta) 38, 40
 Mendaña's fleet, 1595:
  Capitana (San Jerónimo) 66, 67, 81n.3
  San Felipe 66
  Santa Catalina 66
  Santa Isabel (Almiranta) 66, 212
mestizos 2, 3, 39, 110
Meta 53, 60
missionaries 4, 43, 123, 138, 146, 166, 176, 220, 227
 see also Franciscans; padres; individual entries
Moluccas Islands 23, 26, 28–30, 33n.12, 104
Montaigne, Michel de 49, 112
Mourelle de la Rúa, Francisco 99, 109, 181, 182, 227
 Mourelle de la Rúa's ship, 1780:
  Princesa 109, 181, 183, 192, 196, 227
Munilla, Martín de 91, 99, 101n.9, 223, 225
museums 115, 116, 122n.35, 172, 179n.26
 Museo de América 62n.9, 115
 Museo Naval 62n.9, 115, 209n.12
 see also Real Gabinete de la Historia

Navarrete, Martín Fernández de 35n.25, 35n.31
Née, Luis 114, 201, 227
New Guinea 17, 23, 28–31 *passim*, 84, 100, 102n.22, 104, 217, 225
New Hebrides 6, 100n.1
see also Vanuatu
New Spain 22–3, 27–30 *passim*, 84, 100, 102n.32, 104
New Zealand 35n.26, 83, 104, 105, 108, 112, 123, 144n.3, 196
Noble, Miguel 29, 35n.29
'noble savage' 108, 112–13, 121n.26, n.27
Nuñez, Andrés 56, 64n.38
Nuñez de Balboa, Vasco 16, 20

Omai 13n.4, 116, *117*, 119n.9, 122n.38, 219
O Purahi 151, 155, 171, 174
Ortega, Pedro 38, 45–8, 50, 55–6
Ortiz de Retes 22, 30, 31, 34n.16, 35n.34

padres 145n.10, 146–79 *passim*, 227
see also Franciscans; missionaries; individual entries
Pahiriro 140, 151, 152, 159
Palau Islands 23, 30
Pantoja, Juan 121n.26, 147, 149–50, 156, 163, 177n.4, 219, 222n.16, 226
Pautu 143–4, 146, 150–2, 154, 163, 167–8, 219
Philip II (King of Spain) 21, 25, 31, 34n.23, 35n.32, 82, 95
Philip III (King of Spain) 21, 100, 101n.5
Philippines 5, 18, 21, 23, 25–7, 30–4 *passim*, 67, 79, 80, 81n.2, 98, 100, 195
Pigafetta, Antonio 24, 26
Pocock, John 10, 140n.13, 113, 121, 220n.2
Polynesians 4, 16–17, 28, 32n.4, 33n.5, n.7, 42, 63n.14, 70, 72, 81n.7, 110, 123, 132n.3, 140, 142, 178n.23, 179n.30
Prado y Tovar, Diego de 84, 211, 213, 224, 225
Pratt, Mary Louise 12, 15n.9, 111, 120n.18, 19
Ptolemy, Claudius 21–3

Quanchi, Max 12
Quirós, Pedro Fernández de 6–10 *passim*, 66–7, 69–80 *passim*, 81n.5, n.9, 82–102, 112, 119n.5, 161, 225
Quirós's fleet, 1605:
Almiranta 84, 86, 93, 99
Capitana 84, 98, 101n.10, 225
Los Tres Reyes 84
San Pedrico 84
San Pedro y San Pablo 84

Rapa Nui *see* Easter Island
Real Gabinete de la Historia 115, 226, 233n.36, 215
see also museums
Renaissance, The 21, 122n.34, 221n.9
Retes, Iñigo Ortíz de 22, 30–1, 34n.16
Rodríguez, Máximo 9, 115–16, 118, 144–80 *passim*, 210, 226
Roggeveen, Jacob 104, 105, 119n.5, 123, 132n.4

Saavedra Álvaro de 22, 27–9, 34n.16
Salmond, Anne 119n.11, 219
Santa Cruz archipelago 6, 67, 75, 81n.10, 84, 88, 90, 91, 90, 212
Sarmiento de Gamboa, Pedro 38–9, 45, 224
Schouten, Willem Corneliszoon 27, 104
Schouten's and Le Maire's fleet, 1615:
Eendracht 104
Hoorn 104
see also Le Maire, Isaac
scurvy 18, 24, 67, 103
Skelton, Raleigh 33n.9, 34n.17, n.20, 106, 118n.4
slaves 3, 25, 39, 42, 48, 58, 59, 65n.40, 95, 149
see also Africans
Smith, Bernard 136, 208n.1, 212
Sobel, Dava 33n.11
Society Islands
see Tahiti
Solander, Daniel 108, 114
Solomon Islands 6, 17, 19, 23, 36–8, 49, 55, 61, 62n.3, n.4, 66–7, 73, 78, 80–4, 126
Spate, Oskar 16, 19–20, 27, 31, 32n.2, 33n.10, 35n.24, 35n.22, 81n.7, 102n.22, 107
Spice Islands 23, 26, 104
see also Moluccas
spices 20–1, 26, 32, 53, 64n.28
Spriggs, Matthew 42, 81n.4
Stafford, Barbara 109, 112n.21

Tahiti 9, 10–15 *passim*, 34n.16, 37–9, 107–9, 112, 114, 118, 121n.26, 123–4, 129, 133–81 *passim*, 213–22 *passim*, 226

Tasman, Abel Janszoon 104, 105, 119n.5
    Tasman's fleet, 1642:
        Heemskerck 104
        Zeehaen 104
Tautira 116, 117, 147, 151, 153, 167
Tcherkézoff, Serge 32n.3
Terra Australis Incognita 36, 52, 82, 83, 100n.1, 102n.22, 104, 106–7
Tetuanui 143–4, 146, 147, 150, 167, 171, 219
Thomas, Nicholas 13n.4, 17, 33n.5, 209
Thomson, Basil 36, 62n.13, 224
Torre, Bernardo de la 22, 330–1, 34n.16, 35n.32
Torrence, Robin 15n.17, 65n.42
Torres, Luís Vaez de 6, 84, 99–100, 101n.7, n8, 102n.22, 119n.5, 224
trade winds 18, 20, 23, 26, 29–33, 105
Tu 115–16, 138, 140–1, 147, 151–2, 154, 157, 172, 175, 179n.32
Tumai 91–2
Tupou 196, 198, 209n.5, n.14

umete 115–18 *passim*, 122n.37, n.38, 147, 169, 172, 179n.28, n.29
Urdaneta, Andrés de 18, 23, 27, 31, 33n.8, n.16, 35n.25

Van Linschoten, Jan Huyghen 104, 118n.1

Vanuatu 6, 83–4, 85, 100n.1, 108, 161, 211, 214, 216–19, 225
    see also Austrialia del Espíritu Santo
Vázquez, José Antonio 109, 196
Vehiatua 151–5, 157–9, 162, 164–74 *passim*, 177n.11, n.14, 178n.23, 179n.25
Villalobos, Ruy López de 22, 29–31, 34n.16, 34n.23, 35n.32
    Villalobos's fleet, 1542:
        Capitana 30
        San Antonio 30
        San Cristóbal 30
        San Jorge 30
        San Juan de Letrán 30, 31
        San Martín 30
        Santiago 30
Vuna 198–207 *passim*, 209n.16

Wallis, Samuel 8, 107–8, 179n.33, 181, 216, 222n.14
    Wallis's fleet, 1766–68:
        Dolphin 107, 222n.14
        Swallow 107, 222n.14
Williams, Glyndwr 19, 107, 109, 112, 118n.4, 119n.8
Williams, Patrick 31, 34n.23
Wroth, Lawrence 61n.2, 82

Zaragoza, Justo 80n.1, 81n.2, 84, 224